The Provisional Irish Republican Army and the Morality of Terrorism

D1471619

'Even in destruction, there is a right way and
a wrong way – and there are limits.'

Albert Camus, *The Just Assassins*, 1958

The Provisional Irish Republican Army and the Morality of Terrorism

Timothy Shanahan

Edinburgh University Press

Edinburgh University Press Ltd
22 George Square, Edinburgh
www.euppublishing.com

Typeset in 11/13.5 pt Goudy by
Servis Filmsetting Ltd, Stockport, Cheshire, and
printed and bound in Great Britain by
CPI Antony Rowe, Chippenham, Wilts

A CIP record for this book is available from the British Library
ISBN 978 0 7486 3529 0 (hardback)
ISBN 978 0 7486 3530 6 (paperback)

Contents

Plates

Acknowledgements

A number of people deserve thanks for the assistance they provided in the writing of this book. John Menaghan invited me to teach a course in Loyola Marymount University's 1998 Summer in Ireland Program, an experience that compelled me to begin writing this book. During that trip, Shane Paul O'Doherty shared with me the story of his entry into and operations in the Derry IRA, his conversion in prison to non-violence and the life lessons learned. Subsequent trips to Ireland broadened my perspective on 'the Troubles'. I'm grateful to former IRA volunteer Declan Moen who, along with Seán ('John Boy') Ó Muireagáin, graciously took me in when I visited Belfast, introduced me to other republican ex-prisoners, and made real for me the expression 'illegal all-night drinking club'. Whereas they might not be pleased with the arguments of this book, those experiences, while not directly informing the *content* of these arguments, probably tempered their presentation by reminding me that these were young men immersed in events whose direction and meaning at the time were far from clear. Closer to home, my colleagues Jason Baehr and Scott Cameron provided helpful comments on two of the chapters. Terry Dolan assisted with the cover photograph. My editor at Edinburgh University Press, Nicola Ramsey, has been a supportive and gracious counsellor throughout the preparation of the manuscript. Readers for and committee members of EUP provided invaluable comments on the manuscript. Their suggestions significantly improved this book. Brendan O'Leary and John McGarry permitted me to include the diagram that appears in Chapter 1. Oxford University Press granted permission to use the table that also appears in that chapter. My greatest debt is to the many scholars whose works are cited in the pages that follow and from whom I have learned so much. Thank you for being my unwitting teachers, even (or rather, especially) when I found that I could not always agree with you.

Prologue

The Provisional Irish Republican Army was born in December 1969 when the Dublin-based republican movement split into two factions, ostensibly over the traditional republican policy of abstensionism with regard to the Belfast, Dublin and London parliaments, but more consequentially over the issue of whether to pursue an offensive campaign in light of the arrival of the British army in Northern Ireland the previous August. One group within the pre-split IRA, led by Cathal Goulding, was reluctant to supply arms to Catholics in the North for fear of alienating the Protestant working class who were (according to its Marxist ideology) to be included in a cross-community class-based workers' revolution. The other group preferred a more aggressive response. Led by Daithi O'Connaill, Ruairí Ó'Brádaigh and Seán MacStiofáin, it rapidly became the numerically dominant faction in Northern Ireland, attracting younger recruits such as Gerry Adams in Belfast and (later) Martin McGuinness in Derry. It was O'Connaill who proposed the name 'Provisional Irish Republican Army' for the new breakaway group, its name echoing the 'Provisional Government of the Irish Republic' declared at the General Post Office in Dublin in 1916 (White 2006, p. 151). But it was MacStiofáin who best summed up the thinking of the new group: 'You've got to have military victory first and then politicize the people afterwards. To say you've got to unite the Catholic and Protestant working class is just utter rubbish' (Smith 1995, p. 95). Armed struggle, not politics, would be the way forward to a united, independent, all-island Irish state – 'the Holy Grail of republicanism' (Holland 1999, p. 228). The Provisionals began a system-atic bombing campaign the following October. By the year's end they had detonated 153 bombs, mainly in Belfast and Derry. Their bombing

1

campaign escalated rapidly the following year. In January 1971 there were sixteen bombings, followed by thirty-eight in February, thirty-one in March, thirty-eight in April, forty-three in May, forty-four in June, and ninety-four in July. On 6 February 1971, Gunner Robert Curtis became the first British soldier to be killed by the IRA in fifty years. (Although as Warner 2006, p. 329 notes, it wasn't for lack of trying.) The Provisionals' military offensive was in full swing. 'Victory in '71' was declared.

Fast forward thirty-four years. Despite repeated assurances by the Provisional IRA that it would never surrender, would never quit, would never give up one bullet or one ounce of explosives, would never be defeated, and that the armed struggle would continue so long as the goal of a united independent Ireland remained unrealised, it finally capitulated. On 28 July 2005, IRA spokesperson Séanna Walsh (once a cellmate of Bobby Sands in Long Kesh) read a statement announcing the end of the IRA's armed struggle and instructing all units to dump arms (*An Phoblacht/Republican News*, 28 July 2005).[1] Later that day, sounding a bit like the writer of *Ecclesiastes*, Sinn Féin President Gerry Adams called upon republicans to pursue a united independent Ireland by exclusively peaceful means:

> Let us move forward together to re-build the peace process and deliver Irish unity and independence. National liberation struggles can have different phases. There is a time to resist, to stand up and to confront the enemy by arms if necessary. In other words there is a time for war. There is also a time to engage. To reach out. To put war behind us all. (http://www.sinnfein.ie/news/detail/10628)

The next day the British army began dismantling its fortress-like bases in South Armagh, a republican stronghold. On 26 September 2005, the Independent International Commission on Decommissioning verified that the IRA had put its weapons beyond use. On 26 March 2007, Gerry Adams and his ideological antipode, Democratic Unionist Party leader Ian Paisley, agreed to work together to form a coalition government in fulfilment of the requirements of the historic 1998 Good Friday Agreement. On 8 May 2007, Paisley became first minister, and former Derry IRA Commander Martin McGuinness became deputy first minister, in Northern Ireland's new power-sharing parliament. On 31 July 2007 'Operation Banner', the British army's thirty-eight-year operation in Northern Ireland, officially came to an end, as all but a standard deployment of 5,000 troops boarded transport planes for England. The Troubles, it appears, were finally over. It is a fitting time for a retrospective analysis.

The Troubles have been described as 'a little sniping war . . . in the north-western corner of Europe' (Toolis 1996, pp. 3–4), as well as 'the longest war the world has ever known' (Toolis 1996, p. 6). Although literally false, the latter claim undoubtedly conveys something important about the *psychological* impact of the conflict on the people of Northern Ireland. For many of the current residents of Northern Ireland, the conflict existed for nearly their entire lives. Since the beginning of the conflict in 1968, over 3,562 people have died in Troubles-related incidents, almost all of them within the borders of Northern Ireland.[2] An estimated 30,000 people have been injured in the associated violence. Although the number of violence-related deaths in Northern Ireland during the Troubles was no greater than that in a number of other modern liberal democracies, the number of deaths associated with *political violence* was dramatically greater. Between 1969 and 1990 the number of people killed in political violence in Northern Ireland was greater than that in all other European Community countries combined, making it far and away the most violent liberal democracy in the world.

These disturbing facts raise many questions. What were the Troubles all about? How did the conflict arise? What kept the conflict going for so long despite the desire of so many people for peace? What did the IRA want, and why was it willing to inflict so much suffering in order to achieve its aims? Was its armed struggle morally justified? What about others in the conflict, such as loyalist paramilitaries and the British security forces? Were their responses to IRA violence morally justified? The IRA as well as loyalist paramilitaries and the British security forces have been accused of engaging in 'terrorism'. What is 'terrorism' and can acts of terrorism ever be morally justified? How should one approach such questions?

The purpose of this book is to examine such questions seriously and in depth, and to provide reasoned (and reasonable) answers to them. The difficulty of doing so should not be underestimated. As an anonymous graffiti artist editorialised on a Belfast wall in the late 1970s, 'If you are not confused, you don't understand the situation.' A cynic might remark that in the thirty years following, as the conflict became ever more recursively complex, if you are not *really* confused then you really don't understand the situation. In perhaps a tacit rebuke to our pessimistic Belfast graffiti artist, Richard English declares in his masterful examination of the Provisional IRA's armed struggle that, 'contrary to some popular opinion, the IRA is in fact utterly comprehensible: their actions can be systematically explained, and their arguments clearly set out and analysed' (English

2003, p. 338). Bracketing the question of whether *anything* (much less recent Irish history) is 'utterly comprehensible', such an assessment may tend in the opposite direction toward the overly optimistic, especially if the examination is conducted from a single disciplinary perspective. Understanding anything as complex as the Troubles requires the intellectual resources provided by a range of diverse disciplines, each providing a different lens through which to view clearly some aspect of the conflict. English's book is well-informed, balanced and insightful. But whereas he recognises the *question* of the morality of the IRA's armed struggle, he tends to dismiss it as of little interest, writing that 'the most persuasive analysis of the IRA will concentrate less on whether their war was justified than in careful explanation of why it happened' (English 2003, p. 375). Such a declaration begs the question, 'Persuasive for what?' Moral scepticism (at least in their professional work) is fashionable among some academics. For some reason, moral cynicism is supposed to have associated with it an air of intellectual sophistication. I reject these views because I see no need to take such an oppositional approach to understanding. By nature we often want to know not only *why* someone did something, but also whether he was *justified* in doing it. Moreover, the explanatory and the evaluative projects are potentially complementary and mutually illuminating. This book pursues both sorts of projects, although the former project is undertaken in the service of the latter. Its *telos* is fundamentally normative.

Two fundamental issues must be addressed before proceeding further. The first concerns the description of the Provisional IRA's armed struggle as involving the use of terrorism. Can this simply be taken for granted? Certainly most observers outside of the republican movement would say that it can. As Kevin Toolis notes, 'Outside of their Ulster strongholds, the IRA were universally reviled as a terrorist organisation guilty of some of the bloodiest acts in recent political history' (Toolis 1996, p. 25). Indeed, twenty years into its armed struggle one critic judged the Provisional IRA to be 'the most formidable terrorist group in the world' (Patterson 1990, p. 5). Not surprisingly, given the almost universal moral condemnation of terrorism, republicans themselves *never* describe the IRA's activities as terrorism. Instead, efforts to overthrow 'British colonialism' in Ireland are described as 'armed resistance', 'defending liberty by the use of arms', an 'armed uprising', 'armed struggle', 'armed insurrection', an 'armed campaign', a 'guerrilla campaign', 'guerrilla warfare', 'military operations', 'military activity' and, of course, 'war'. 'Terrorism' is notably absent from this list.

Part of the difficulty here is that terrorism is a contested concept that often functions as a term of reproach to describe any violence of which one disapproves. Consequently there is no absolute consensus on the precise meaning of this term. In 1988, Schmid and Jongman estimated that there were well over a hundred definitions of terrorism in the scholarly litera-ture. That there are many more now suggests either that consensus is impossible or that many consider the formulation of an adequate defini-tion of terrorism to be indispensable for understanding the phenomenon it describes, and therefore worth trying to formulate correctly. Despite the profusion of definitions of terrorism, according to virtually all of them at least some of the Provisional IRA's activities qualify as acts of terrorism. I could simply leave it at that, and proceed to discuss the IRA's armed strug-gle as including the use of terrorism. But in order to ground the discussions that follow, it is useful to state explicitly the precise concept of terrorism (including state terrorism) I will be using. Here is my proposed definition:

> (T) 'Terrorism' is the strategically indiscriminate harming or threat of harming others within a target group in order to advance some political, ideological, social, economic, or religious agenda by influencing members of an audience group in ways believed to be conducive to the advancement of that agenda.

Space prohibits me from explicating and defending this definition in detail here. Given this definition, however, it follows that many of the IRA's acts were acts of terrorism. For example, over the course of thirty years the IRA detonated innumerable bombs in pubs, in automobiles and in buildings, each of which was intended to indiscriminately harm those within a target group in order to advance the political and ideological agenda of achiev-ing a united independent Ireland, free from British control, by influencing others, especially British politicians and their constituencies, in ways believed to be conducive to the advancement of that agenda. Such acts satisfy the conditions of (T), and hence are correctly described as acts of terrorism. The definition has teeth because not all acts undertaken by the IRA qualify as acts of terrorism according to this definition, including some that are routinely described as acts of terrorism. Jonathan Stevenson (1996, p. 51) describes the IRA's killing on 27 October 1979 of Queen Elizabeth II's cousin, Lord Louis Mountbatten, as an example of 'terrorism par excellence'. Yet this was hardly an indiscriminate killing. It was care-fully planned as a 'spectacular' guaranteed to make headlines. Indeed, the IRA itself explicitly described this as 'a discriminate operation to bring to the attention of the English people the continuing occupation of our country' (*An Phoblacht/Republican News*, 1 September 1979). Consequently, some care will need to be taken to distinguish IRA actions that constitute acts of terrorism from those that do not.

The characterisation of the IRA's armed struggle as involving the use of terrorism is one preliminary issue. Another issue that must be addressed here concerns the proposal to undertake a moral evaluation of the IRA's armed struggle, including its use of terrorism. I can well imagine some readers experiencing acute puzzlement at this point. How can one seriously propose an inquiry into the *morality of terrorism*? Isn't this just perverse? Post-9/11, post-7/7, and post- all the terrorist violence that has followed these high-profile events, isn't asking about the morality of terrorism on a par with asking about the morality of child molestation or of genocide? Is there really any room for debate or inquiry about such matters? In proposing an inquiry into the morality of the acts of a terrorist organisation, has common sense and basic decency simply gone off the rails? In short, why continue reading?

To many people, treating the morality of terrorism as if it were an open question meriting serious discussion betrays either a fundamental misunderstanding of the nature of terrorism, or a moral sense dulled by prolonged isolation in the ivory tower (or both). They would agree with Peter Simpson that

> the first thing to say about terrorism is that it is an evil and a crime . . . To doubt this is to betray a certain confusion if not corruption of mind . . . If we are to have any hope of understanding the phenomenon of terrorism or of how to deal with it, we must all *start* with the fact that it is evil. (Simpson 2005, p. 197; emphasis added)

It is not difficult to sympathise with this position. Most people would be morally outraged were a loved one to become a victim of terrorism, and rightly so, it seems. So this a priori judgement against the very possibility of morally justified terrorism has a powerful gut-level reaction in its favour. This view has the added benefit of simplicity, which, *ceteris paribus*, is always to be welcomed. Terrorism is always, necessarily, morally wrong. Period. Yet as powerfully attractive as this simple view might be, matters are seldom so simple, and all else is seldom equal.

First, many conventional military operations satisfy the definition of terrorism articulated above. For example, the RAF's area fire-bombing of Hamburg on 27 July 1943, and the US Army Air Force's detonation of atomic bombs over Hiroshima and Nagasaki on 6 and 9 August 1945, qualify as acts of terrorism according to this definition. Were such actions morally justified? Many believe that they were. But if so, then it is reasonable to ask under what *other* sorts of conditions might acts that qualify as terrorism be morally justified. On the other hand, if a blanket moral rejection of terrorism would logically entail a moral rejection of these acts of conventional warfare, then those acts, and others like them, were morally wrong, and consistency demands that they should be described as such without attempting to maintain an incoherent moral distinction between acts of terrorism and those acts of war.

Second, it could be (and often has been) argued that although it is 'regrettable' that acts such as area bombing and dropping atomic bombs had to be undertaken, they were necessary in order to prevent the even greater harm that would have resulted from a Nazi invasion of Britain, and a full-scale US ground invasion of Japan, respectively. Sometimes, it seems, it is necessary to cause great harm in order to prevent even *greater* harm, or in order to bring about some greater good. In other words, sometimes the end really does justify the means, even when the means are truly terrible. Although professional ethicists sometimes reject this reasoning as irredeemably odious and symptomatic of an impoverished moral sense, in fact we (and they) often are willing to act in ways that in isolation might seem morally forbidden if we judge the likely outcome to be sufficiently valuable. Likewise, some actions that might have seemed morally risky when contemplated beforehand are lauded as morally brilliant after they have (perhaps with a healthy dose of luck) achieved some great good. In short, we are sometimes willing to judge the morality of actions by their actual consequences, even when bringing about these consequences requires causing great harm. But if so, then there is no reason to suppose that all acts of terrorism *have* to generate more terrible than good consequences. Whether some acts of terrorism can be justified by their consequences is a matter that has to be carefully examined rather than decided a priori.

Finally, it is commonly taken for granted that acts of terrorism necessarily violate fundamental human rights, and therefore that no acts of terrorism can ever be morally justified. If these assumptions could be shown to be correct, this would effectively settle the matter of the morality of terrorism. Human rights must always be respected. But what if there are situations in which 'achieving effective respect for the fundamental human rights of the members of one group . . . requires the violation of the fundamental human rights of the members of another group' (Held 1991,

p. 75)? If rights violations can be morally justified in such situations, it follows that not all rights violations are necessarily morally wrong, even from a perspective that values respect for rights. But if so, then a space has been created within which it is possible to ask whether some acts of terrorism that violate human rights might be morally justified for the sake of achieving greater effective respect for rights.

The absurdity of inquiring into the morality of terrorism, it seems, is not as self-evident as it might at first have appeared. Our moral intuitions are perhaps an important source of moral *data*, but rational evaluation of the morality of actions requires the judicious application of moral *theories* (Shanahan 2003). Whether acknowledged or not, every moral evaluation presupposes some principle or standard in relation to which actions are assessed. *Moral theories* are these standards made explicit and rendered more precise. They provide explanations for what makes an action right or wrong (their explanatory function), and they provide guidance for determining whether a contemplated course of action should be pursued (their prescriptive function). It is noteworthy that included in the IRA's carefully crafted statement of its abandonment of the armed struggle is an assertion about the unqualified moral legitimacy of that struggle: 'We reiterate our view that the armed struggle was *entirely* legitimate' (emphasis added). The IRA's leadership did not elaborate nor explain how this judgement was reached. The major aim of this book is to deploy the concepts, theories and resources of moral philosophy in order to evaluate the IRA's claim of unqualified moral legitimacy. With due care to identify relevant similarities and differences, the conclusions reached here can be extended to understand the morality of other terrorist campaigns.

These preliminary remarks presage how I intend to proceed. Chapter 1 critically examines the 'standard republican narrative' which attempts to explain and legitimate the Provisional IRA's armed struggle by framing it as a heroic struggle against a foreign invader. My concern is to calibrate that account against the facts in order to have a historically accurate interpretation that can serve as a basis for the discussions of later chapters. Fundamental to the republican movement's ideology are the convictions that 'blood sacrifice' is causally efficacious, that the armed struggle was 'necessary' and that it is the 'destiny' of the Irish people to achieve a united independent sovereign state. Chapter 2 critically examines these elements of 'republican metaphysics'. Chapter 3 undertakes a critical examination of a wide range of republican arguments in support of the claim that 'the Irish people' are entitled to an independent self-governing state. In each case the republican arguments are found to be less rationally persuasive than their advocates take them to be.

Republicans insist that the use of 'physical force' (including what most observers would classify as acts of terrorism) is morally justified in the pursuit of their political goals. Assessment of this claim requires the careful application of moral theories to the IRA's armed struggle. Chapter 4 explores whether the IRA's armed struggle can be morally justified in terms of traditional Just War Theory. Chapter 5 examines the morality of that struggle in relation to consequentialist moral considerations. Chapter 6 considers whether the IRA's campaign might be morally justified in relation to a concern for rights. In each case I will argue that the IRA's use of terrorism was not (or was not obviously) morally justified – not because this is a moral truth knowable a priori, but because this conclusion emerges from a charitable application of fundamental moral theories to the IRA's armed struggle. I will also consider various 'possible worlds' in order to address the further question of whether it *could* have been morally justified had its world been different in certain specific respects.

Although the focus of this book is the morality of the IRA's armed struggle, that struggle was conducted in symbiotic relation with other groups with their own diametrically opposed agendas. Understanding and evaluating the IRA's armed struggle requires some understanding and evaluation of the activities of these other groups as well. Chapter 7 examines and critically evaluates British counter-terrorism in Northern Ireland. Chapter 8 explores the related issue of the British state's alleged use of terrorism in its fight against the IRA. An Epilogue extends the book's examination of the morality of terrorism by briefly considering how the conclusions reached here might have broader significance.

In writing this book, decisions had to be made about its intended audience and hence about how much background material to include. It became apparent that I could not provide a general introduction to recent Irish history, *and* a primer on moral philosophy, *and* delve as deeply as I desired into a moral analysis of the conflict, while staying within my page limits. Fortunately, plenty of other books cover the first two tasks quite well, permitting me to concentrate on the third task. Consequently, this book presupposes in the reader a basic familiarity with the conflict in Northern Ireland, and to a lesser extent a basic familiarity with the methods of analytic moral philosophy. For those lacking such backgrounds, I suggest that they first read a reliable introductory text on the Northern Ireland conflict, such as *Making Sense of the Troubles*, by David

McKittrick and David McVea (2002). Following that, they might read the best scholarly treatment to date of the Provisional IRA, namely, Richard English's book *Armed Struggle* (2003). Both of these are substantial books. Readers who wish to acquire just the basics so that they can begin fully enjoying the present book as soon as possible might wish to consult the considerably shorter works covering roughly the same ground by Feeney (2004) and O'Brien (2004), respectively. Excellent books on analytic moral philosophy abound. *Applying Moral Theories*, by Charles Edwin Harris Jr (2006), is a particularly elegant and readable introduction to the most important moral theories.

The formerly unthinkable can now be thought. The Northern Ireland Troubles can finally be referred to in the past tense. As one scholar has observed, 'if Northern Ireland's conflict really is starting to slip into history there is more need than ever for its story to be fully and truthfully told' (Wood 2006, p. 345). A critical examination of the morality of the IRA's armed struggle is one element of this story that has so far not been 'fully and truthfully told'. My hope is that by doing so in this book we will be in a better position to comprehend, evaluate and respond appropriately to other conflicts whose histories lie still in the future.

CHAPTER I

The Meaning of August 1969: Calibrating the Standard Republican Narrative

The turmoil of August 1969 is remembered by Northern Irish Catholics as if it had a clear meaning. That meaning is accepted not just by republicans but by many who oppose them yet who trust themselves to understand the fundamental anxieties that perpetuated the IRA campaign . . .

(Malachi O'Doherty 1998, p. 35)

INTRODUCTION

In its July 2005 statement declaring an end to the armed struggle, the leadership of the IRA reiterated its view that 'the armed struggle was entirely legitimate'. Assessing statements of legitimacy requires normative analysis. But normative analysis requires first establishing the relevant non-normative facts. Thus, determining whether the IRA's armed struggle was morally legitimate requires first securing an accurate factual understanding of that armed struggle itself. Doing so might seem straightforward, but certain 'myths' promulgated by the republican movement have served to obscure the fundamental nature of the IRA's campaign. Consequently, identification and evaluation of these myths must precede the normative project of later chapters. I will not argue that these myths are false in all respects, but rather that they contain partial-truths at best and that the reality is considerably more complicated. Although along the way I will try to make clear why it matters for the moral evaluation of the IRA's armed struggle that we have an accurate understanding of the relevant facts, the full importance of the 'demythologising' project of this chapter will only become evident later.

The Standard Republican Narrative

Republicans prefer to explain themselves by telling a story. It is a story that has been repeated many times, and is always presented as being simply an objective description of historical and political events.[1] According to what I will henceforth call 'the standard republican narrative', Ireland has always been a single nation. Prior to the Norman invasion in 1169, the Irish had their own system of law, culture and language, and their own political and social structures. Ireland was subdued by superior arms in the twelfth century and has been controlled by England ever since, but its spirit of freedom has never been extinguished. In each generation Irish patriots have taken up the cause of Irish freedom and have passed on the torch to others.

Although modern Irish republicanism traces its political origins to the movement of the United Irishmen of the 1790s, the 1916 Easter Rising was its defining event. The Rising was crushed after a week, but the exe-cution of sixteen of its leaders awakened the Irish people to the liberation struggle. In the all-Ireland general election of 1918, the Sinn Féin politi-cal party won seventy-three seats in the Westminster Parliament (com-pared to only twenty-six for the Unionist party and a paltry six for the Irish Parliamentary party) – a landslide representing an overwhelming popular mandate for an Irish Republic. Nonetheless, Britain refused to grant the Irish people their democratic right to freedom. In the Irish War of Independence from 1919 to 1921, the Irish Republican Army fought Britain to the negotiating table. In 1921 Ireland was partitioned into the Free State, comprising twenty-six counties and having dominion status with the UK, and Northern Ireland, comprising six of the nine counties of the historic province of Ulster. The consent of the Irish people for this artificial arrangement was never sought nor freely given, making both Northern Ireland and the Free State illegitimate political entities.

Following partition, Northern Ireland was essentially a one-party state, with the Ulster Unionist Party (UUP) controlling all aspects of life in the Six Counties, despite the fact that the unionist community constituted no more than 20 per cent of the entire Irish nation. The British government actively fostered political division between Irish Catholics and Irish Protestants through an arrangement that politically, economically and socially privileged the latter. Because Northern Ireland had been inten-tionally created as 'a Protestant state', the Unionist government at Stormont in Belfast enforced institutionalised discrimination against Catholics. Although Catholics constituted an overwhelming majority in

Ireland, for almost fifty years they were an oppressed minority within an artificially contrived sectarian North East Irish statelet.

Inspired by Dr Martin Luther King Jr's civil rights movement in the United States and by student protests in France, in January 1967 Catholics in the Six Counties organised their own civil rights movement with the formation of the Northern Ireland Civil Rights Association (NICRA). Their modest demands included equal voting rights, an end to gerrymandered voting districts, fairness in the allocation of housing, an end to discrimination in employment, and a repeal of the draconian Special Powers legislation of 1922 – put in place to control the Catholic community. Despite the reasonableness of these demands, they were viewed by unionists as a threat to their privileged position, who then responded with violence. Peaceful civil rights demonstrators were attacked by members of the B Specials, a brutal sectarian part-time police force, and by armed loyalists. The Protestant-dominated police force of Northern Ireland, the Royal Ulster Constabulary (RUC), simply watched.

August 1969 was the flashpoint. On 12 August 1969, during a 15,000-strong Protestant Apprentice Boys march in Derry intended to trumpet Protestant superiority over Catholics, B Specials attempted to enter the densely populated Catholic Bogside area of the city, but were prevented from doing so by barricades erected by residents who feared that their homes were about to be attacked. Catholics used petrol bombs to keep the police at bay. Two days of rioting followed, which became known in the nationalist community as the 'Battle of the Bogside'. Catholics established 'Free Derry' in the Bogside, a self-policed 'no-go' area, preventing state security forces from entering. The violence quickly spread to Belfast, where Catholics rioted in solidarity and in order to further stretch police resources. Protestant mobs responded by launching a pogrom, setting fire to hundreds of Catholic homes. Catholics living in Belfast's Bombay Street were forced out of their homes and saw their entire neighbourhood burned to the ground. The RUC responded to the deteriorating situation by spraying the remaining Catholic homes with bullets from heavy-calibre Browning machine guns mounted on armoured vehicles. Eight Catholics were killed in the violence.

Faced with the prospect of a collapse into anarchy of its oldest colony, on 14 August 1969 the British government at Westminster sent troops to Derry to restore order. Additional troops were sent to Belfast the next day. Because the army's official mission was to restore stability to the province, the soldiers were at first warmly welcomed by Catholics, who believed that they would provide protection from loyalist mobs and the sectarian police force. It soon became evident, however, that far from being neutral, the army was firmly on the side of the Protestant establishment, a fact that became painfully obvious when the British army enforced a curfew in nationalist areas on 3–5 July 1970, and then interned hundreds of innocent nationalists on 9 August 1971, and yet again when British paratroopers murdered fourteen unarmed Catholic civil rights demonstrators in Derry on 'Bloody Sunday', 30 January 1972. After that, the army's true role as an army of occupation could no longer be doubted.

The violence of August 1969 was the watershed for the IRA. A small remnant of the old IRA still existed, but in the aftermath of the failed Border Campaign of 1956–62, it had become run down. Armed with just a few old pistols and rusty rifles, it was powerless to protect Catholics in Belfast from loyalist mobs. A revitalised IRA arose in response to the urgent need to defend the Catholic community, but there was disagreement about how best to do this. Some favoured uniting the Catholic and Protestant working classes in common cause against the state. Others emphasised the need to reorganise and rearm in order to first defend Catholics, and to then go on the offensive against the British occupation to demand a complete British withdrawal from Ireland – the only real guarantee of lasting safety for Catholics. The IRA split in December 1969, with the former group becoming known as the Official IRA, and the latter group becoming known as the Provisional IRA. Whereas the former continued its quest for a socialist workers' revolution, the latter took a more traditional military approach to the plight of Catholics in the North. Hence the Provisional IRA arose as a direct response to the state-sponsored violence of 1968–9, and ultimately as a necessary response to injustices resulting from British colonial rule in Ireland. Initially choosing only non-violent means to secure freedom for the Irish people, republicans quickly met with a repressive response from the British government. It was only then that they exercised their right as Irish people to defend their liberty by the use of arms. To symbolise its origins as a response to the state's violence against Catholics in August 1969, the Provisional IRA chose as its emblem a phoenix rising from the ashes, representing the resurrection of the IRA from the ashes of burnt-out Catholic Belfast. Its subsequent military operations throughout the 1970s, 1980s, and 1990s were extensions of this basic moral mandate.

Although republicans had been active in political initiatives on behalf of the nationalist community from the beginning, in the wake of the hunger strikes in 1981 Sinn Féin emerged as a real political force in the 1980s, carrying on the work of the civil rights movement in its demand for equal rights for nationalists, making substantial electoral progress, and defining a workable peace strategy in key documents such as 'A Scenario for Peace' (1987) and 'Towards a Lasting Peace in Ireland' (1992). Yet without justice there can be no peace. Calls for the IRA to disarm could not be heeded because that would leave the nationalist community in the Six Counties defenceless against state-sponsored unionist death squads. The IRA will never give up the armed struggle until the Irish nation has achieved its God-given destiny as united, independent and free. As Bobby Sands, the courageous 1981 H-Block hunger striker declared, *Tiocfaidh ar la* ('Our day will come').

THE PROVISIONAL IRA's ARMED STRUGGLE IN FOCUS

I have rehearsed the standard republican narrative in some detail because it is essential for understanding the preferred public image of the republican movement. In order to have a factual basis for later discussions, however, it is important that the accuracy of this account be assessed. In a historiographic movement known as 'revisionism', some Irish historians in the mid-twentieth century, sceptical of traditional narratives and committed to re-examining original sources in a detached, objective and non-politicised manner, began applying critical scholarly tools to standard nationalist histories of Ireland in order to determine, so far as possible, what really happened in Ireland's history, and why (Boyce and O'Day 1996; Brady 1994; Hutchinson 1996). The standard republican narrative has not been immune to revisionist re-evaluation (O'Malley 1983, pp. 295–8), and has not emerged unscathed.

The Civil Rights Movement and the IRA

According to Sinn Féin's official history of the conflict in Northern Ireland, the civil rights movement's 'peaceful demand for basic rights . . . was met with violence from the forces of the sectarian state' as nationalist neighbourhoods in Belfast and Derry were attacked by the RUC and by unionist mobs. Hence, 'once more the peaceful pursuit of change in the form of the Civil Rights Movement had been met with violence from the British state and so it was that the armed struggle gained predominance again as the republican strategy' (http://www.sinnfein.ie/history).

In this account, the rise of the civil rights movement and the resumption of the IRA's armed struggle were distinct but causally related events, with the former predating the latter. The civil rights movement arose in response to state-sanctioned discrimination against Catholics. Violent attacks against civil rights activists and the nationalist community demonstrated that an armed struggle was necessary to secure the reforms demanded by Catholics in the Six Counties. The implication appears to be that the IRA had the same goals as the civil rights movement, such that had the authorities responded appropriately to the modest demands of the civil rights movement, there would have been no need for the IRA to restart the armed struggle, and consequently it would not have done so. Thus, according to republican ex-prisoner Anthony McIntyre, writing in the mid 1990s, 'the republican movement and its activities, including the use of political violence, is not . . . mainly . . . a dynamic towards a united Ireland, but is . . . a dynamic for reform within the North of Ireland' (McIntyre 1995, p. 98). Likewise, republican Patrick Magee attempts to set the record straight by insisting: 'people talk about fighting for a united Ireland, but really that was always just a means to political ends: . . . to extend democracy as much as you can, and [to get] political strength and the strength of your communities' (English 2003, p. 339). Civil rights, not a united Ireland, was the raison d'être that made the IRA's armed struggle necessary.

The relationship between the IRA, the civil rights movement and the resumption of the armed struggle is more complex than either the standard republican narrative or these glosses on it suggest. The least controversial element of that narrative is the claim that Catholics in the northeast of Ireland were victims of significant discrimination. Since the seventeenth century, Protestants loyal to the British Crown had been in the majority in six of the nine counties of Ulster. The creation of Northern Ireland in 1921 gave this demographic fact added political potency. In 1966, Northern Ireland had a population of 1.5 million: 65 per cent Protestant, 35 per cent Catholic. Their majority status allowed Protestants to impose their will on the Catholic minority with relative impunity. Catholics were treated as second-class citizens, with priority for jobs, housing and opportunities for political representation given to Protestants. Some scholars have disputed that discrimination against Catholics was as extensive as the data concerning inequalities suggest (Hewitt 1981), or even that there was discrimination at all (Barritt and Carter 1962; Calvert 1972; Wilson 1989). It is undeniable, however, that there were vast differences in unemployment rates, civil service appointments, housing conditions and electoral representation between Catholics and Protestants, and that discrimination played a significant role (Smith and Chambers 1991; Whyte 1983). Gerrymandered electoral boundaries, in particular, ensured that unionists would remain in power, and that Catholics would be essentially powerless to effect significant social change legislatively (Tonge 1998).

Some Catholics concluded that if positive change was going to occur, it would have to come about as a result of their own efforts to organise and mobilise the Catholic populace. In January 1967 the Northern Ireland Civil Rights Association (NICRA) was formed as an umbrella organisation bringing together various groups concerned with civil rights, including the Campaign for Social Justice, trade unionists, liberal Protestants, middle-class nationalists and the 'Republican Clubs' (especially the Wolfe Tone Societies; English 2003, p. 85). NICRA's stated agenda was entirely reformist, insisting on 'British Rights for British Subjects' (NICRA 1978). Its very title implied a tacit recognition of the legitimacy of the Northern Ireland state. Its demands included equal voting rights, an end to gerrymandered voting districts, fairness in the allocation of housing, an end to discrimination in employment and a repeal of the Special Powers Act of 1922. Entirely absent from the stated agenda was the republican demand for an end to partition. As one civil rights organiser later put it, 'NICRA was a reformist organisation, out for limited change in the North, not an end to the northern state, much less a transformation of Irish society north and south' (McCann 1992, p. 179).

In its first eighteen months NICRA accomplished little (Jackson 1999; Purdie 1988). Its members wrote letters to MPs in the House of Commons and published a series of pamphlets setting out their case that Catholics in the province were severely disadvantaged – all to no discernible effect. In mid-1968, NICRA organised a series of peaceful street demonstrations to publicise its complaints. Despite the fact that such demonstrations were not overtly nationalist, and indeed appeared to give Protestants just what they wanted – a willingness on the part of Catholics to end their 'rejectionist' stance toward the Northern Irish state – loyalists reacted with alarm. Catholic-led civil rights marches were seen by loyalists as making territorial claims. As they saw it, to march in Ulster is to stake a claim on territory (a deeply entrenched view that is still made manifest every summer during the 'marching season' in Northern Ireland when the issue of which parades are permitted to proceed through which neighbourhoods dominates the news, and often leads to violence).

This was a view shared by many unionists. In their view, the civil rights movement, far from being non-sectarian and concerned solely with reform, was nationalist to the core. Empowering Catholics was seen as a first step on a slippery slope that would end with the abolition of partition. Some unionists declared that NICRA (or the CRA) was just the IRA in disguise, and that the civil rights campaign was merely a cleverly constructed Trojan horse for armed republicanism to renew its attempt to achieve a unified Ireland by taking advantage of a destabilised North. Shortly after a 5 October 1968 civil rights march in Derry, Minister of Home Affairs William Craig told the *Irish News* that 'there is little doubt in police circles that [the civil rights movement] is, in fact, a Republican front' (Purdie 1988, pp. 33–4). As the Ulster Unionist Party politician John Taylor later explained, 'It was seen by myself and fellow Unionists as a new means of overthrowing Northern Ireland and forcing Northern Ireland into a united Ireland. It was seen as a nationalist plot to overthrow the state' (Taylor 1999, p. 51).

This unionist view is clearly at odds with the standard republican narrative's account of the relationship between the civil rights movement and the IRA. Although the assertion that the IRA was a cuckoo in the nest of the civil rights campaign has often been dismissed as a predictable manifestation of 'unionist paranoia', it should not be so breezily rejected. A number of scholarly analyses have argued that the IRA was, in fact, deeply involved in the civil rights movement from the start – although how deeply it was involved, and to what effect, are matters of some dispute. Alvin Jackson concludes that 'though republicans were influential in moulding the civil rights agenda, this is very far from saying . . . that NICRA was merely a sophisticated ruse, a libertarian camouflage for violent nationalism' (Jackson 1999, p. 367). Henry Patterson claims that northern republicans assumed a 'key role' in the creation of NICRA in January 1967 (Patterson 1997, pp. 112–13). Bob Purdie writes that 'NICRA had been founded as a direct result of an initiative taken by a section of the Republican Movement' (Purdie 1988, p. 34) and that 'agitation on civil rights was seen as a means of undermining Unionism and as a step toward a united Ireland' (Purdie 1988, p. 38; cf. Purdie 1990). Thomas Hennessey (2005, p. 129) credits the IRA itself with the creation of the civil rights movement in Northern Ireland. Finally, Richard English states unequivocally that 'the Northern Irish civil rights movement . . . originated from within the old IRA . . . with the explicit intention of bringing down the Northern Ireland state' (English 2003, p. 82).

Additional considerations of a strategic nature bolster these historical judgements. A civil rights campaign could serve the IRA's purposes in at least two ways. First, for those in the pre-split IRA wedded to a Marxist ideology (who would later become the Officials), a civil rights movement might precipitate an internal collapse of the sectarian state. Ulster unionism and Protestant working class loyalty to Northern Ireland benefited from and relied upon systematic discrimination against Catholics, making the Northern Irish Protestant state itself fundamentally unreformable. A campaign for 'reform' would therefore necessarily be a campaign to undermine the sectarian state itself. The state would be unable to grant reforms without alienating the Protestant working-class, which would by this means come to see that it, too, was being exploited by the unionist state, thereby causing that state's collapse.

Second, for those in the pre-split IRA who favoured a more traditional military approach (who would later become the Provisionals), a civil rights campaign could help to create the conditions for the renewal of the armed struggle. As early as August 1966 the IRA's Army Council had decided to promote a civil rights campaign in Northern Ireland in order to harness the power of Catholic frustration in an assault on the unionist-dominated state. Secret IRA documents that fell into the hands of Unionist politicians indicated clearly that although the IRA was still primarily a military organisation, arming and training for violent conflict, political agitation would henceforth assume increased importance (Purdie 1988, p. 37). In the aftermath of a military campaign (the IRA's Border Campaign of 1956–62) that had failed due to lack of popular support, what better way to 'provoke repression from the police and the B Special constabulary . . . and [to thereby] provide the space for the IRA to emerge as a "people's" defence force' (Patterson 1997, pp. 89–90)? In short, 'the emergence of a mass civil rights movement seemed to offer rich opportunities, which [the IRA] was eager to seize' (Patterson 1997, p. 115).

Additional evidence supports this interpretation. White notes that Ruairí Ó Brádaigh and other veterans of the 1950s 'believed that the ground was being laid for a full-scale guerrilla campaign . . . The civil rights movement had mobilised people. If it was built on the back of this mobilization, an IRA campaign might succeed' (White 2006, p. 148). Provisional IRA Chief of Staff Seán MacStiofáin later wrote that the pre-split IRA leadership at the time believed that the civil rights movement could be manipulated to allow the IRA to undertake 'offensive action . . . on the main national objective of ending British Rule' (MacStiofáin 1975, p. 113). This suggests that even if, *pace* some unionists, the civil rights movement was neither entirely the creation of IRA strategising nor completely controlled by the IRA at the highest levels, it was nonetheless skilfully exploited by the IRA for its own political agenda.

The relationship between the civil rights movement and the resumption of the IRA's armed struggle was thus more complicated than the standard republican narrative suggests. That narrative implies that the civil rights movement had been ruthlessly crushed by the state, thus demonstrating the necessity of an armed struggle to secure the sought-after reforms. Yet this claim is dubious for several reasons.

First, as a movement aimed at securing civil rights for Catholics in Northern Ireland, the civil rights movement was arguably a success. By early 1970 most of its original demands had been met (although the introduction of internment in 1971, and the introduction of even more sweeping emergency legislation in 1973, meant that *complete* satisfaction of Catholic demands for civil rights would always be a moving target). Significantly, the satisfaction of most of the civil rights movement's demands *preceded* the escalation of the IRA's bombing campaign, suggesting that the latter had different aims than the former. Steve Bruce, writing in 1994, put the issue with characteristic bluntness: 'The persistence of republican violence after the legitimate grievances of the minority have been addressed and redressed proves that this conflict is not about civil rights; it is about ethnic power' (Bruce 1994, p. 46).

Second, if the speculation reported above about republican motivations for involvement in the civil rights movement from the start is correct, then *from the IRA's standpoint* the civil rights movement was not a failure at all, because it *succeeded* in the way that mattered most. Its explicit challenge to Protestant privilege invited state violence against Catholics that the IRA could and did exploit by gaining mass support from the nationalist community. As a surrogate agent provocateur the civil rights movement was a grand success.

Finally, the 'failure' of the civil rights movement was a success for the IRA in another important respect. Most of NICRA's original demands were eventually met. (Indeed, the key civil rights demand of one-man-one-vote in local elections had been granted even before the Provisionals had come into existence.) But for the civil rights movement to have been seen by most Catholics as having significantly succeeded in its demands would have undercut one of the main republican arguments for the necessity of a united independent Ireland. The civil rights movement had as its explicit aim the reform rather than the destruction of the Northern Irish state. To the extent that Catholics in the Six Counties recognised the legitimacy of this state, sought reforms within it and succeeded in winning such reforms, to that extent republicans would lose the ability to persuade Catholics that the improvement of their condition required achievement of the core republican goal of a united independent Ireland. The prospect of Catholics in the Six Counties embracing 'British Rights for British Subjects' would have constituted a complete rejection of the republican ideal. As a leading republican admitted in 1988, 'repression we can cope with, reform we can't' (Patterson 1990, p. 20).

State Violence and the Rise of the Provisional IRA

According to the standard republican narrative, the pre-split IRA played no significant role in the violence erupting in Derry and Belfast in August 1969. It simply *couldn't* have played any significant role, nor even have *tried* to play a significant role, because in the aftermath of the failed Border Campaign it had become run down and was equipped with only a few aged and practically useless weapons. It was caught on the wrong foot and was simply overwhelmed by the sheer momentum of events. The Provisional IRA arose in December 1969 in response to state violence the previous August. As the Sinn Féin history of the conflict tenselessly reports, in 1969 'the IRA, in response to the Battle of the Bogside in Derry, unionist pogroms in Belfast and the introduction of internment without trial, goes on the offensive' (http://www.sinnfein.ie/history).[2] In other words, the IRA re-emerged as an active guerrilla army following, and *in reaction to*, state violence. The implication is that had the state not engaged in illegitimate violence against the Catholic community, the IRA would not have re-emerged and felt it necessary to adopt an offensive posture against the state.

This version of the events of late 1969 has been repeated so often that it goes largely unquestioned, especially by working-class Catholics, the republican movement's main audience. Malachi O'Doherty, himself a witness to many of the events unfolding in Belfast at that time, notes that:

the rioting of those days is recalled as a pogrom in which the state, supported by loyalists, ran wild and attacked and murdered innocent Catholics . . . [who] realised that they were defenceless and open to attack from Protestants and the state. Therefore they needed the IRA, and the IRA needed guns. (O'Doherty 1998, pp. 35, 38)

21

In this recounting (which O'Doherty himself rejects), the Provisional IRA was 'born out of the volition of history' (O'Doherty 1998, p. 37).

The accuracy of this aspect of the standard republican narrative can be questioned. First, it is worth noting that in the period immediately preceding the eruption of violence in Northern Ireland, membership in the IRA steadily increased from about 657 Volunteers in 1962, to 763 in 1963, to 807 in 1964, to 923 in 1965, to 1,039 in 1966 (Dixon 2001; Hennessey 2005), indicating that the pre-split IRA was not quite as 'run down' as the standard republican narrative suggests. Second, the question of whether IRA violence was simply a consequence of antecedent state violence merits closer examination. The important question here is whether the IRA simply reacted to, or instead had a hand in provoking, the state violence that erupted in August 1969 and which it subsequently exploited so effectively.

On the one hand, some scholars otherwise unsympathetic to republican self-justifications have been willing to give them the benefit of the doubt on this issue. According to M. L. R. Smith, although the IRA was certainly hoping for an end to the honeymoon period after British troops arrived in August 1969, there is little evidence to suggest that the IRA intentionally provoked the army into overreacting. In Smith's view, the IRA discouraged rioting because 'they did not wish to cause hardship to the residents from whom they derived their support and who they aspired to protect' (Smith 1995, p. 93). Whether the IRA was as concerned to safeguard the nationalist community as this explanation requires will be considered shortly.

On the other hand, Henry Patterson is more sceptical. He notes that, outdated or not, the IRA had guns in the Lower Falls on the night of 14–15 August 1969, and that in an atmosphere of inter-communal rioting the mere presence of such weapons served to incite the Protestant mobs to greater violence and encouraged the RUC to respond with superior firepower. He concludes that 'the frenzied, systematic burning of Catholic houses in the Lower Falls, Clonard and the Ardoyne was not inevitable. The IRA's use of guns contributed powerfully to the remorseless intensity of the Protestant onslaught in these areas' (Patterson 1997, p. 128). O'Doherty (1998, p. 38) sounds a similar note: 'It is impossible to know now if a combined force of police and loyalist mobs would have attacked the Falls Road, had hundreds of people there not been organised by republicans into overrunning the police, but it seems unlikely.'

Given the confusion and the rapid proliferation of rumours at the time, it is impossible to produce a definitive answer to the question of who committed the first act of violence in August 1969 (although Hennessey 2005, pp. 237–85 comes as close as anyone is likely to in doing so). Based on the available evidence, however, it appears that the pre-split IRA contributed to, encouraged and ultimately exploited the state violence of August 1969. The Provisional IRA did not arise simply as a consequence of state violence in 1968–9 in order to protect the nationalist community. Elements of the Provisional IRA were already in place at this time, and these individuals recognised the potential of, and seized the opportunity afforded by, the violent clashes of 1968–9 in order to resurrect the centuries-old ideal of an armed struggle in pursuit of a united independent Ireland. Contrary to the scenario implied in the standard republican narrative, the IRA was there at the beginning of the conflict, and rather than simply responding to state violence, it actively encouraged it as a way of creating the conditions necessary for completing the unfinished business of 1916–21. In short, the evidence supports the conclusion that 'the Provos were revolutionaries, whose desire to engage in a war existed before, and helped to create, the conditions within which it could lastingly be fought' (English 2003, p. 146).

The Essential Defensive Function of the Provisional IRA

According to the standard republican narrative, the first and most fundamental function of the Provisional IRA was defence of the Catholic community from unionist pogroms and state violence. Gerry Adams has written that by 1972 the IRA constituted 'a defensive force of unprecedented effectiveness' (Adams 1986, p. 53). In 1997 a leading Sinn Féin politician referred to the Provisional IRA as 'the defenders of our people for the last twenty-five or thirty years' (English 2003, p. 339). Calls over the years for the IRA to decommission its weapons could not be heeded because it would leave the Catholic community defenceless against the state violence of the security forces, and at the mercy of state-sponsored loyalist death squads.

That the Catholic community in Northern Ireland has at various times needed defence can be taken as a given. Whether the Provisional IRA provided this defence, or created a greater need for it, are distinct issues. It is often taken for granted that the Provisional IRA did provide such defence. For example, according to M. L. R. Smith, 'The Provisionals derived genuine popular kudos from fulfilling such a practical function . . . [the Provisional IRA's] popularity, in the main, was not forced but rested on the legitimacy acquired from its protective role' (Smith 1995, p. 93). The assumptions here seem to be that the Provisional IRA *saw itself*, and was seen *by the Catholic community*, as an effective defence force, and that it *was* in fact effective as a defence force. Each of these assumptions merits examination.

Begin with the third of these assumptions. What evidence is there that the IRA provided an effective defensive shield for Catholics, either at the outbreak of the Northern Ireland conflict or over the decades to follow? Clearly the pre-split IRA did not prevent loyalist mobs from attacking peaceful civil rights marchers in October 1968, or from destroying Catholic neighbourhoods in Belfast in August 1969. The Provisional IRA did not prevent the British army from ransacking Catholic homes during the Falls Road curfew in July 1970; nor did it resist the imposition of internment without trial throughout the Six Counties in August 1971; nor did it take up defensive positions when British paratroopers began killing unarmed civil rights demonstrators in Derry in January 1972. Ironically, although the incidents just mentioned loom large in the standard republican narrative, in none of them did the IRA provide effective defence. Indeed, in the first three years of the Provisional IRA's existence, 171 Catholic civilians were killed by loyalists or by the security forces (http://cain.ulst.ac.uk/sutton/index.html), the very people from whom the Provisional IRA claimed to be providing effective protection for Catholics.

The incident that occupies pride of place in republican accounts of the IRA as a nationalist protector is the brave defence of St. Matthew's church in the Short Strand area, a small Catholic enclave in Belfast surrounded by Protestant neighbourhoods. On 27 June 1970, loyalist mobs armed with petrol bombs threatened to burn down St. Matthew's and were poised to kill the priests inside as well. Provisional IRA Belfast Commander Billy McKee and other members of the IRA took up arms to defend the church. In the ensuing gun battle, three Protestants were shot dead, one IRA volunteer was killed and McKee was seriously wounded, but the church was saved. The IRA had redeemed itself for August 1969. As *An Phoblacht/Republican News* declared a decade later,

> The heroic defence of the Short Strand in June 1970 showed the fruits of all the reorganising and training that had followed August 1969, and that when it came to it the Irish Republican Army could and would defend the oppressed nationalist people. (*An Phoblacht/Republican News*, 28 June 1980; in English 2003, p. 135)

As (perhaps) the only unequivocal instance in which the Provisional IRA fulfilled its self-described role as a protector of the nationalist community, this action has become far more important for republican propaganda purposes than the event itself was at the time, considered purely as a defensive action. Even here, however, caution is warranted. Many Protestants, at the time and even decades later, viewed this as nothing more than carefully cultivated republican propaganda, arguing that republicans were in fact the primary aggressors in this incident and that, far from acting as defenders, they had in fact provoked the violence in which they were then embroiled (Hennessey 2007; Taylor 1999).

The evidence that at the outbreak of the Troubles the IRA was effective in defending Catholics turns out to be considerably less substantial than is often supposed. The assumption that the IRA continued in the years and decades to follow to function as an effective defensive shield rests on an even slimmer foundation, as some Provisionals have on occasion been willing to admit. As one ex-IRA man explained,

> As a functional, practical strategy did the IRA protect Catholics, did they succeed in protecting Catholics, from loyalist attack by its activities in 1974, '75, '76? I would say no. Did they make it worse for Catholics? I would say no. At least they were promoting themselves as somebody who would do something . . . The IRA, who were supposed to be defenders, could never actually defend . . . So the only way to appear to be defending, to appear to be active, was to take other people out. (English 2003, pp. 173–4)

In order to support the assumption that the Catholic community would have been on the receiving end of *more* violence had the IRA not been there to defend it, one would need to compare the actual world with a possible world in which the IRA did *not* take on the role of defender of the Catholic community, and indeed did not engage in any acts of violence at all. Charting the topography of possible worlds is notoriously difficult. We can never know for sure how much violence would have been inflicted on the Catholic community in a possible world in which the Provisional IRA did not exist or did not attempt to defend it by 'taking people out'. Nonetheless, there are grounds for offering a somewhat less sanguine judgement.

First, one can consider how much overall death, destruction and misery have been visited upon the Catholic community given the fact that the IRA *has* (according to its own account) served as a defensive force to protect this community. Since 1968, approximately 1,534 Catholics have been killed in Troubles-related violence (http://cain.ulst.ac.uk/sutton/index.html). It is impossible to know how many Catholics have been injured in Troubles-related violence, but because the number of Catholic fatalities represents roughly half of the total death toll for the Troubles, and about 30,000 injuries have been attributed to Troubles-related violence, a figure of approximately 15,000 injuries to Catholics is perhaps a not unreasonable estimate. The actual totals in both cases may be significantly higher than this. Clearly the IRA has not been *directly* responsible for every Catholic death and injury in the conflict, although the data suggest that the Provisional IRA is the organisation most directly responsible for the greatest number (341) of Catholic Troubles-related deaths in Northern Ireland. By contrast, the Ulster Volunteer Force (UVF), a Protestant paramilitary organisation, comes in a distant second as directly responsible for 278 Catholic Troubles-related deaths. The British army comes in third as directly responsible for 253 Catholic Troubles-related deaths (http://cain. ulst.ac.uk/sutton/index.html).

Direct responsibility for Catholic deaths is one way of gauging the effectiveness of the Provisional IRA as a Catholic defence force. But one also has to consider how many of the Catholic deaths from loyalist paramilitaries and from the British army would have occurred if the IRA had not been a factor. As O'Doherty avers, 'In strict literal terms, I think you can only judge the Provisionals as having provided defence if you can argue that more Catholics would have been killed by Protestants and the army if there had been no IRA' (O'Doherty 1998, p. 70). If we are comparing the actual world with a possible world in which the IRA was not a causal factor at all, it is hard to imagine that the Catholics of the Northern Ireland of this possible world would have experienced anything close to the violence that the Catholics of the actual Northern Ireland experienced. The reason is straightforward:

> If defence is protection, marked by the reduction of casualties . . . then what the IRA did for the Catholic community was the precise opposite, for it plunged Catholics into a war with the British army and escalated the sectarian tensions . . . putting them in danger from murderous loyalists. (O'Doherty 1998, p. 72)

O'Doherty sums up his assessment of the IRA as a defensive force by observing, 'the fact is that the Provisionals articulated not defence but defiance, and the cost of that defiance was increased casualties among the Catholic working classes' (O'Doherty 1998, p. 73). Charles Townshend sounds a similar note: 'In fact the defenders brought down more trouble on the people they claimed to be protecting' (Townshend 1999, p. 208).

Second, one can look at particular incidents involving violence against Catholics and ask whether there is any reason to suppose that any of those *specific* incidents would have occurred had the IRA not acted as it did. Three examples that figure prominently in the standard republican narrative can be cited to suggest that, *sans* the IRA's provocations, Catholics would not have experienced the violence that they did in these incidents. (1) Within four months of the split in the IRA in December 1969, the Provisionals launched a bombing campaign against commercial targets. The British army responded by enforcing a curfew in nationalist areas in Belfast on 3–5 July 1970, in which Catholic homes on the Falls Road were ransacked in a search for weapons and explosives; eight Catholics were killed in the ensuing violence. (2) The Provisional IRA intensified its urban bombing campaign in the spring and summer of 1971. In an effort to quell IRA activity, the British government introduced internment without trial on 9 August 1971. At 4:15 that morning, thousands of British troops entered the Catholic areas of Belfast and Derry, breaking down doors and dragging off suspected terrorists. Of the 342 suspects rounded up that morning, all were Catholic. Many of those taken in for questioning were beaten, brutalised and tortured to extract information. (3) During the last two weeks of January 1972, the IRA was increasingly active in Derry, firing hundreds of rounds at the security forces. On 27 January a soldier was shot at Bligh's Lane, and the IRA killed two young RUC officers in Derry when it riddled their car with bullets (English 2003, p. 148). Intelligence reports for 28 January reported that 'the IRA are determined to produce a major confrontation by one means or another during the march' scheduled for two days later (Hennessey 2007, p. 266). On 29 January there were intense exchanges of gunfire between the army and the IRA in Derry. The following day, Sunday, 30 January 1972, with tensions running high as a result, British paratroopers killed thirteen unarmed civil rights marchers in Derry who were demonstrating against internment without trial – which had been introduced in an effort to contain IRA violence. Moreover, despite denials by the IRA that its members engaged the paratroopers on Bloody Sunday, the best available evidence indicates that shots had been fired (by members of either the Official IRA, or the Provisional IRA, or both) at the paratroopers moments *prior* to the commencement of their ill-fated arrest operation (Hennessey 2007, pp. 280–5, 348). It is *possible* that the Falls Road curfew, internment without trial and Bloody Sunday (or their equivalents) would have happened without the provocative IRA activities that immediately

27

preceded each of them, and *nothing said here should be read as absolving the British army of direct responsibility for its actions.* But there is no reason to suppose that these events *would* have happened without the prior provocations supplied by the IRA.

Finally, one can compare the levels of violence against Catholics during those periods when the IRA has been on ceasefire and after it had abandoned its armed struggle, on the one hand, with the level of violence against Catholics when the IRA was most actively involved in its armed struggle, on the other. The year that began with Bloody Sunday also marked the peak of intensity of the IRA's offensive campaign and the single most violent year of the conflict. In 1972 there were 10,628 shootings, 1,853 bombings and 479 people killed in Troubles-related violence in Northern Ireland, with 234 of these deaths directly attributable to the Provisional IRA. This was also the year that Catholic deaths from Troubles-related violence peaked, with 239 Catholics being killed. In 1994, thirty-six Catholics died from Troubles-related violence. In the three years following the IRA's 1994 ceasefire, Catholic deaths from Troubles-related violence dropped to seven, ten and eight deaths, respectively. Since the 2005 announcement of the end of the IRA's armed struggle, there have been just three Catholic Troubles-related deaths (http://cain.ulst.ac.uk/sutton/). Correlation is not necessarily causation. Striking and dramatic correlations, however, often provide clues that permit cautiously drawn causal inferences, especially when combined with more direct evidence. The evidence reviewed above strongly suggests that the assumption that the Catholic community was safer thanks to the Provisional IRA is quite simply false. More disturbingly, it seems clear that the IRA's 'defensive' efforts were a primary cause of Catholic casualties.

Not every organisation lives up to its aspirations. It could be argued that although the IRA was not especially *effective* in providing defence to Catholics, it nonetheless had that as a primary *goal*, and that it continued to be a primary raison d'être for its existence. This considerably more modest claim is vulnerable to the observation that the IRA had decades to assess the causal consequences of its operations and their impact on the community it claimed to represent and defend. The most obvious consequence of its operations, besides the death and destruction inflicted on the security forces and their perceived collaborators, was the death and destruction visited upon the Catholic community in direct or indirect reaction to IRA violence. The connection between its operations and their actual effects on the nationalist community was presumably as well-known to the

IRA leadership as it was to those outside the movement. By itself this does not show that the IRA did not have as a primary goal the defence of the nationalist community. But it does present a puzzle: if the IRA's strategy of violence so obviously had the effect of *increasing* violence against the Catholic community to whose protection it had pledged itself, and upon which it depended for vital support, why did it take so long for the IRA to abandon that strategy?

The idea that the leadership of the Provisional IRA simply did not notice the correlation between its operations and the violence inflicted on the Catholic community can be set aside as implausible. This leaves three broad classes of explanations. Perhaps the IRA was locked into a military strategy from which it could not escape, despite the consequences for those it claimed to protect. As Smith (1995, p. 13) speculates, the deeply ingrained traditional republican 'romantic' preference for an armed struggle took on a life of its own, encouraging violence not apparently related to the achievement of political or practical objectives. Although there is probably some truth in this, ultimately it makes the IRA's activities irrational, which is belied by their otherwise eminently rational character.

A second possibility is that the IRA leadership really did think that it was defending the Catholic community. Although in the short-term the bombings, sniper attacks and assassinations that constituted the bulk of the Provisional IRA's activities invited retaliation against ordinary Catholics by the security forces and by loyalist paramilitaries, it might be thought that such activities were necessary for creating the conditions for the 'ultimate' defence and protection of the nationalist community. That is, 'since the Provisionals believed that ultimately only in the framework of a united Ireland could Northern Catholics be properly protected, then they may have seen little contradiction in the provocation of the security forces in this manner' (Smith 1995, p. 99). If so, then they appear to have been mistaken. Catholics in Northern Ireland are now safer than they have been in thirty years, despite the failure of the republican movement to achieve its cherished political goals.

A third, more sinister possibility is that engaging in activities that consistently drew violence into their community over some three decades was intentional and part of a well-planned strategy. Patterson suggests as much when he writes that the Provisional IRA correctly calculated that its 1971 bombing campaign against commercial targets owned by prominent Unionist businessmen 'would lead to increased pressure on the Unionist government and the British state for a policy of repression'

(Patterson 1997, p. 151). This repression – 'saturating Catholic areas, house searches, large-scale screenings of the population, and so on' (Patterson 1997, p. 152) – ensured that the nationalist community remained thoroughly alienated from the state, and hence that any accommodation short of ending partition would be considered unacceptable. The introduction of internment without trial in August 1971, rather than catching the IRA by surprise, was the result of an IRA strategy designed to bring about precisely that result. By forcing the premature introduction of such a repressive measure the IRA guaranteed that British information about IRA members would be out of date, and hence that many ordinary Catholics would be caught up in the internment sweep (Alonso 2007). They might be detained, abused and thoroughly alienated from the state as a result, but their anger could be used to the IRA's gain.

In other words, while publicly posing as the Catholic community's selfless defender, much IRA violence had as its aim to use that community (along with loyalist paramilitaries and the state's security forces) for its own agenda. Ensuring that the Catholic community remained thoroughly alienated from the state, and that it believed that the state was so thoroughly, essentially, fundamentally unreformable that only its destruction would suffice to alleviate their plight, would prevent the constitutional nationalists of the SDLP (Social Democratic and Labour Party) from making palatable the 'Catholic unionist' sop of reform within the illegitimate northern statelet.

Some former IRA volunteers have been remarkably forthright in admitting that drawing violence into their community was part of a deliberate strategy. As Sean O'Hara explains, describing the rationale of attacks on soldiers in Derry in 1971,

> If we provoked them enough, if we attacked them enough, at some point it wasn't just us they were going to be shooting at, it was the people . . . They had to shoot civilians and we knew that. And we agitated and agitated until we got to that situation. We had to move the violence to a new level, right? And the only way that we could do that was causing thems [sic] to commit the outrageous, to shoot innocent civilians . . . As soon as they shoot somebody, you cry 'Foul, they are shooting innocent people.' Which, in a sense, they were, but the situation was engineered . . . We needed the whole situation to be escalated. The thing was always planned. (Alonso 2007, p. 76)

That this was the IRA's strategy in *Derry* in 1971, where the following year would begin with the tragedy of Bloody Sunday, makes this admission all the more remarkable.

Some of the Provisionals' own public pronouncements also suggest that IRA violence was intended to provoke counter-violence from the state, rather than to protect Catholics, or even to score conventional military victories. Shortly after its formation the Provisional IRA announced that 'as soon as it became feasible and practical, the IRA would move from a purely defensive position into a phase of combined defence and retaliation' (MacStiofáin 1975). The language here is significant, albeit easily overlooked. 'Retaliation' is not usually considered, by itself, to be a legitimate military, much less defensive, objective. This could perhaps be charitably read as a warning that the Provisionals would enact revenge for any further atrocities committed against Catholics, but it could also be read as indicating that an aim of IRA operations would be to invite retaliation on the part of the security forces as a way of escalating, or at least maintaining, a sufficiently high level of conflict in order to sharpen the divisions between oppressors and oppressed, and to guarantee that no peaceful settlement of the conflict that did not meet their requirements would be forthcoming. If this latter reading is correct, then the provocation of counter-violence was intentional from the start. Hennessey (2005, p. 337) is unsparing in his assessment that 'it was the Provisional IRA that, more than any other single factor post-1969, transformed the nature of the Northern Ireland conflict from a tribal dispute into a cycle of sub-state and counter-state violence'. If this was the IRA's deliberate strategy, then it was wildly successful for over three decades.

Finally, it is worth considering the question of the Catholic community's embrace of the IRA as its official protector. Although for a brief time at the beginning of the Troubles the Provisional IRA was considered by some within the Catholic community to be engaged in its defence, that such defence had never been the primary activity of the IRA became more evident to Catholics as the conflict wore on. As Rogelio Alonso notes, 'many in the Catholic community perceived that far from being their protector, what the IRA really wanted to do was create the conditions in which they could then present themselves as the only organisation capable of offering such protection' (Alonso 2007, p. 49). Like all effective marketing of non-essentials, the best way to get others to 'buy' what one is selling is to convince them of their need for one's product or services, even if (unbeknownst to them) that need was created precisely in order to sell those services. The Provisional IRA had as its supreme goal from the beginning to force the withdrawal of British troops from the Six Counties as a necessary precondition for the creation of a united independent Irish nation-state. If achieving this goal meant drawing violence into the Catholic community, then, as the Catholic community itself eventually realised, the Provisional IRA was willing to do that.

The Provisional IRA and Sectarian Violence

According to the standard republican narrative, Provisional IRA violence, unlike state and loyalist violence, is not sectarian in nature. Republicans venerate Theobald Wolfe Tone (1763–98), a Dublin Anglican, who founded the United Irishmen as a secret society uniting Protestant, Catholic and Dissenter (that is, Presbyterian) in order 'to break the connection with England, the never failing source of all our political evils' (Douglas et al. 1999, p. 22). As one Provisional, echoing Tone, put it, 'We have no fight with the Protestants, in fact we detest these terms "Protestant" and "Catholic". . . Our fight is with the English for our God-given right to nationhood' (Smith 1995, p. 98). On 17 January 1976 *Republican News* carried a statement from the Provisionals declaring that 'the Irish Republican Army has never initiated sectarian killings, and sectarianism of any kind is abhorrent to the republican movement and to its philosophy' (English 2003, p. 173). Violence by the state's security forces and by loyalist paramilitaries, by contrast, is routinely described as sectarian in nature, as illustrated in these statements from three different republican web pages: 'For nationalists, life under Stormont rule meant institutionalised discrimination, electoral gerrymandering, human rights abuses and sectarian pogroms instanced by a sectarian state' (http://www.sinnfein.ie/history). 'In the mid-1960s . . . the peaceful demand for civil rights was met with violence from the forces of the sectarian state' (http://www.sinnfein.ie/introduction). 'Almost 700 people, 90.5% nationalists, have been victims of sectarian assassinations perpetrated by loyalist paramilitaries' (http://sinnfein.org/). Such statements could be multiplied almost indefinitely. State and loyalist violence is consistently described as sectarian; republican violence never is. Some commentators support this interpretation. According to Robert W. White, writing in 1993, 'Examination of who it is the IRA attacks (primarily police officers and soldiers) . . . suggests that IRA violence is not the product of sectarian motives' (White 1993, p. 90).

The fundamental difficulty in assessing this element of the standard republican narrative lies in distinguishing between IRA attacks on Protestants qua Protestants, and IRA attacks on Protestants who were selected for attack solely because of their membership in the security

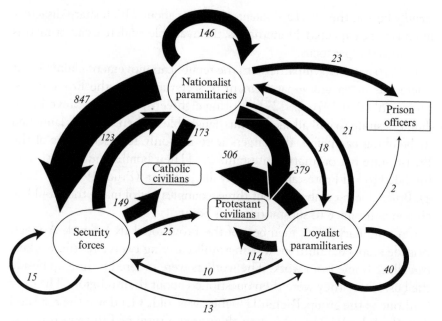

Figure 1.1 Troubles-related deaths in Northern Ireland, 1969–89. (Source: O'Leary and McGarry 1996, p. 25. Reprinted by permission of Thomson Publishing.)

forces. Not all violence is lethal, but as a first step toward resolving this difficulty, consider the overall shape of Troubles-related deaths in the first two decades of the conflict, as shown in Figure 1.1. During the first two decades of the Troubles, members of the security forces were by far the main victims of republican paramilitary attacks, constituting more than half of all fatalities attributed to republicans. From the very beginning, the RUC was viewed by republicans as a thoroughly sectarian Protestant police force more concerned with protecting Protestants and harassing Catholics than with enforcing the law. Apart from the brief 'honeymoon' period when British troops first arrived in Belfast and Derry in August 1969, the British army, including the locally recruited Ulster Defence Regiment (UDR), had been considered by republicans to be a foreign occupying force and as a legitimate target for attack. Because the security forces consisted overwhelmingly of Protestants, republican attacks on security forces were typically perceived by loyalists as sectarian attacks, as attacks on Protestants qua Protestants – or what Stevenson (1996, p. 51) calls 'sectarianism by proxy'. However, whether republican attacks on the security forces were in fact sectarian ultimately depends not on the *victims' identity* but on the *attackers' intent* – an issue about which sharp disagreement is to be expected. Nonetheless, the available evidence can bring this issue into sharper focus.

In 1976 a writer sympathetic to the republican movement claimed that 'there was never any great element of sectarianism in the Provisionals' campaign' (Bell 1976, p. 127). Writing eighteen years later, Steve Bruce didn't hesitate to call all such claims 'laughable': 'when the IRA launched its bombing campaign, the targets were not only representatives of the British state but ordinary Protestants . . . [Their bombs and bullets] were intended to kill Protestants and they did just that' (Bruce 1994, pp. 123– 4). Bruce doesn't elaborate, but three examples out of many that could be chosen will suffice to substantiate this point.

On 5 January 1976, members of the Provisional IRA South Armagh Brigade stopped a minibus in Kingsmills carrying twelve textile workers travelling home from work. The workers were ordered to line up beside the bus, where they were then questioned about their religion. The only Catholic of the group, Richard Hughes, was told, 'Get down the road and don't look back.' The IRA men then fired a total of 136 rounds in less than a minute at the remaining men. Ten men died at the scene; one man survived, despite receiving eighteen gunshot wounds. On 17 February 1978, an IRA bomb killed twelve people at the La Mon House Hotel, in County Down. The victims had been attending the annual dinner dance of the Irish Collie Club. IRA volunteers hung an incendiary bomb on a window of the hotel's restaurant. When it exploded, the bomb sent a massive fireball through the restaurant, destroying everything and everyone in its path. A dozen people, all Protestants, were literally burned alive. On 8 November 1987, the IRA struck in Enniskillen, County Fermanagh, at the annual Remembrance Day ceremonies commemorating the Protestant dead of two world wars. As local Protestants gathered for the laying of poppy wreaths at the war memorial, the IRA detonated a huge bomb hidden in a nearby building, sending tons of debris into the crowd. Eleven people were killed and sixty more people were seriously injured. (The IRA later explained, unconvincingly to many, that the bomb had been triggered prematurely by a British army radio signal.) None of these three operations involved attacks on the security forces. All of those killed were Protestants. These and many other examples suggest that IRA violence was often directed at Protestants qua Protestants in precisely the same way that much loyalist violence was directed at Catholics qua Catholics.

Table 1.1 Victims of Republican and Loyalist Paramilitaries: 1969–89

Status of Victim	Agency Responsible			
	Republican		Loyalist	
	No.	%	No.	%
Security Forces	847	52.7	10	1.4
Republican Paramilitary	146	9.1	21	3.0
Loyalist Paramilitary	18	1.1	40	5.7
Catholic Civilian	173	10.8	506	71.8
Protestant Civilian	379	23.6	14	16.2
Other Civilians	22	1.4	12	1.7
Prison Officers	23	1.4	2	0.3
TOTAL	1,608	100.1	605	100.1

Source: Adapted from Bruce 1992, p. 277. By permission of Oxford University Press. © Oxford University Press.

Despite the sectarian nature of much republican violence, there is nonetheless a perception that loyalist violence was significantly *more* sectarian than IRA violence. Niall Ó Dochartaigh writes that 'both in their actions and in their rhetoric, loyalist paramilitaries emphasised their hostility to Catholics as a group . . . and regarded virtually all Catholics as legitimate targets' (Ó Dochartaigh 2005, p. 254). Consequently, whereas most of the deliberate killings carried out by the IRA were of members of the security forces, virtually all of the killings attributed to loyalists were of uninvolved Catholic civilians. This perception appears to be borne out by the data for some time periods, as Table 1.1 shows. In the first two decades of the conflict, republicans were responsible for 72.7 per cent of the fatalities due to paramilitaries. Of these, 52.7 per cent were suffered by the security forces, whereas Protestant civilians constituted only 23.6 per cent of the fatalities. By contrast, loyalists were responsible for 27.3 per cent of the fatalities due to paramilitaries. Of these, only 1.4 per cent were suffered by the security forces, whereas Catholic civilians constituted 71.8 per cent of the fatalities attributed to loyalist paramilitary attacks. Although between 1989 and 1993 the Loyalist Volunteer Force (LVF) and Ulster Freedom Fighters (UFF) killed twenty-six members of the IRA, Sinn Féin and relatives of republican families (and indeed out-killed the IRA in 1992–3), the *majority* of loyalist killings still involved innocent Catholics who appear to have been chosen precisely because of their religious identity (Taylor 1999, p. 213).

However, such data cannot unproblematically be taken to show that loyalist violence was more sectarian than republican violence, because it is impossible to know how many security personnel were killed by republican paramilitaries, at least in part, because they were presumed to be Protestants. Bruce assumes that this number is substantial because republican violence was *fundamentally* sectarian:

> In so far as republicans are more likely than loyalists to confine their killing to 'legitimate' targets, this is . . . because so many Protestants are legitimate targets that the desire to kill Protestants is fully satisfied, and the capacity to kill fully utilised, without going beyond that very long list of candidates. (Bruce 1994, p. 125)

Alas, this is pure speculation.

Regardless of how sectarian IRA violence in fact was, it is safe to say that it was considerably more sectarian than the standard republican narrative concedes. But there remains the question of the IRA's motivation for sectarian killings. How did such killings relate to the IRA's agenda?

At the simplest level of analysis, the sectarian nature of much Provisional IRA violence was a predictable consequence of its self-appointed role as a Catholic defence force. To 'defend' Catholics qua Catholics meant 'taking people out', which in Northern Irish society meant taking action against Protestants (Smith 1995, p. 120). When ordinary Catholics were targeted by loyalist paramilitaries simply in virtue of being Catholic, as they increasingly were in the 1980s, this seemed to republicans to require retaliation in kind against Protestants.

A second explanation appeals to the relative availability of targets. As the British government instituted its policy of Ulsterisation from 1976 on, giving the locally recruited RUC and UDR more of the day-to-day responsibility for security in Northern Ireland, the availability of security force targets who were more likely to be Protestants increased as the availability of British soldiers (whose religious identity was less uniform) decreased. British soldiers also tended to be more heavily armed, equipped with better backup in case of trouble, and considerably more lethal themselves, making them less attractive as routine targets.

A third explanation considers the political benefits of targeting ordinary Protestants. Doing so could be useful for ensuring swift retaliation from loyalist paramilitaries. Padraig O'Malley suggests a Protestant backlash served the interests of the IRA, not only by providing opportunities for the IRA to promote its image as the protector of the minority community, but also by making the province appear more ungovernable, thus cleverly manipulating Protestants in a way that was inimical to their own interests (O'Malley 1983, p. 290). M. L. R. Smith offers a similar analysis. Provoking loyalists into violent retaliation could provide political benefits to the IRA in at least two ways: 'first, by provoking loyalist attacks, Catholics would continue to seek [the IRA's] protection and second, communal hostility polarised society and eroded the political middle ground which destroyed any hope for an internal settlement within Northern Ireland . . .' (Smith 1995, p. 122). He concludes that, 'the bulk of the circumstantial evidence suggests that some Provisionals were deeply involved in the sectarian war' (Smith 1995, p. 123) – a judgement that, given the evidence discussed in this section, is perhaps unduly cautious.

PEACE AND THE REPUBLICAN AGENDA

According to the standard republican narrative, the republican movement has always sought a peaceful resolution to the conflict in Northern Ireland, and clearly spelled out the conditions necessary for a peaceful resolution of the conflict in key policy documents such as 'A Scenario for Peace' (1987) and 'Toward a Lasting Peace in Ireland' (1992). Unfortunately, the British consistently rejected these conditions. Given this British 'rejectionist' stance, the IRA was left with no choice but to continue the armed struggle until its demands had been met.

This way of putting it makes it sound as if peace per se was the goal of the republican movement. A more accurate statement would be that the republican movement had as its goal the long sought-after Irish republic, which would (in its view) *entail* peace, but until that goal was reached peace was counter-productive to the revolutionary struggle. Rather than seeking a peaceful resolution of the conflict, the main business of the Provisional IRA for most of its existence was to ensure that Northern Ireland would *not* be peaceful, because peace would mean that 'the national question' could lay idle. Continued conflict would ensure that the republicans' main agenda item could never be ignored. It follows that the peace process should be disrupted whenever it threatened a political settlement short of the ending of partition. This is precisely what the republican movement did for several decades.

This alternative to the standard republican narrative might be called the Prolonged Ideological Resistance to Accommodation (or PIRA) interpretation.[3] According to this view, although one of the *root causes* of the conflict in Northern Ireland was a grossly unjust social organisation that systematically disadvantaged Catholics through institutionalised injustices, the primary cause of the *prolongation of the conflict* was republican paramilitary activity whose chief goal was to prevent any resolution of the conflict short of the establishment of a united, independent Irish nation-state. This is *not*, I hasten to add, meant to imply a moral judgement, because it is not a necessary moral truth that keeping a conflict going is always morally unjustified, and there are conceivable situations in which doing so is perhaps a moral imperative. The question of the morality of the republican movement's 'armed politics' is a distinct issue that is simply not addressed in the interpretation just sketched. The point here is to be clear about the republican movement's adversarial relationship to a peaceful resolution of the Northern Ireland conflict during the first three decades of the Troubles. Although the republican movement did eventually join with the peace-makers, for the preceding three decades peace was viewed as counter-productive to the revolutionary struggle.

CONCLUSIONS

My aim in this chapter has been to assess the accuracy of the standard republican narrative in order to arrive at a more accurate account of the Provisional IRA's armed struggle. The weight of the evidence suggests that the pre-split IRA was instrumental in the origins of the civil rights movement, that the movement had its own non-republican agenda aimed at improving the conditions of Catholics in Northern Ireland, but that the full potential of this movement to achieve this goal was thwarted when what was to become the Provisional IRA exploited it in order to advance its own ideological agenda. Like the car bomb, which the Provisional IRA accidentally invented in December 1971 and then used to such devastating effect, the IRA was in part responsible for the civil rights movement, probably did not at first fully anticipate its far-reaching propaganda potential for underwriting the armed struggle, but once its potential was clear moved quickly to capitalise on this discovery. Its relationship to the violence of August 1969 followed a similar pattern. The Provisional IRA did not arise simply as a consequence of state violence. Elements of the Provisional IRA were already in place in 1969, and these individuals recognised the potential of, and seized the opportunity afforded by, the violent clashes of 1968–9 in order to resurrect the centuries-old ideal of an armed struggle in pursuit of a united independent Ireland. The Provisional IRA's credentials as a Catholic defence force are dubious, to put it mildly, as it seems to have welcomed violence into the Catholic community in order to ensure that 'the national question' remain front and centre. Although there is some difficulty in determining precisely how sectarian was IRA violence, it is safe to say that it was considerably more sectarian than the standard republican narrative concedes. Finally, rather than working to achieve peace in Northern Ireland, the republican movement had an interest in ensuring that peace apart from the achievement of its political goals would remain elusive. With this more accurate understanding in hand, we can next go on to critically examine the metaphysical basis for the republican movement's faith in the efficacy of armed struggle and blood sacrifice in pursuit of the Irish people's destiny to achieve a united, independent, Irish nation-state.

Blood Sacrifice and Destiny: Republican Metaphysics and the IRA's Armed Struggle

I am dying . . . because what is lost in here is lost for the Republic and those wretched oppressed whom I am deeply proud to know as the 'risen people' . . . I may die, but the Republic of 1916 will never die. Onward to the Republic and liberation of our people.

(Bobby Sands, on the first day of his hunger strike in the Maze Prison, 1 March 1981)

INTRODUCTION

Within the republican world view, the Provisional IRA's armed struggle is seen as the contemporary manifestation of the tradition of heroic self-sacrifice inaugurated by Theobald Wolfe Tone and the United Irishmen in the 1790s, epitomised in the executions of Patrick Pearse and the other leaders of the 1916 Easter Rising, and given its definitive expression in the death of Bobby Sands and nine other martyrs of the 1981 H-Block hunger strike. Such acts were not merely instrumental; their true nature can only be properly understood as essentially spiritual offerings whose efficacy must be located on an entirely different ontic plane. Moreover, that the republican movement undertook an armed struggle against the British occupation of Ireland, rather than pursuing some less violent alternative strategy, was simply dictated by the circumstances. Given those circumstances, no other course of action was possible. Finally, it is the Irish people's God-given destiny to achieve the Republic declared in the 1916 Proclamation. Such an achievement is viewed not merely as a good, or even the greatest good, but as an *absolute good* such that its achievement would justify whatever sacrifices and hardships must be made en route to its realisation. It is the special

40

responsibility of the IRA to lead the Irish people to their divinely appointed destiny.

My aim in this chapter is to critically examine these aspects of the traditional republican world view. Doing so is important for the project of this book for several reasons. First, if the republican faith in 'blood sacrifice' entails spiritual transactions taking place beyond the realm of mundane experience, such that the most important causal effects of suffering and death are inaccessible to ordinary observation and analysis, then the project of Chapters 4, 5, and 6 of this book (which are grounded in the empirical details of the IRA's armed struggle) are hopelessly wide of the mark. Second, 'ought implies can' remains a bedrock of moral evaluation. If what happens of necessity is beyond the realm of moral evaluation, then moral evaluation of the IRA's armed struggle, conceptualised as the inevitable consequence of historical circumstances, makes about as much sense as normative assessment of the fact that planets move in elliptical orbits. Finally, if the IRA's armed struggle has a transcendental moral sanction in virtue of its role in actualising Ireland's God-given destiny, conceived as an absolute good meriting any cost, then the application of such pedestrian moral theories as Just War Theory, consequentialism and the morality of rights is moot, and the central project of this book is deeply misguided and doomed to failure. In sum, if any of the elements of the republican world view sketched above are accepted, moral analysis can gain no purchase on the IRA's armed struggle. Clearly, therefore, these aspects of the republican world view need to be critically evaluated.

The proposal to do so might seem quixotic. Republicans have often been described as having their own insular (in the sense both of 'island' and 'self-contained') world view that brooks no dissent from within, and recognises as valid no critique from without. One either professes allegiance to the republican 'political theology' or one doesn't. If one does, it will seem self-evident that the IRA's armed struggle is morally justified, and therefore not in need of critical evaluation. If one doesn't, it will seem just as self-evident that its armed struggle lacks moral justification. Either way, it appears, moral evaluation of the IRA's armed struggle is irrelevant. The flaw in this reasoning is that the supposed dilemma it describes depends on conflating the psychological and the logical. Republicans believe that their armed struggle was morally justified, and they are unlikely to be reasoned out of this view. Their adversaries are equally convinced that the IRA's armed struggle was *not* morally justified, and will resist any attempt to suggest otherwise. True enough. But from these facts about people's beliefs nothing whatsoever follows about whether that armed struggle *was* morally justified. The latter requires critical evaluation of the arguments for and against the claim of moral justification. First one must attempt to understand the IRA's armed struggle as accurately as possible, and then apply fundamental moral theories to the understanding thereby achieved.

The present chapter begins to bridge the gap between these two tasks by critically examining the conditions for the possibility of moral analysis of the IRA's armed struggle. The difficulty of doing so should not be underestimated. World views, replete with internally self-justifying explanations, are notoriously resistant to external critique. The republican world view is no exception. But there are ways of breaching its defences. One strategy for penetrating the insular republican world view is to realise that even islands must rest on deeper foundations, hidden from immediate view but accessible through careful excavation. What the apparently disparate republican notions of 'blood sacrifice', 'necessity' and 'destiny' have in common is a reliance on peculiar understandings of *causation*. The attempt to understand causation is a fundamental concern of metaphysics. The central task of this chapter is therefore to assess the republican world view by examining its metaphysical foundations, focusing especially on the role that notions of 'cause' play in this world view.

Blood Sacrifice and Martyrdom

Within the republican world view, the IRA's armed struggle is viewed as having been characterised by hardship, sacrifice and a courageous willingness of its volunteers to pay the ultimate price on behalf of the Irish people. When six Provisional IRA volunteers were killed on active service in February 1972, *Republican News* announced (echoing the 1916 Easter Rising rebel Sean MacDiarmada), 'They died so that we can live' (Alonso 2007, p. 7). Their heroic willingness to sacrifice themselves for the republican cause had deep historical roots. Despite overwhelming odds, Irish patriots such as Theobold Wolfe Tone (1763–98), Robert Emmet (1778–1803), and Patrick (Padraig) Pearse (1879–1916) took up arms against British oppression and willingly laid down their lives for the Irish nation. Pearse, in particular, memorably articulated the core republican conviction that self-sacrifice is ennobling and redemptive. Three years before the 1916 Easter Rising, he wrote that 'bloodshed is a cleansing and a sanctifying thing, and the nation which regards it as the final horror has lost its manhood. There are many things more horrible than bloodshed; and slavery is one of them' (Edwards 2006, p. 179). He described the death of Emmet, who was hanged, drawn and quartered for his role in the rebellion of 1803, as 'a sacrifice Christ-like in its perfection', and went on to assure his readers that Emmet's attempt 'was not a failure, but a triumph for that deathless thing called Irish Nationality' (Smith 1995, p. 12). In a graveside funeral oration for the Fenian (Irish Republican Brotherhood member) Jeremiah O'Donovan Rossa on 1 August 1915, Pearse ended with stirring words that have been echoed by republicans through the years:

> Life springs from death; and from the graves of patriot men and women spring living nations. The Defenders of this Realm . . . have left us our Fenian dead, and while Ireland holds these graves, Ireland unfree shall never be at peace. (Moran 1994, p. 146)

Pearse, perhaps more than any of the other leaders of the 1916 Rising, embraced the idea of the efficacious power of blood sacrifice. His martyr's death would do more to advance Irish freedom than mere military victory ever could, because 'it served to win the battle on the eternal plane where a new Ireland, resurrected, pure, Gaelic and Catholic, unspoiled by England . . . could emerge triumphant over its eternal enemy to assume its rightful place' (Moran 1991, p. 17).

Moved by the examples of Pearse and his compatriots, in his poem 'Easter, 1916' William Butler Yeats has often been seen as giving the romantic element of the republican struggle its definitive expression:

> We know their dream; enough
> To know they dreamed and are dead;
> And what if excess of love
> Bewildered them till they died?
> I write it out in a verse –
> MacDonagh and MacBride
> And Connolly and Pearse
> Now and in time to be,
> Wherever green is worn,
> Are changed, changed utterly:
> A terrible beauty is born.[1]

Transmuting defeat into victory, in Yeats' poetic vision the martyrs of Easter 1916 have been transfigured.[2] The parallels with traditional Christian imagery could hardly be more complete.

As Ian McBride notes, 'Pearse's hold over nationalist remembrance is inescapable. It was 1916 that facilitated the retrospective ordering of earlier rebellions into a cumulative sequence of inspirational defeats; and it was Pearse who defined the ideal of sacrificial martyrdom for future generations' (McBride 2001, p. 35). The Easter Rising of 1916, in particular, has assumed a mythic status within the republican movement. The event is celebrated annually and the IRA's leaders regularly invoke the spirit of the event in their public declarations. In its first public statement, the Provisional IRA in December 1969 announced: 'We declare our allegiance to the thirty-two-county Irish republic proclaimed at Easter 1916' (English 2003, p. 386). In its 1986 Easter message, the IRA insisted that its members 'are the inheritors of 1916 because they have the same spirit of freedom which motivated the 1916 rebels' (Smith 1995, p. 30). This spirit reached its apotheosis in the republican hunger strike in 1981 when ten men in the H-Blocks starved themselves to death in demand of recognition of their status as political prisoners. In the republican world view, theirs was just the most dramatic example of the daily sacrifices the men and women of Óglaigh na hÉireann have made, as acknowledged in the official statement announcing the end of the IRA's armed struggle: 'We [the leadership of the Provisional IRA] are very mindful of the sacrifices of our patriot dead, those who went to jail, Volunteers, their families and the wider republican base' (An Phoblacht/Republican News, 28 July 2005). This image of self-sacrifice as central to the IRA's struggle is not confined to official republican statements. Even some commentators not otherwise sympathetic with the IRA's goals recognise that the republican movement can only be understood as acting from a theology of blood sacrifice in which death brings life, defeat brings victory, and 'in mimetically dying on behalf of Ireland the republican martyr seeks to redeem both his country and himself' (Moran 1991, pp. 9–10).

The Necessity of an Armed Struggle

According to the standard republican narrative, the Provisional IRA arose in direct response to the state-sponsored violence of 1969, and its armed struggle was a *necessary* response to the social, economic and political injustices inherent in British colonial rule in Ireland. As one IRA volunteer explained,

> I don't think there was any other way we could have went. Armed struggle was forced upon us . . . It wasn't something the IRA went out to create. It was something that happened, we were the products of the sort of political climate that we're living in. (Alonso 2007, p. 83)

This view is also evident in some remarks of Danny Morrison, who at the time (1982) was the National Publicity Director for Provisional Sinn Féin: 'In Sinn Féin's case, elections are only one part of the overall struggle. The main struggle, the main thrust – *and this goes without saying* – is the armed struggle, because that's the only way to get the Brits out of Ireland' (in O'Malley 1983, pp. 275–6; emphasis added). In 1984 Gerry Adams described the Provisionals' bombing of the Conservative Party's annual conference at the Grand Hotel in Brighton as 'an inevitable result of the British occupation of the six counties' (*Irish News*, 13 October 1984). Two years later he described IRA violence as 'a necessary form of struggle' (Adams 1986, p. 64). Ruairí Ó Brádaigh, the first Provisional IRA Chief of Staff (and later President of Republican Sinn Féin), spoke for all republicans in August 1993 when he declared, 'As long as the British are in occupation of any part of Ireland, there will be a revolutionary movement to oppose them and that, in part, will of necessity include an armed wing, or armed struggle' (O'Brien 1999, p. 278). In 1994, a Sinn Féin writer stated confidently that 'the existence of injustice, allied to the absence of any real prospect of redress, made political violence inevitable' (*An Phoblacht/Republican News*, 8 December 1994). In 1995, republican ex-prisoner Anthony McIntyre wrote that British state strategies in Northern Ireland 'inevitably meant that the existing political conditions left no political space for nationalists to campaign in an exclusively peaceful manner' (McIntyre 1995, p. 105). In 2000, IRA bomber Patrick Magee explained, 'I believe that the IRA actions over the last thirty years were justified . . . There was simply no other way . . . Every generation of republicans has had to turn to violence' (English 2003, p. 342). Such statements could be multiplied almost indefinitely. The IRA's armed struggle, in this view, was an unavoidable product of Ireland's troubled history. Necessity rules the republican universe.

Ireland's Destiny

Regardless of temporary setbacks, apparent defeats and the occasional need to withdraw from action in order to re-strategise, within the republican world view ultimate victory is nonetheless guaranteed, because it is the destiny of the Irish people to overcome British oppression and to achieve the long-sought-for sovereign, united Irish republic. Although this destiny is obvious to republicans, it was not always obvious to all of those on whose support they depended, so there was a perennial need to rally ordinary Irishmen and Irishwomen to the eternal cause. The Proclamation of 1916, which the Provisional IRA considered to be its foundational document, is replete with the language of divine sanction, the fullness of time, and the blessings and protection of 'the Most High God'. It ends with the stirring declaration that, 'in this supreme hour, the Irish nation must, by its valour and discipline and by the readiness of its children to sacrifice themselves for the common good, prove itself worthy of the august destiny to which it is called'. In 1919–21 many responded to this call. The result was independence (of a sort) for twenty-six of Ireland's thirty-two counties. Liberating the remaining six counties remained the unfinished business of the Irish War of Independence. To the 'Irregulars' of the Irish Republican Army, defeated in the Irish Civil War (1922–3), to the IRA of the 1940s and 1950s (whose 'Border Campaign' fizzled out in 1962), and then (after the split in 1969) to the Provisional IRA, was bequeathed the duty to be the vanguard of this sacred destiny in the current age. As Bobby Sands wrote in his journal on the first day of his hunger strike in the Maze Prison in 1981, 'I may die, but the Republic of 1916 will never die. Onward to the Republic and liberation of our people'. The Provisional IRA's motto – *Tiocfaidh ar la* ('Our day will come'), bequeathed to the republican movement by Sands – captures this confident sense of historical destiny.

REPUBLICAN METAPHYSICS EXAMINED

The cogency of the republican world view is not self-evident. Because a world view is essentially an *interpretation* of reality that extends beyond the observable facts, direct empirical confirmation or refutation is impossible. Nonetheless, it does not follow that world views cannot be critically evaluated, or that facts are unimportant in their evaluation. First, at a minimum, to be cogent any world view has to be *consistent* with the observable facts, and ideally should also account for those facts by situating them in an explanatory framework that renders those facts more intelligible than they otherwise might be. In this sense it has to adequately 'fit the facts'. A world view can be understood as an inference to the best explanation. Hence a world view can fail by being incongruent with the observable facts or by failing to explain those facts as well as do other, competing explanatory frameworks.

Second, a world view can be evaluated by excavating the metaphysical presuppositions upon which it depends, and then evaluating these metaphysical elements in relation to one another. Because metaphysics refers to aspects of reality that are, by definition, inaccessible to ordinary observation, a simple comparison between a proposition expressing a metaphysical claim and 'the facts' is out of the question. But it is possible to ask whether a given metaphysical view is internally coherent. Not all metaphysical views 'hang together' equally well, in the sense of asserting mutually consistent claims about reality. Consequently, any world view can be evaluated by asking whether it provides the most reasonable explanation of the observable facts, and also whether it relies upon presuppositions that are mutually consistent. Both of these methods of evaluation are available and relevant for assessing the cogency of the republican world view.

Blood Sacrifice and Martyrdom Examined

Begin with the notion that blood sacrifice and martyrdom are efficacious in advancing the republican agenda. There are essentially three ways in which this can be understood. First, such acts can be understood as essentially symbolic acts that attract the favourable attention of those unfamiliar with one's agenda, arouse the emotions of those already predisposed toward one's agenda, and serve as a kind of moral extortion against those opposed to one's agenda. For example, had the British authorities not executed the leaders of the 1916 Easter Rising, their rebellion might have become a mere footnote in Irish history. By executing those leaders, however, their deaths acquired a powerful symbolic value that stirred the sentiments of the Irish population, resulting in widespread support for the republican goal of Irish freedom, manifested a few years later in the Irish War of Independence. Likewise, the 1981 hunger strikes were an enormously effective tactic insofar as they garnered worldwide attention for the republican movement, inspired many people to join the IRA, and secured enough votes for Bobby Sands to be elected to Parliament, all of which, in the short-term at least, can be interpreted as advancing the republican agenda. Thus:

Acts of blood sacrifice ➜ Psychological effects ➜ Advancement of the
and martyrdom   on a target audience   republican agenda

The sort of causation operative here is the just ordinary kind that social scientists might study. The questions associated with it are the usual ones that preoccupy social scientists attempting to understand the psychology and sociology of mass movements and societal trends.

47

Second, blood sacrifice and martyrdom could be considered efficacious in advancing the republican agenda by way of their influence in an eternal, timeless plane, according to which the very act of shedding blood in this world sets in motion unseen spiritual forces operating in a transcendent realm of value, eventually resulting in the advancement of the republican agenda back in the empirical world. Again, pictured schematically:

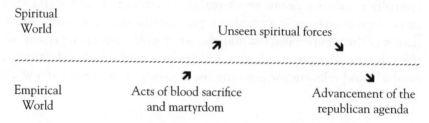

Spiritual World | Unseen spiritual forces

Empirical World | Acts of blood sacrifice and martyrdom | Advancement of the republican agenda

Acts of blood sacrifice and martyrdom in the empirical world initiate a causal sequence that passes through another, spiritual, realm before re-entering this world to issue in politically meaningful effects. Practical considerations about popular support and electoral victories play little or no role in this view. Instead, 'the would-be martyr is a gnostic who possesses a truth and destiny denied the masses' (Martin 1968, p. 97), namely, the truth that acts of blood sacrifice have their greatest significance through a kind of hidden 'moral causation' that eventuates in the desired political outcome. Although some 'hard men' of the republican movement (including some former hunger strikers) would deny that this spiritualised interpretation of blood sacrifice significantly informed their actions, the frequently casual concern with the practical political effects of many republican acts of self-sacrifice suggests that, historically at least, something like this picture comprises an important element of traditional republican metaphysics.

Third, the two accounts described above can be (and usually are) combined to form a two-level composite picture such that blood sacrifice and martyrdom are efficacious in advancing the republican agenda by operating on both a mundane *and* a spiritual plane:

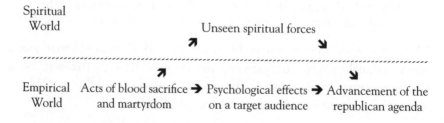

Spiritual World | Unseen spiritual forces

Empirical World | Acts of blood sacrifice and martyrdom → Psychological effects on a target audience → Advancement of the republican agenda

In this composite view, blood sacrifice and martyrdom have causal power as symbolic acts that attract attention, arouse emotions and engage the wills of those predisposed to be moved by such acts, *and* the very act of shedding blood in this world sets in motion unseen forces operating in a transcendental realm of value, with both chains of causation resulting in the advancement of the republican agenda in the empirical world.

Is this third, two-level composite view, cogent? Acts of self-sacrifice and martyrdom have had, let us suppose, some positive effects in advancing the republican cause. The question, then, is how best to account for such effects. In particular, the explanatory role of each causal chain in the two-level composite picture must be considered. The two-level picture posits two distinct causal chains issuing in the same observable effects. One problem with this composite picture is that there is no reason to suppose that *both* of these causal chains are necessary to fully explain the observable effects. It follows that one of these sets of causes is explanatorily superfluous. An application of Ockham's Razor would counsel us to excise one of the causal chains in the two-level picture. Yet the two causal chains cannot be considered co-equal because they do not have comparable evidential support. Specifically, whatever advancement of the republican agenda has resulted from acts of self-sacrifice and martyrdom appears to be adequately explained simply in terms of the observable causes operating in the empirical world. The causal chain in the mundane, empirical world is well-established and can hardly be denied. To jettison it is to reject basic social science methodology (to say nothing of ordinary empirical observation) as fundamentally misguided. The postulated causal chain running through the spiritual world, on the other hand, has no such credentials of explanatory success. One can easily imagine excising this part of the two-level composite view without loss of explanatory power. It is, as Williams James might say, a 'fifth wheel to the coach'. It does no work, and can easily be elided without loss.

This argument can be bolstered by considering more closely the actual efficacy of republican self-sacrifice and martyrdom, when it occurs, in advancing the republican agenda. With two distinct causal chains having the same political ideal as their intended effect, it might be reasonable to predict that republicans would by now have advanced much further toward the realisation of their ultimate goal of a united independent Ireland. In fact, however, the realisation of that goal appears as far off as ever, despite multiple (four, if we include the armed struggle and electoral politics as well) deliberately initiated causal chains having that as their intended effect. Consequently, in the two-level composite picture republicans need to account for the failure of multiple distinct causal chains rather than the failure of just one. This consideration provides some grounds for concluding that one of the postulated causal chains either does not exist, or if it does exist then it has failed to pull its weight.

A final consideration also weighs against the two-level composite picture. If the actual efficacy of acts of self-sacrifice and martyrdom in advancing the republican cause has been roughly proportional to the degree of publicity such acts have received, and all such acts are supposed to be equally efficacious in the spiritual realm, then this would suggest that the causal influence (if any) of such acts via a transcendental plane is insignificant. In fact, this does seem to be the case. The blood sacrifice and martyrdom of the 1916 rebels, and of the 1981 hunger strikers, received enormous publicity and were such as to move many to embrace the republican agenda. The blood sacrifice and martyrdom of other republicans (for example, those who died between 1916 and 1981) pursuing the same agenda, but minus the enormous publicity, were much less influential in advancing the republican cause. If acts of blood sacrifice and martyrdom are thought to be causally efficacious by way of transactions occurring in a transcendental realm of value, then such correlations become anomalous, suggesting that such supposed spiritual transactions are causally inert, or at least that the significance of such influences must be judged as more modest than republicans assume.[3]

A problem with the transcendental interpretation of the significance of blood sacrifice and martyrdom, then, taken either in isolation or as part of the two-level composite picture, is its explanatory poverty. But a different sort of problem afflicts the idea of blood sacrifice and martyrdom in both its empirical *and* transcendental interpretations. It is sometimes taken for granted that *actual* blood sacrifice and martyrdom, as distinct from an *ideology* of blood sacrifice and martyrdom, has been central to the republican movement. For example, Sweeney (1993, p. 432) poses the following question as the central problematic of his inquiry into 'Irish hunger strikes and the cult of self-sacrifice': 'Why do so many republicans choose a death of self-sacrifice?' His question takes for granted that many republicans *have* chosen self-sacrificial death. This can and should be questioned, although apparently it rarely is.

How important has *actual* self-sacrifice and martyrdom been within the republican movement? We can set aside the deaths of those republicans who died while assembling bombs, were shot by the security forces, were killed by loyalists, or were killed by other republicans. Such deaths count as self-sacrifice only in the most attenuated sense, because presumably such individuals did not intentionally will their own deaths any more than does any person engaged in dangerous military activities. Self-sacrifice to be such must be deliberate. It is undeniable that historically the *themes* of blood sacrifice and martyrdom have been important elements in the republican movement, and that much about that movement would be unintelligible without this recognition. But an exaggerated emphasis on the actual practice of self-sacrifice can lead to a distorted understanding of the republican movement.

For example, Moran notes that the spirit of self-sacrifice is most clearly seen in the cult of martyrdom associated with republican hunger strikes, emphasising that 'since 1916 nearly 9,000 Irish republicans have gone on hunger strike' (Moran 1991, p. 20). This certainly sounds impressive, until one looks more closely at the percentage of hunger strikes that actually resulted in self-immolation. Approximately 1,000 hunger strikes took place between 1916 and 1922. Of these, just four (0.4%) resulted in deaths.[4] Of the more than 8,000 prisoners who went on hunger strike on 14 October 1923 in opposition to the 1921 Anglo-Irish Treaty, just three (<0.04%) died before the strike was called off five weeks later (Sweeney 1993).[5] Two more republicans (Seán McNeela and Tony D'Arcy) died on hunger strike in 1940, as did Seán McCaughey in 1946, Michael Gaughan in 1974 and Frank Stagg in 1976. And, of course, ten republican prisoners (seven Provisional IRA and four Irish National Liberation Army (INLA)) died on hunger strike in 1981. In sum, of the more than 9,000 republican prisoners who, according to Moran, since 1916 have gone on hunger strike, twenty-two have starved themselves to death. Assuming that these figures are correct, this means that only 0.2 per cent of those Irish republicans who went on hunger strike succeeded in self-sacrifice. Some of those who embarked on self-immolation were prevented from carrying out their martyrdoms by family interventions, and most who fasted for more than thirty days probably suffered at least some long-term disabilities as a result. Even so, this suggests that precious few of those who undertook hunger strikes actually achieved the republican ideal of martyrdom.

Understanding the limited significance of *actual* self-sacrificial martyrdom within Irish republicanism is essential for bringing the republican movement in general, and the IRA's armed struggle in particular, into clearer focus. Reflecting an important element of republican self-understanding, in *Rebel Hearts: Journeys within the IRA's Soul*, Kevin Toolis sympathetically writes: 'In an obscure rain-sodden corner of northwestern Europe there was still a small group of believers who were prepared to lay down their lives for a cause' (Toolis 1996, pp. 25–6). Indeed, from reading republican literature one might suppose that republicans have spent most of their time, energy and resources engaging in symbolic acts of self-sacrificial martyrdom (and in community welfare projects).

Certainly the IRA nurtured its members' self-conception as potential martyrs for a noble cause. Yet the military dimension of the armed struggle was always central to the republican movement, and the IRA was first and foremost a *paramilitary* organisation which treated its members' lives as a military resource to be used strategically, no less than bullets and Semtex. Their primary value lay not in their deaths (although the republican movement was always willing to capitalise on their deaths), but rather in their capability of carrying out death-dealing operations. As Steve Bruce laconically observes, 'While they may do other things, paramilitaries are fundamentally concerned with killing people' (Bruce 1992, p. 276). Republicans are fond of quoting Terence McSwiney, Lord Mayor of Cork, who died in December 1920 in Brixton Prison after a seventy-four-day hunger strike: 'It is not those who inflict the most but those who suffer the most who will conquer.' Yet the IRA practised killing its enemies with a passion that was never invested in martyrdom. Despite hallowed traditional republican ideology and much influential propaganda, 'blood sacrifice' within the republican movement overwhelmingly meant sacrificing *other* people's blood.

Republican Necessitarianism Examined

Fundamental to any systematic conception of the world is a view of the nature and extent of *causation*. Why do events happen as they do? How much control over events does anyone have? To what extent could events have been different than they were? 'Necessitarianism' is the general philosophical view according to which all events are *necessary*, and hence could not be other than what they are. 'Causal determinism' is the necessitarian view according to which all events are rendered unavoidable by their antecedent *causes* (Taylor 1992, p. 55). Given specific antecedent causes, specific effects necessarily follow. Events, in this view, have a momentum of their own whose outcomes are thereby rendered inevitable.

Causal determinism *seems* to be presupposed in republican explanations of the necessity of the IRA's armed struggle.[6] This presupposition takes several different forms. Malachi O'Doherty notes that the republican movement benefited by presenting IRA violence as manifesting 'automaticity' (*sensu* Schelling 1966), that is, a kind of uncontrollability that must be accommodated and assuaged rather than reasoned with, much as one might try to mollify, rather than to engage in calm philosophical conversation with, an angry Doberman. Promoting this image permitted Sinn Féin politicians to argue that IRA violence was a straightforward product of circumstances, and therefore that only the correction of those circumstances – the end of partition and a British departure – could quell that violence.

The most obvious flaw in this presentation is that it appears to be inconsistent with the degree of control the republican movement exerted over the timing of IRA violence. When it sensed that its political objectives could be advanced by a temporary or permanent cessation of operations (as in, for example, 1972, 1975, 1994, 1996 and 2005), it could and did adjust the level of violence accordingly. Yet, as O'Doherty notes, 'If the violence can in fact be switched on and off to suit electoral purposes, it clearly isn't the passion of the aggrieved in action; rather, it is the tool of a thinking movement' (O'Doherty 1998, p. 158).

Likewise, the major circumstance said to render IRA violence inevitable – the British occupation of Ireland – was a *constant* throughout the Provisional IRA's campaign, yet the *intensity* of that campaign appeared at times to be carefully modulated to perceived political opportunities. Such a pattern is more consistent with agents making careful cost/benefit analyses and deciding on a course of action on that basis than with violence as a primal juggernaut rolling on until the conditions sustaining its existence have been radically altered.

There are additional reasons to be sceptical about the inevitability of IRA violence. As argued in the previous chapter, the republican movement was itself largely responsible for the cycle of violence in Northern Ireland, such that had it chosen a different strategy for achieving its political goals, the circumstances to which it was supposedly constrained to respond might well have been quite different. To the extent that circumstances constrained the republican movement's options, the agents of the republican movement themselves must take significant responsibility for this narrowing of possibilities.

Even when one's possibilities have been narrowed, however, perhaps through the effects of one's own choices, it is rarely the case that all options but one have been precluded. Circumstances, including those of one's own making, may restrict the choices available, and in that sense one can be described as a 'product of circumstances', yet within those circumstances there is typically room for genuine choice. Applying this alternative 'libertarian' view to the IRA's armed struggle casts it in a very different light. Robert W. White (1993, p. 64) expresses the relevant point nearly perfectly: 'Post-1969 Republicans are a product of events that force[d] them to make political choices'. Especially after internment in 1971 and Bloody Sunday in 1972, nationalists in Northern Ireland were faced with a political choice: 'on the one hand, they could continue to endorse peaceful agitation in the face of extreme state violence. On the other hand, they could embrace the appeals of . . . the Provisionals, who argued that the only method of bringing about change in Northern Ireland is through physical force' (White 1993, p. 83). White's characterisation of nationalists in Northern Ireland was true as well of those nationalists who were also republicans. At some level the individuals in question themselves realised this. A recurring theme in White's interviews with those who joined the Provisional IRA was that their 'involvement in political violence resulted from a conscious decision [to embrace what they] believed to be the most effective approach to bringing about political change' (White 1988, pp. 82–3; 1993, p. 93). Thus the IRA's armed struggle, from the birth of the Provisionals in December 1969 to the announcement of the end of the armed struggle in July 2005, took the path it did because numerous individuals made *decisions* among alternative possible actions that led to certain previously possible worlds being forever consigned to the realm of the impossible, thereby narrowing the range of subsequent possible future worlds. Although one must always choose from among the options that circumstances have provided (and there is no guarantee that history will be generous in providing alternatives), there are always at least *some* alternatives in any given situation.

This abstract assertion can be given flesh for a range of actors in the Northern Ireland conflict. Unionists could have instituted significant reforms prior to being forced to do so by the civil rights movement. They could have been far more open to giving nationalists avenues for pursuing their political objectives non-violently. The leaders of the civil rights movement could have chosen not to engage in deliberately provocative marches, such as the 1969 Burntollet march. Rather than splitting to form the Provisional IRA, those republicans who did so could have continued to follow the path taken by (what would become) the Official IRA, namely, the attempt to unite the Catholic and Protestant working classes.

In 1968–9 the future leaders of the Provisionals could have thrown their support behind those nationalists (some of whom went on to form the SDLP in 1970) who were also (albeit less impatiently) committed to Irish reunification, but who argued that reunification must be achieved through the consent of a majority of the people of Ireland, north and south, rather than by physical force. Much later, when the futility of the armed struggle had become abundantly clear, the leaders of the Provisionals could have joined, rather than derided, those in the Irish Independence Party. The IIP, formed in 1977, rejected British rule in Northern Ireland more strongly than did the more accommodationist SDLP, yet it eschewed armed struggle (Murray and Tonge 2005). Although by 1982 it had been eclipsed by Sinn Féin, for a few years it represented an alternative political approach. In sum, there was no necessity for the Provisional IRA to come into existence, and once in existence, there was no necessity for it to continue its armed struggle for three decades. It existed because many individuals, both in the leadership and also in the rank-and-file, rejected the alternatives.

Even after the Provisional IRA came into existence as a paramilitary organisation, significant options remained. Its leaders could have decided to restrict its activities to defence, as the Catholic Citizens' Defence Committee and the Catholic Ex-Servicemen's Association (CESA) did. The CESA was organised by Phil Curran in West Belfast in 1971 following the introduction of internment without trial. Its stated aim was the protection of Catholic neighbourhoods. The plan was to build and maintain a militia that would be prepared to defend Catholic neighbourhoods if they were again attacked by Protestant mobs. The CESA was paramilitary in nature but unarmed. At its most active in 1972 it could claim a membership of 8,000. An armed struggle to achieve a united independent Ireland was no part of its agenda. The fact that few have ever heard of the CESA testifies to the success of the republican movement in marginalising such groups, and hence polarising the de facto choices available to the Catholic community between the non-violent, political approach of the 'Catholic unionist' SDLP and the militant republican Provisionals. Alternatively, the Provisional IRA could have followed the lead of the Official IRA, which called a ceasefire in 1972 and ('officially', at least) restricted its paramilitary actions to defence and retaliation.

Another alternative, rarely considered or discussed, is that the leadership of the Provisional IRA could have decided to pursue a middle path between, on the one hand, non-violent civil rights agitation and, on the other hand, an armed struggle intended to expel the British presence from

Ireland. Even if it was true, as republicans typically claimed, that only violence could bring about genuine reforms in Northern Ireland, it does not follow that that violence had to be directed at first dismantling the Northern Irish state. The leadership of the IRA could have decided to wage an armed struggle directly for meaningful reform in Northern Ireland, rather than indirectly by attempting to end partition. It is interesting to speculate what the consequences might have been had the leadership of the Provisional IRA developed a comprehensive account of the requirements for genuine equality in Northern Ireland that did *not* require an end to partition, and then announced that it would engage in an armed struggle against the ruling government until that government had done all that it could to facilitate a transition to a genuinely just society. The Provisional IRA (unlike, for example, the ANC in South Africa) did not take this path, but had it done so the character of the conflict in Northern Ireland would have been quite different, and certainly much shorter.

Finally, even if the Provisional IRA was expressly formed in order to wage an armed struggle against the British presence in Ireland (that is, if that was its raison d'être, such that it would be a contradiction to talk about a *Provisional IRA* that was *not* dedicated to that goal), it could have eschewed an urban bombing campaign – virtually guaranteed to produce enormous foreseen but unintended collateral damage – in favour of an exclusive emphasis on the precision targeting of British military personnel. Such a strategy would presumably have resulted in far fewer civilian casualties, albeit more Provisional casualties. Again, had they chosen this path, the conflict in Northern Ireland would have looked quite different.

Contrary to the presupposition enshrined in the republican world view, therefore, an armed struggle was not *obviously* inevitable; rather, it depended fundamentally on the choices made by numerous individuals within the movement, but especially by the Provisional IRA's leadership. None of the crucial events in the Northern Ireland conflict would have taken place without the decisions made by specific individuals, each of whom could have chosen otherwise. As Richard English (2006, p. 377) stresses, 'the choices made – on all sides – were choices to which there were alternatives . . . there was nothing inevitable about the IRA's violence: not all working-class Catholics responded to Bloody Sunday in 1972 by joining the Provisionals and killing people.' Rogelio Alonso (2007, p. 64), likewise, notes that, 'other alternatives did, therefore, exist, in contrast to those who claim, deterministically, that the armed struggle was the only way'. Although every party to the conflict made choices that had important ramifications, Thomas Hennessey places particular emphasis on the choices made by the IRA: 'The single most disastrous decision that produced . . . two and a half decades of conflict was the decision of the Provisional IRA's Army Council in January 1970 to begin a war – their war – against the British state' (Hennessey 2005, p. 394). The IRA undertook its armed struggle despite the availability of radically different alternatives, not as the inevitable result of causes that left open one and only one possible course of action. Precisely because it was not inevitable, but fundamentally depended on the choices made by individuals, the Provisional IRA's armed struggle is a candidate for moral evaluation, and questions about the morality of that armed struggle remain live issues meriting normative analysis.

'Ireland's Destiny'?

Causal determinism is one manifestation of republican necessitarianism. A belief in destiny is another. A core republican conviction is that it is the Irish people's God-given destiny to achieve the united independent thirty-two-county Irish republic proclaimed in 1916, and it is the special responsibility of the Provisional IRA to spearhead this quest. Moreover, this destiny is understood to ground a right to political self-determination for the Irish people as a whole. Because it is a God-given destiny, ultimately nothing can prevent its realisation. As Anthony D. Smith notes, the idea of *destiny* carries far more emotional freight than notions of 'the future': 'destinies are predetermined by histories; destinies chart a unique course and fate; destinies speak of transcendence, perhaps immortality' (Smith 2001, p. 30). For republicans, the belief that 'Our day will come' expresses a necessary metaphysical truth whose negation represents not merely a *falsehood* (as if it were a merely contingently true statement), but rather a metaphysical *impossibility*. Failure to achieve Ireland's destiny is inconceivable.

Difficulties arise as soon as we begin to ponder the meaning of the word 'destiny' and what it might mean to struggle or fight for this destiny. One meaning of destiny is what *will*, necessarily, happen, no matter what; that is, what is fated to happen. Understood in this first, modal, sense, there would be no need to do anything to bring about Ireland's destiny; the Irish people's destiny *will* be fulfilled because it is the inevitable, predetermined fate beyond human control or influence that will necessarily come to be, irrespective of human decisions or actions. Presumably one's God-given destiny is not something that anyone could take away, deny or prevent from being realised, although conceivably individuals might be able to impede or delay its realisation. Understood in this sense, if a united independent Ireland is truly destined to be and therefore inevitable, it will come to pass even if the Army Council of the Provisional IRA renounces armed struggle and applies for enlistment in the British army.

Sometimes, however, the word 'destiny' is used to convey not what will, necessarily, happen, but rather what is *meant* to happen, in the sense of what is right, or fitting, or morally required, such that there is a *moral imperative* to bring the destined event to fruition. Understood in this second, voluntarist, sense, action is called for, but if republican metaphysics is assumed, then agents never act freely. If agents never act freely, then assertions of moral responsibility (which seem to presuppose the ability to choose from among alternative courses of action) appear confused. More on this below.

In addition to their individual difficulties, the two meanings of destiny do not easily fit together in the context of the IRA's armed struggle. Certainly it would be nonsensical to insist on a right to a united independent Ireland, conceived as one's *destiny*. As Paul Gilbert observes, 'Just as a nation's history is what fate has made it, so its destiny is what it is fated to become. Destiny, thus conceived, can confer no rights or duties . . .' (Gilbert 1998, p. 167). To make matters worse, rather than consistently adopting one meaning or the other, republican metaphysics incoherently mixes these two meanings: a united independent Ireland is both inevitable *and* requires action. I'll say more about this apparent contradiction below.

Republican claims about 'Ireland's destiny' suffer from an additional problem that might be called the problem of non-exclusivity: they must compete with an alternative – and indeed, diametrically opposed – vision of political destiny. As Margaret Moore notes, in the seventeenth century Ulster-Scots considered themselves to be a divinely chosen people with a divine mission in Ireland, namely that of 'carrying the torch of Christian civilization to backward Catholics' (Moore 2001, pp. 180–1). More recently, evangelicals such as Ian Paisley have articulated their own view of destiny according to which, in the struggle between good (evangelical Protestantism) and evil (Roman Catholicism), good will ultimately triumph:

> The Almighty does not make mistakes; He alone is infallible. Our presence in Ulster is no accident of history . . . We have an historic and a Divine Commission. We are the defenders of Truth in this Province and in this island . . . Ulster is the

last bastion of Evangelical Protestantism in Western Europe; we must not let drop the torch of Truth at this stage of the eternal conflict between Truth and Evil . . . We are a special people, not of ourselves, but of our Divine mission. Ulster arise and acknowledge your God. (Whyte 1990, pp. 107–8)

The point in quoting Paisley here is not to suggest that his view of destiny is superior to that of the republican movement, but rather to highlight the essentially intractable problem of adjudicating between mutually exclusive visions of (Northern) Ireland's destiny. Insisting on a God-given destiny for Ireland in the context of the conflict in Northern Ireland inevitably begs the question: which God and whose destiny? Given the conflicting, irreconcilable visions of (Northern) Ireland's destiny, such beliefs are in principle incapable of resolution.

Is the Republican World View Internally Coherent?

In addition to problems of 'fit' between elements of the republican world view and various empirical facts, there are also tensions *internal* to that world view. Causal determinism is typically understood to be incompatible with the existence of free will and genuine moral responsibility. Consequently, a belief in the inevitability of all events is inconsistent both with praising republican martyrs for their sacrifices and with blaming the 'Crown forces' for opposing the republican agenda. If causal determinism is embraced, then neither party really had any other alternative, in which case genuine praise and blame are simply irrelevant.

Likewise, a belief that an armed struggle is necessary in order to realise the right of the Irish people to a united, independent Irish republic sits uneasily with the belief that the Irish people are destined to achieve this political goal. If this destiny is inevitable, what can be the point of insisting on the necessity of an armed struggle to achieve this destiny? One could perhaps propose an alternative, deflationary notion of destiny such that Ireland's destiny can only be achieved through concerted collective effort, but then the confident assertion that Ireland's destiny *will* be achieved loses much of its power to inspire and motivate.

One way of attempting to resolve this tension would be to distinguish between the *realisation* of a given event and the *date* of its realisation. Thus Ireland's ultimate destiny is assured, but through actions such as armed struggle one can hasten its arrival. Engaging in or supporting the armed struggle thereby becomes a moral imperative. The problem with this approach is that it tends to have considerably less motivational power than either the assurance that Ireland's destiny is guaranteed, or the assurance that the responsibility for achieving Ireland's destiny lay squarely in one's hands. On the one hand, if one knew that Ireland's destiny was assured and that at best one's sacrifices would merely shave a few weeks or months off its date of arrival, there might be a tendency to sit back and let others do the heavy lifting (that is, to participate in dangerous operations and to risk injury, death or lengthy prison sentences). On the other hand, if one believed that Ireland's destiny lay squarely in one's hands, and therefore that its realisation was entirely contingent upon effort and good fortune, then confidence in its achievement would be eroded. Destiny, in this latter interpretation, begins to look a lot more like other more pedestrian goals that come about in direct proportion to the effort exerted on their behalf. Whatever assurances talk of 'destiny' was supposed to convey would thus be reduced to the simple effects of hard work and luck. The republican belief in destiny, like the related beliefs in blood sacrifice and causal determinism, faces serious problems to which there is no obviously satisfactory solution.

Paramilitaries and Politics: the Evolution of Irish Republicanism

I have been concerned so far in this chapter to identify and evaluate some of the key metaphysical elements of the traditional republican world view and to suggest some alternative perspectives. But belief in the timelessness of metaphysical truths should not be confused with the degree of consistency with which one acts in accordance with them. The republican movement underwent a significant evolution over the course of almost four decades of conflict, during which time articulations of its traditional ideology were subtly moulded to fit the changing circumstances. It is important that this dynamic element be acknowledged and examined as well. I will briefly describe this evolution before commenting on how these changes have generated additional conceptual tensions within the republican world view.

In the broadest terms, the evolution of the republican movement can be characterised as a gradual shift in emphasis from paramilitary to political activity, embodied in the activities of the IRA and Sinn Féin, respectively, although it is important not to exaggerate the exclusivity (until the abandonment of the armed struggle in 2005) of one or the other of these strategies. The two strategies, like the membership of the Provisional IRA and Provisional Sinn Féin, overlap a great deal. When it became clearly understood by the republican leadership in the mid 1970s that they could not compel the British to leave Northern Ireland through the use of physical force alone, armed struggle and political manoeuvring became entwined in a complicated dual strategy of exerting military pressure through acts of violence designed to make the British presence in Northern Ireland prohibitively expensive, both politically and economically (the 'long war' strategy), while at the same time attempting to gain strength politically within Ireland. This strategy crystallised at the Sinn Féin *Ard Fheis* in Dublin on 31 October 1981, when Danny Morrison asked: 'Who here really believes we can win the war through the ballot box? But will anyone here object if, with a ballot paper in one hand and the Armalite in the other, we take power in Ireland?' (*An Phoblacht/Republican News*, 5 November 1981). The dual military/political approach of 'the Armalite and the ballot box' became the two-pronged republican strategy through the 1980s and into the 1990s. Yet even at the height of the armed struggle in the early 1970s the aim was not to achieve a conventional military victory over the British (which would have been impossible in any case, given the disparity in the resources available to each side), but rather to inflict so much suffering on those with the power to influence British policy in Northern Ireland that the British government would be forced to negotiate with the IRA on terms that republicans found acceptable. The IRA's campaign was always 'armed politics'.

An additional, perhaps equally important, function of the violence was to ensure that the republican agenda received prominent media coverage. IRA bombs functioned to send a 'violent, loud, persistent and adamant message' that the armed struggle had not ended (Bell 1976, pp. 203–4). Politics and armed struggle, in this integrated approach, became distinct but interrelated *tactics* in the republican movement's 'total strategy' (Smith 1995, p. 152). As Gerry Adams revealingly explained, 'The tactic of armed struggle is of primary importance because it provides a vital cutting edge. Without it, the issue of Ireland would not even be an issue. So, in effect, the armed struggle becomes armed propaganda' (Adams 1995, p. 63).

According to the republican movement's own internal analysis in the late 1960s, the Border Campaign of 1956–62 fizzled and failed through lack of popular support. Generating and maintaining popular support for the next phase of the armed struggle was therefore imperative in pursuit of the core republican goal of a united independent Ireland. For most Catholics this ultimate goal was all well and fine, but the more immediate and pressing issue was the need for adequate housing, decent jobs, voting rights and basic safety. As Niall Ó Dochartaigh (2005, p. 11) notes, as violence erupted in the late 1960s, 'It was not so much that Northern Catholics turned enthusiastically towards the ideal of a united Ireland but rather that they turned decisively away in these years from what they came to regard as a malevolent state.' The state's perceived malevolence proved to be a godsend for the republican movement by generating support, recruits and propaganda for the armed struggle.

Unfortunately, from the republican perspective, by the early 1970s the civil rights movement had succeeded all too well. By 1971 NICRA had achieved its major objectives. The awarding of public housing, formerly the responsibility of local authorities, had been placed under the jurisdiction of a new Central Housing Executive to ensure equitable allocations. The gerrymandered, Unionist-dominated City Council in Derry had been abolished. The B Specials had been disbanded. Equal voting rights for all citizens had been the law since 1969. In short, most of the demands of the civil rights movement had been met. Although hardly a civil rights paradise, significant reform had been achieved in Northern Ireland. How could the Catholic community be persuaded to continue to support an armed struggle when their condition, and the issues they most cared about, seemed to be improving?

The answer was 'social republicanism' (Patterson 1997). As Smyth notes,

> The traditional [republican] preoccupation with national unity was forced to make room for an increasing emphasis on unemployment and urban social problems. The eventual realisation that there was no swift military victory in sight brought about a focus on social problems as a means of maintaining mass support for a 'long war'. (Smyth 1991, p. 136)

The connection between resolving social problems and maintaining mass support for a long war was not automatic, however; it had to be forged. Enter the republican propaganda machine.

Consider this revealing statement from a Sinn Féin Republican Lecture Series of the early 1980s:

> the IRA and Sinn Féin play different but convergent roles in the war of national liberation. The Irish Republican Army wages an armed campaign in the occupied six counties . . . Sinn Féin maintains the propaganda war and is the public and political voice of the Movement . . . The exploited masses must be made to identify with

the national liberation struggle because they see a successful conclusion of the war as being essential for their own social and economic liberation. (O'Brien 1999, p. 128)

This statement suggests a neat division of labour. The task of Sinn Féin is to make sure that the masses recognise themselves as exploited and come to view their own economic well-being as ineluctably linked with the success of the IRA's armed struggle to end the British occupation. In other words, the political side of the republican movement had to constantly emphasise that there could be no 'real' answer to the problems of working-class Catholic existence in the Six Counties so long as the British occupation continued (Patterson 1997). On the military side, by maintaining a steady level of violence, foreign investment in Northern Ireland would remain minimal and the economy would remain depressed, keeping unemployment high. Ensuring the continued presence of the British army would guarantee that Catholics remained cognisant that Ireland was an occupied country. By provoking excessive reactions from the security forces, the IRA could ensure that the Catholic community remained deeply alienated from the state. It would then be relatively simple to argue that only the achievement of the republican goal of a united independent Ireland could guarantee the well-being and security that were so clearly missing in the British statelet.

Just as the Catholic community had to be persuaded that achievement of the republican goal was the only way to secure their rights and safety, the armed struggle could be represented as a direct consequence of the denial of the rights and safety of Catholics. It was not enough to create conditions that entailed the necessity of the IRA's armed struggle and to then hope that ordinary Catholics would make the connection between the two. The connection between the well-being of Catholics and the armed struggle had to be made explicit. This is where the political dimension of the republican movement became essential. Sinn Féin's new role 'was to inject political meaning into [the Provisionals'] campaign in order to depict the violence as a direct outgrowth of public discontent, rather than being independent, or merely a cursory reflection of it' (Smith 1995, p. 147). Such an image proved useful for external fund-raising purposes as well, especially among the Irish-American diaspora for whom the belief that the IRA was the conscience of a beleaguered community provided a powerful moral incentive to open wallets. The primary motivation for the republican leadership's social agenda was not, however, a desire to eradicate the conditions of poverty or privation suffered by the Catholic community. Social republicanism, although it may have had the effect of improving the well-being of some Catholics, was conceived and motivated primarily in instrumentalist terms in the service of the republican movement's ideological goal of achieving a united independent Ireland.

The shift from an almost exclusively military strategy in the early 1970s, to the dual strategy of 'the Armalite and the ballot box' in the 1980s, to the increasingly political orientation of the republican movement in the 1990s, to the final abandonment of the armed struggle in 2005, suggests a dynamic movement capable of change, albeit undertaken slowly and painfully. It is not difficult to understand why. Blood sacrifice and martyrdom begin to look like merely tactical manoeuvres to a public that had become sceptical, if not cynical, about the republican movement's assurances that its cause is righteous. There have been no more republican hunger strikes since 1981. The de-emphasis and then final abandonment of its military strategy fits uneasily with the republican movement's earlier assurances that an armed struggle is absolutely necessary. To be united, independent and free is still Ireland's God-given destiny. But only God knows when this destiny will be achieved. The republican world view, with its metaphysics of martyrdom, necessity and destiny, was forced to yield to more pragmatic considerations. In the 1970s the immediate aim of Irish republicanism was to make Northern Ireland ungovernable. Three decades later its aim was to govern, first in Northern Ireland, and then (eventually) in the Republic of Ireland. As Gerry Adams, speaking to reporters in Dublin on 3 May 2007, prophesied, 'We're going to be in government in the north; we want to be in government in the south. We are an all-island party.' Those who sought to destroy the establishment now aspired to become part of it.

CONCLUSIONS

The Provisional IRA's armed struggle was embedded in, and drew moral confidence from, an ideology according to which that armed struggle was absolutely necessary, blood sacrifice and martyrdom were ennobling, spiritually efficacious acts, and ultimate victory was assured. This ideology, in turn, rested on deeper metaphysical foundations whose presuppositions can be identified, examined and evaluated. Despite the historical centrality of a belief in the efficacy of blood sacrifice and martyrdom, such acts were neither as obviously efficacious nor nearly as common as traditional republican ideology would suggest. Contrary to the republican insistence that the armed struggle was absolutely necessary, in fact a range of alternatives existed, suggesting that much of the enormous suffering caused by the Provisional IRA's armed struggle was not inevitable. The core republican belief in 'Ireland's destiny', while perhaps inspiring to the movement's adherents, appears to be in serious tension with other elements of the republican world view. To the extent that one emphasises the metaphysical inevitability of achieving the ultimate republican goal of a united independent Ireland, to that same extent the claim that an armed struggle was necessary to achieve this goal appears gratuitous. Finally, the Provisional republican movement has undergone a dynamic development such that commitment to traditional republican ideology, while still integral to republican self-conception, indoctrination and propaganda, has in practice yielded to pragmatic considerations based on judgements of political exigency. Throughout the evolution of the republican movement, however, one thing has remained constant: an unwavering belief in the inalienable right of the Irish people to an independent, united Ireland free from British control. It is the reason for all the bombs, bullets, suffering, injuries and deaths. The next chapter critically examines a range of arguments in support of this belief.

CHAPTER 3

Republicanism's Holy Grail: 'One Nation United, Gaelic and Free'

I believe and stand by the God-given right of the Irish nation to sovereign independence and the right of any Irishman or woman to assert this right in armed revolution.

(Bobby Sands, on the first day of his hunger strike in the Maze Prison,
1 March 1981)

INTRODUCTION

The fundamental republican conviction that the establishment of a united independent Ireland free from British control is a value worth dying (and killing) for is represented in various diverse media, including funeral orations, wall murals, political speeches, books, newspaper articles, prison journals, T-shirts, songs, websites, coffee mugs, commemorations and posters, as well as in the actions of republicans themselves, including political activism, hunger strikes and bombings.[1] These disparate expressions do not add up to an explicit, systematic defence of the core republican conviction. Nor has the republican movement produced such a defence. Yet in the absence of such a defence, the moral justification of the IRA's armed struggle appears to be precariously ungrounded.

My aim in this chapter is to bring together and critically examine arguments that attempt to establish a right of the Irish people to a united independent thirty-two-county Irish state. For clarity I distinguish among three different kinds of argument, although in practice republicans move freely from one sort to another, depending on the rhetorical context. First, there are arguments that take for granted that achieving a united independent thirty-two-county Irish state has *intrinsic* value. Such a value can be identified and exhibited, but as an intrinsic value it requires no justification in terms of a more fundamental good. These arguments reached their zenith in the view expressed most passionately by Patrick Pearse, who considered the Irish nation to be a mystical entity, something 'holy in itself' whose freedom was 'a spiritual necessity' which 'transcends all corporeal necessities' (Smith 1995, p. 10). Second, there are arguments that treat the establishment of a united independent thirty-two-county Irish state, not as an intrinsic good, but rather as the necessary precondition for achieving something else of fundamental value. As an *instrumental* value, a united independent Ireland is conceived and represented as a means to an end, not as an end in itself. Finally, *procedural* arguments attempt to justify the establishment of a united independent thirty-two-county Irish state democratically by arguing that such a state should exist simply because it represents the democratically expressed will of the people of Ireland. My aim is to identify the most important examples within each argument class and to determine which of these, if any, succeeds in establishing the purported right. Doing so turns out to be more difficult than many republicans and their supporters have supposed.

Arguments for a United Independent Irish State as an Intrinsic Good

What arguments can republicans marshal in support of their claim that the Irish people have an inalienable right to a sovereign state encompassing the entire island of Ireland? Consider this statement from the Sinn Féin website (http://www.sinnfein.ie/history):

> Throughout history, the island of Ireland has been regarded as a single national unit. Prior to the Norman invasion from England in 1169, the Irish people had their own system of law, culture and language and their own political and social structures. Following this invasion the island continued to be governed as a single political unit, as a colony of Britain, until 1921.

This statement makes a number of striking claims that are worth examining more closely because they provide the basis for common republican arguments for the right of the Irish people to a united independent Irish state.

The Geographical Unity Argument

Remarkably, this short passage *twice* reminds readers that Ireland is an island. This geographical factoid was broadcast in the title of Frank

67

Gallagher's book, *The Indivisible Island* (1957), and was given official status in Article 2 of the Free State's 1937 Constitution (unchanged until 1998), which stated that 'the national territory consists of the whole island of Ireland, its islands and the territorial seas'. Implicit in such descriptions of Ireland as an island is that it has a natural unity and integrity marked out by its geography. Partition in 1921 artificially divided a territory that was naturally one. Republicans seek to restore Ireland's wholeness. In short, the fact that Ireland is surrounded by water is assumed to ground a right of the Irish people to a united independent 'all-island' political state.

The 'Geographical Unity Argument', as it might be called, depends on the truth of the following proposition: the people of every geographically distinct region (for example, an island or other well-defined landmass) have a right to national self-determination as a people taking the form of whatever political governance it desires simply in virtue of inhabiting that geographically distinct region, but people occupying merely a part of a geographically distinct region do not. Call this 'the principle of geographical political entitlement'. Bracketing the difficult question of what criteria should be used for distinguishing geographically distinct regions, we can proceed directly to asking whether this principle is true.

The most reasonable answer is: not obviously. As Dermot Quinn notes, it depends on a form of simple 'geographical determinism' according to which 'the island of Ireland [is] one, therefore the governance of Ireland should be one' (Quinn 1993, pp. 65–6; cf. Murray and Tonge 2005, pp. 165–6). He rejects such geographical determinism as a simple non sequitur. Peter Simpson explains in more detail why this presupposition is problematic:

> Those . . . who strive for the unity of Ireland by force . . . seem to regard this unity in a mythical and even mystical way, as if the geographical integrity of Ireland somehow required its political unity, to violate which is to violate some natural right and justice. But it is absurd to suppose that the just and good could be defined by reference to the limits of the sea, as opposed to the objective needs of the people who live within those limits . . . This is to confuse things existing in different orders. (Simpson 1986, p. 80)

Terry Eagleton adds that 'the bald fact that Ireland is "divided" . . . is no more to be mourned than the fact that Europe is . . .' (Eagleton 1999, p. 51). In addition, although the principle of geographical political entitlement might entail that Ulster Protestants cannot legitimately claim shared nationhood with the British island across the Irish Sea (a bonus from the republican perspective), it would also entail that any Scottish and Welsh aspirations to independent nationhood are *necessarily* invalid (a conclusion that most republicans would reject). Individually and collectively, I take such considerations to be decisive.

The Single Nation Argument

Republicans assert that Ireland is and always has been a single nation. As Gerry Adams puts it, 'Ireland is historically, culturally, and geographically one single unit' (Adams 1986, p. 88). Furthermore, according to republicans it is Ireland's status *as* a genuine nation that establishes the right of the Irish people as a whole to their own united independent political state. This 'Single Nation Argument' presupposes both (1) that the people of Ireland constitute a single nation, 'the Irish people', and (2) the principle that if a group of people constitute a single nation, they are (in virtue of that fact alone) entitled to their own self-governing political state (call this 'the nation-state principle').[2] Both of these assumptions deserve critical examination.

Begin with the assumption that the people of Ireland constitute a single nation, 'the Irish people'. Is this true? The answer to this question depends on answering several more fundamental questions, starting with: what is a nation? Notoriously, the term 'nation' as it appears in ordinary language is ambiguous, as it may refer to either (1) a relatively large group of people organised under a single, usually independent government (a 'country'), or (2) a people, usually the inhabitants of a specific territory, who share common customs, origins, history and frequently language. Paul Gilbert (1993) refers to these as the 'statist' and 'culturist' conceptions of nations, respectively. Obviously, a group of people could constitute a nation in either the statist or the culturist sense without constituting a nation in the other. For example, 'the German people' inhabit a specific territory in Europe and share common customs, origins, history and language, and thus constitute a single 'cultural nation'. Yet from 1949 to 1990, there were three distinct 'German' political states: the Federal Republic of Germany (West Germany), the German Democratic Republic (East Germany) and (arguably) Austria. On the other hand, since 1949 the People's Republic of China has been one 'political nation', ruled from Beijing, but consisting of a number of 'cultural nations', such as Han Chinese (who tend to be secular), Tibetans (mainly Buddhist), the Xinjiang people (mainly Muslim), and so on. Likewise, the former USSR was one political nation consisting of many cultural nations, many of which *became* political nations (again or for the first time) following the break-up of the Soviet empire. Clearly, the referents of 'political nations' and of 'cultural nations' may, but need not, coincide.

What of 'Ireland'? Clearly, Ireland is not a single nation in the *political* sense, because the people of Ireland are governed by two distinct governments (in Dublin and in London), have two distinct systems of laws, and so forth. Is it a nation in the cultural sense? In support of the claim that it is, republicans can appeal to certain historical and sociological facts. They can argue that Ireland has throughout its history possessed a 'cultural unity' based on a common language, laws, religion and traditions. For example, it could be pointed out that there was a monarchy in Ireland under the High King for more than five centuries before there were monarchies in England or France. These kingships were sufficiently powerful to repulse the threat posed by Viking invaders in the eighth, ninth and tenth centuries. It was not until 1169, when the Normans invaded Ireland from England, that a foreign power finally succeeded in usurping Irish control. Even then, Irish culture in the form of Gaelic traditions and laws continued throughout the island until the seventeenth century when the English established the plantation system, confiscating land in Ulster from Catholics for newly-arrived Scottish Presbyterians as well as for themselves. The Penal Laws in the eighteenth century further consolidated foreign control over Ireland by breaking up the estates of Catholic landowners. Despite such attempts at domination, however, Irish culture has survived and Ireland continues to constitute a distinctive cultural nation. This is as true in the Six Counties as it is in the South. Hence, Ireland is a single cultural nation.

One serious problem with such claims is their questionable historical accuracy. Ellis (1986) stresses that Gaelic society in Ireland before the Norman invasion in the twelfth century had extensive connections with the Scottish Highlands and possessed no concept of a unified Irish state. Ireland in the twelfth century was an island of independent chiefdoms frequently at war with one another for local control and power – wars that continued for the next four-hundred years, with Irish chieftains gladly aligning themselves with the invaders when it suited their purposes. O'Leary and McGarry (1996) simply reject what they consider to be the crude nationalist myth of a distinct and continuous Irish identity:

The inhabitants of Ireland, *pace* Irish nationalists, have not shared one singular ethnic or national identity for over a millennium. Ireland, *pace* Irish nationalists, had no modern or medieval history of political unity. The *peoples* of Ireland have only been unified under one state as part of another state, i.e., under the Act of Union. (O'Leary and McGarry 1996, p. 102)

A second problem with such claims is that they fail to take into account the distinctive cultural self-identification of Protestants in Northern Ireland, many of whom would reject the claim that they are simply part of one Celtic people, 'the Irish', who share a common cultural heritage. Consider this statement from the Ulster Unionist Party (UUP), which represented most Protestants in Northern Ireland for half a century:

Ulster (Northern Ireland) has always been distinct from the rest of the island of Ireland. It is a hybrid of Scots and Irish culture and was marked as a place apart in the ancient Celtic legends. Scots culture became the predominant influence with the last great wave of migration which occurred before most European settlers arrived in North America. (http://www.uup.org)

Some Ulster Protestants have gone even further to construct an alternative 'myth of origins and descent' (Smith 2001, p. 29), according to which they are the descendents of the primordial people of Ulster, the Cruthin, as opposed to the Gaels who ruled elsewhere in Ireland (Wood 2006). Such historical reconstructions are best understood as desperate attempts to urge Protestants to take pride in their distinctive cultural identity, rather than as sober history lessons. Even without the aid of such historiographic legerdemain, however, most Protestants in Northern Ireland consider themselves to be fundamentally British rather than Irish or Celtic. In their view, it was the founders of the Irish Free State in 1921 who severed historic economic, cultural and ancestral ties with Britain to declare a new, artificially created state. The north chose to remain a loyal part of the British nation to which it has always belonged. Consequently, unionists can claim that there are in fact *two* nations in Ireland: an Irish nation south of the border and a British nation that includes Ulster or, alternatively, a distinctive Ulster nation (Gallagher 1995). In short, the historical claims made by republicans can be challenged by offering an alternative historical account that emphasises the economic, cultural and ancestral linkages between Northern Ireland and Great Britain, while emphasising corresponding cultural differences between Northern Ireland and the rest of the island to the south.

Despite their disagreements about the correct way to characterise nationhood in Ireland, the arguments so far assume that there are objective features of cultures that suffice to mark out distinct nations. The problem to which these differing 'objectivist' conceptions of nationhood point is acute. Sharing a common culture is always a matter of degree and depends in part on how heavily some cultural elements are weighted relative to others. Republicans emphasise common elements in Irish and Ulster Protestant histories to emphasise Irish cultural unity. In response, Protestants highlight differences between Ulster and the rest of Ireland (but in common with Great Britain) to emphasise unity within a distinctively British culture. Ultimately, republicans can simply assert that 'Irishness' is known intuitively. Smyth notes that, 'An essential component of traditional Irish Nationalism is . . . the subordination of political and social ideas to a conception of Irishness which is grasped by intuition rather than by reason' (Smyth 1991, p. 136). Protestants, however, can likewise claim an intuitive grasp of a distinctive Ulster Protestant culture. But if so, then attempts to ground claims for authentic nationhood solely on historical facts about cultural integrity become deeply problematic. More generally, when different communities occupying the same area privilege different aspects of culture, a purely objective determination of cultural nationhood may be impossible.

Some scholars have attempted to circumvent the problems facing objectivist accounts by interpreting 'nations' subjectively, that is, as essentially an *idea* embraced by a group of people – but nonetheless as being no less *real* despite existing *only* in people's imaginations. For example, Krejci and Velimsky (1981, p. 45) write that, 'The subjective factor of consciousness is the ultimate factor which eventually decides the issue of national identity'. Benedict Anderson elaborates on this approach by proposing that a nation be defined as 'an imagined political community – and imagined as both inherently limited and sovereign' (Anderson 2006, p. 6). It is *imagined* because even in the smallest of nations, all the members cannot and never will meet one another face to face, yet each has the idea of a common community. It is *limited* because even the largest of nations has finite boundaries, beyond which lie other nations. It is imagined as *sovereign* because nations dream of being free. Finally, it is a *community* because 'the nation is always conceived as a deep, horizontal comradeship' (Anderson 2006, pp. 6–7).

Conceiving of nations as 'imagined communities' appears to circumvent some of the problems facing objectivist accounts of nations, especially the vexed (and perhaps inherently irresolvable) question of *how much* cultural unity based on common language, laws, religion and traditions must be shared among a group of people in order for that group to constitute a nation. In Anderson's view, by contrast, a group of people constitute a nation simply if they believe or imagine that they do. A moment's reflection, however, makes clear that this apparent advantage is illusory, because a communal subjectivist view that makes a nation solely a matter of shared ideas faces precisely the same kind of problem facing objectivist views: sharing ideas is just as much a matter of degree as is sharing aspects of culture; hence the extent to which any group of people think of themselves as constituting a nation can *also* vary by degree. Moreover, which elements of identity the individuals in a group deem most important to their collective identity as a nation can vary greatly from one individual to the next. Sharing the *idea* of a common community, no less than sharing a common culture, depends in part on how heavily some notional elements are weighted relative to others. In the absence of a non-arbitrary (objective?) criterion for *how much* shared belief is sufficient to constitute nationhood, and for *which* beliefs matter, the 'imagined community' proposal faces its own version of the very same primary theoretical problem plaguing objectivist accounts.

Anderson's notion of nations as 'imagined communities' suffers from other defects as well. Such an approach can easily lead to the facile conclusion that all that matters for a group of people to constitute a nation is that they think they do (as assumed, for example, in Colley 1992). Thus according to David Miller, 'nations exist when their members recognise one another as compatriots, and believe that they share characteristics of the relevant kind' (Miller 1995, p. 22). Likewise, Steve Bruce, citing Anderson's book *Imagined Communities* in support, maintains that 'what matters for ethnic identity is what people believe to be the case, not what actually is the case . . .' (Bruce 1994, p. 142). In addition to dichotomising reality into facts versus beliefs (as if there were no facts about people's beliefs, or no beliefs about facts), this radically subjectivist understanding of nationhood entails the reductio ad absurdum that any group (or even pair) of people who believe, for whatever reason, that they constitute a nation, ipso facto do so. Extra-mental reality, in this view, has absolutely no bearing on the issue.

Viewed from a wider perspective, the problems attending objectivist and subjectivist accounts of nationhood are hardly surprising, because the various cultural criteria emphasised by objectivists – common customs, origins, history and language – although assumed to exist independently of one's beliefs, only exist *as criteria* for nationhood by being interpreted as such. Which customs matter, how far back in time to trace one's origins, the narrative one chooses to impose on historical events, and the seriousness with which one takes linguistic forms to be culturally significant are all matters of judgement. As brute, un-interpreted facts (if this is even conceivable) such elements would be incapable of grounding claims to nationhood. Clearly, beliefs play an important role in constituting nations. W. B. Yeats was no doubt correct when he noted that a nation cannot exist without 'a model of it in the mind of the people' (Gilbert 1998, p. 57). Yet recognising the *necessity* of shared beliefs for constituting nationhood does not entail that such beliefs, by themselves, are *sufficient* for constituting nationhood. As Richard English rightly notes, 'Nations may be invented, but not all inventions work or become popular: successful nationalisms build on prior foundations which, to some degree, determine the shape and appearance of each nation in question' (English 2006, p. 20). Objectivist and subjectivist accounts each err through exclusivity.

These considerations suggest that a satisfactory account of 'nations' should be sensitive to the subtle interplay between objectivist and subjectivist elements by acknowledging the distinctive contributions of each. Catholic and Protestant identities in Northern Ireland are based on real differences in customs, origins, history and language, as objectivists would insist. Yet such cultural elements only become constitutive of nationhood when they are valued and appropriated by individuals perceiving one another as sharing these elements in common. Such collective self-identification is often self-reinforcing: publicly emphasising one or another aspect of the culture with which one identifies helps to bring about, for others already inclined in that direction, the very cultural identification upon which one insists. Marching in loyalist parades, painting the Union Jack on curb-stones and wearing bowler hats and orange sashes simultaneously draws upon objectively existing cultural resources, and propagates the ideas associated with such resources, among the Protestant faithful. Commemorating the 1916 Rising, greeting one another in Gaelic and patronising distinctively Gaelic sporting events draw upon equally real cultural resources and serve an analogous function for the nationalist community. In this sense, nationhood is always a work in progress. As Terry Eagleton remarks, 'political nationalism . . . tends to define, remodel and reorganize ethnicities for its own ends' (Eagleton 1999, p. 47). A satisfactory account of nationhood should take into account the symbiotic relationship between these distinct factors.

In a number of publications, Anthony D. Smith has developed a more promising approach that combines objectivist and subjectivist considerations without one-sidedly privileging either. According to his 'ethno-symbolic' view, nations have as their foundations distinctive *ethnie*, defined as 'named human populations with shared ancestry myths, histories and cultures, having an association with a specific territory and a sense of solidarity' (Smith 1986, p. 320). Such *ethnie* provide the objective foundation for claims to nationhood, but are not, by themselves, sufficient to constitute nationhood. Such elements must be suitably appropriated by a reflexively self-identified community before they can function in this capacity. A nation, in Smith's view, is thus 'a named and self-defined human community of shared history and destiny, possessed of a homeland whose members cultivate shared myths, memories, symbols and traditions' (http://www.axess.se/english/2005/06/theme_smith.php).[3] Nations are thus a form of objectively grounded, collective cultural identities that may coexist and compete with one another within the boundaries of a common political community.

Arguably this is the case in Ireland. The Troubles can perhaps be best understood as an 'ethnic conflict' in which religious belief per se serves primarily as a central organising principle grounding community identity, rather than as itself the basis for the conflict (Ó Dochartaigh 2005, p. 7). Despite speaking the same language with roughly the same local accents, and sharing the same geographical area and much history, Catholics and Protestants tend to value and invest with meaning different cultural resources. Catholics in the Six Counties tend to identify with the history, myths, memories, symbols and traditions of Ireland. Protestants in Northern Ireland tend to identify with the history, myths, memories, symbols and traditions of Ulster, conceived as having a distinctive British culture. Their respective national identities are not, however, purely notional, because they are grounded in history, in stories and memories passed from one generation to the next, in symbols that persist and evolve through time, and in traditions that bind the other cultural elements together. The ethno-symbolic approach renders intelligible the distinctive republican and loyalist wall murals (examples of which are reproduced in the photos section of this book) that for much of the conflict in Northern Ireland identified and marked off Catholic and Protestant neighbourhoods in Belfast and Derry. Prominent among these in Catholic areas have been murals depicting those killed on Bloody Sunday, the 1981 hunger strikers and the 1987 'Loughgall Martyrs'. As Alonso notes, 'Remembering the dead heroes of the republican cause has nurtured a martyrology which has been used in an attempt to obtain the sympathy of the nationalist community, and, in this way, to provide a source of collective identity' (Alonso 2007, p. 81). These collective identities could then be used to maintain that Catholics and Protestants constitute distinct cultural nations within Ireland, rendering more acute the claim of each to possess a right to political self-governance.

Does Cultural Nationhood Entail a Right to Political Self-Governance?

Suppose that it is at least sometimes possible to identify bona fide cultural nations in one of the senses discussed above. Can the identification of a people as a cultural nation be used to ground a right to political self-governance?

It is often simply assumed as a self-evident truth that nationhood entails a right to national self-determination, and hence to political self-governance. As an IRA spokesperson confidently declared in 1990, 'We demand the basic right of every nation to national self-determination. The denial of that right by armed might will always legitimise and give rise to armed struggle in pursuit of that right' (English 2003, pp. 339–40). Speaking on behalf of Sinn Féin four years later, Gerry Adams declared in no uncertain terms that 'the right to national self-determination is inalienable, unassailable and absolute. It cannot be defined or qualified other than by the Irish people themselves' (O'Brien 1999, p. 304). Various international human rights covenants grandly declare that 'all peoples have the right of self-determination. By virtue of that right they freely determine their political status and freely pursue their economic, social and cultural development'.[4] It is just as frequently assumed that if all peoples necessarily have this right simply in virtue of being 'a people', then a fortiori peoples who have lived under colonial domination have a right to political self-determination. To many this has seemed nearly self-evident. According to Ronald Beiner, 'To make no concessions to the normative force of nationalist thought would entail not only embracing the nineteenth-century empires within Europe . . . but also denying the moral legitimacy of the politics of anticolonialism in the twentieth century' (Beiner 1999, p. 4; emphasis in original).

Paul Gilbert attempts to justify this assumption *definitionally*. In his view, all nations *by definition* are entitled to independent statehood, because a nation just *is* the kind of group that has a right to statehood by virtue of the kind of group it is (Gilbert 1998). He thus proposes an inversion of the standard view:

> instead of following Weber's definition of a nation as what tends to independent statehood, we should think of it as a group of a kind that has, other things being equal, the *right* to statehood. Then disagreements about what nations there are will be disagreements over what sorts of groups have these rights. (Gilbert 1998, p. 16)

As clever as this proposed inversion of the question is, however, it simply shifts rather than solves the fundamental problem. Rather than asking, as formerly, whether every nation has a right to political self-determination, the problem now becomes how to identify those groups that do have a right to political self-determination. The problem has simply been relocated rather than resolved.

Against the assumption that every nation has a right to political self-determination it can be pointed out that nearly every state that currently exists contains within it a number of different cultural nations. If the very fact of being a cultural nation entails a right to statehood, then we face the prospect of a runaway proliferation of states of ever-diminishing size. Likewise, as Eagleton points out,

> a nation-state may be forged out of a whole number of ethnicities; some ethnic groups may aspire to nationhood but not statehood; some of them – the Celts, for example – may have several nations but not several nation-states . . . some peoples, like the Arabs, have a number of political states, and so forth. (Eagleton 1999, p. 48)

But if so, then whether a people is entitled to political self-determination is a contingent affair not intrinsically linked to its cultural nationhood. As Judith Lichtenberg observes, 'This is not merely a practical problem. It is a sufficient reason to deny that cultures per se have a right to statehood. A culture must provide very good reason why it *needs* a state' (Lichtenberg 1999, p. 174). There is no self-evident necessary connection between cultural nations configured along ethnic lines and self-governing nation-states that requires that they exist in a one-to-one correspondence with each other. As Eagleton memorably puts this point, 'The Irish *qua* Irish have no more right to collective self-determination than have the freckled, red-haired or bow-legged' (Eagleton 1999, p. 44).

77

The Historical Grievance Argument

Daniel Philpott writes:

> A group that was once invaded, annexed, or robbed of its land through diplomatic subterfuge and continues, through literature, stories handed down, and the brave acts of dissidents, to tend the memory of its glorious, innocent, free, untrammelled past, staving off the homogenizing intentions of its oppressors, has suffered a historical grievance. (Philpott 1995, p. 376)

Irish Catholics could be viewed as having suffered a historical grievance in precisely this sense, a fact repeatedly emphasised by the republican movement (see, for example, the Sinn Féin statement at http://www.sinnfein.ie/peace/document/79). As Ian McBride notes, 'the eight-centuries-of-British-oppression version of Irish history' which sustained the Provisional IRA's propaganda war in Northern Ireland had already long been part of the political culture of the Republic (McBride 2001, p. 39). Moreover, in Northern Ireland 'the deep-rooted structures of economic and occupational inequality between the Catholic and Protestant communities provided a material substratum for the *reproduction* of a communal nationalism of grievance' (Patterson 1997, pp. 185–6; emphasis added). In this way, injustices in the past continue to resonate in the present, engendering a communal sense of grievance that demands political redress. If a territory has been unjustly seized from its rightful owners, then the rightful owners of that territory have a legitimate historical grievance grounding a right to political sovereignty over that territory. It could be argued that having suffered a historical grievance of this sort constitutes the strongest case for establishing a territorial claim (Brilmayer 1991). Call this 'the historical grievance entitlement principle'.

Unfortunately, there are a number of serious problems with this irredentist principle. Taken literally, it would at most establish that the *previous* occupants of Ireland are entitled to exercise political sovereignty over all of Ireland. Because the previous occupants from whom parts of Ulster had been seized are all long dead, none of them are in a position to claim this right. In order to use such a principle to establish that their currently living descendents have such a right, one would need to show that the right belonging to the previous occupants of Ireland transfers unproblematically to their present-day descendents. It is not at all clear how this is to be accomplished (Thompson 2001). In addition, Unionists can dismiss the aforementioned historical grievance entitlement principle with a counter-principle of their own according to which 'the land of Ulster belongs to those who are on it and not under it' (Gallagher 1990, p. 12). Call this the 'on it not under it principle'. It is not obvious why this principle must be less valid than the historical grievance entitlement principle, with which it is apparently locked in an irresolvable stalemate.

Problems also arise when one examines the notion of 'rightful owners' more closely. Irish Catholics (for the most part) tended the land of the Six Counties prior to the arrival of the English and Presbyterian 'planters' in the seventeenth century. But the Irish Catholics of seventeenth-century Ulster were themselves descendents of still earlier tribes and peoples, who usurped the land from its previous occupants, and so on back in time through the murky mists of pre-history. Thus, the same argument that would negate the right of the British to control of the Six Counties in favour of their previous Irish Catholic owners would also negate the right of *those* particular Irish occupants in favour of those whom *they* displaced. Once the historical grievance entitlement principle is put in play, there is no principled reason to stop moving the territorial entitlement further and further back in time until one reaches the absurd conclusion that the only people with a genuine right to ownership of the land now constituting the Six Counties are the original settlers who arrived there some 10,000 years ago. Yet even this conclusion is problematic if, as some scholars insist, 'there was no single, original Gaelic or Irish race, just as there were no discernible natives in the sense of an original people than whom all others and their descendents are less truly Irish' (English 2006, p. 26). Consequently, it could be argued that people of English and Scottish descent in Ulster have as much right to consider themselves its legitimate owners as do presently existing Irish Catholics. Ironically, the historical grievance argument fails by proving too much.

Ulster Protestants could go further than this by arguing that whether or not Ulster was primordially Irish or English or Scottish (or 'Celtic') is beside the point. What matters is that the distinctive cultural identity of Ulster Protestants as a people was formed in what is now Northern Ireland. They have an interest in not being severed from their formative territory, an interest grounded in the deepest layers of their identity. This interest can be used to construct an alternative to the republican argument. According to Chaim Gans, 'given the centrality of historical territories in the formation of national identities, there seems to be an inherent link between these territories and the right to national self-determination' (Gans 2001, p. 72). But if so, then Ulster Protestants could argue that they have a right to a Northern Ireland that remains part of the UK because of the unique historical importance of that land in the formation of their distinctive identity as a people.

Unfortunately, this unionist argument fares no better than its republican counterpart because it leaves too many questions unanswered. For example, Gans himself goes on to ask,

> When can a territory . . . justly be said to be 'of formative value' to the historical identity of a given people? Should we adopt objective, uniform criteria . . . Or should we ascribe any importance to the subjective feelings of the people whose right is in question . . .? (Gans 2001, p. 61)

He wisely prescinds from offering answers to these questions. Additionally, suppose that a land has been historically important in forming the identities of *two* distinct groups – precisely the situation in the historic province of Ulster, which *includes* Northern Ireland but *is included in* Ireland as a whole. In this case can either group have an exclusive claim to that land? Insofar as two peoples can each claim the right to self-determination on the same historically significant parcel of territory, such rights will be jointly unrealisable so long as the right self-determination is held to entail a right to territorial sovereignty (Makinson 1989). Finally, because people develop attachments to territories, attempting to rectify past injustices may create new, equal or greater injustices (Waldron 1992). The historical grievances of Irish Catholics may be entirely legitimate. By themselves, however, they do not provide any clear entitlement to political sovereignty over all of Ireland.

Arguments for a Right to a United Independent Irish State as an Instrumental Good

On Being an Oppressed Minority

Arguments that treat a united independent Ireland as an intrinsic good fail to establish the conclusion that the Irish people as a whole have a right to political self-determination. Perhaps arguments that take this goal as an *instrumental* good can fare better. Instrumentalist arguments treat the attainment of a united independent Ireland, not as an end in itself, but rather as the necessary precondition for the attainment of other goods or for the removal of certain evils. For example, republicans maintain that the oppression of Catholics in Northern Ireland follows directly from their status as a minority within that society, and hence that this oppression can *only* be ended by the ending of partition and the political reunification of Ireland. An article entitled 'No Civil Rights Without National Rights' in the 26 August 1993 issue of *An Phoblacht/Republican News* expressed this view well when it declared that 'no reform short of its abolition can remedy the fundamental injustice of the six county state' (Wood 2006, p. 174). Call this the 'Oppressed Minority Argument'. Again, in order to be clear about what is required to make this argument convincing, it is helpful to render explicit its crucial premise: being a minority within a society entails being oppressed by the majority, and thereby entitles the minority group to its own political state. This premise deserves careful examination. There are at least three serious problems with it.

First, although having minority status can facilitate oppression of a group, it is neither necessary nor sufficient for such oppression. The reason is straightforward: 'minorities are not always oppressed, and the oppressed are not always minorities' (Eagleton 1999, p. 53), as the situation in South Africa during the era of apartheid made clear. Besides, if it were true that having minority status somehow *entailed* being oppressed, then the very same argument for abolishing Northern Ireland in order to end the oppression of Catholics there would also support an argument *against* abolishing Northern Ireland, since ending partition would necessarily make an oppressed minority of the Protestants who found themselves living in a reconstituted thirty-two-county Irish state. If having minority status really entailed being oppressed, then ending partition would simply substitute the oppression of one group for that of another.

Second, being oppressed does not, by itself, entail a right to one's own political state, because although one way to end the oppression might be to form one's own political state, it is not necessarily the only way to do so. In the present context this is critical, because although *one* way of ending the perceived oppression of Northern Irish Catholics might be to dismantle the Northern Irish state (although this, by itself, doesn't guarantee that result), there may be other ways of achieving this desirable goal that *don't* require dismantling the Northern Irish state. *Pace* republican assertions, radical reform might be sufficient.

Third, Catholics in Northern Ireland were undoubtedly discriminated against but were not necessarily oppressed. It is uncontroversial that historically Catholics in Northern Ireland suffered significant discrimination at the hands of the Protestant majority and that their minority status was an important factor permitting this discrimination. Discrimination, however, does not entail oppression. Catholics in the Six Counties were not denied religious freedom nor (after reforms had been put in place) were they denied basic socio-economic rights or opportunities for political representation. Describing Catholics in Northern Ireland as 'oppressed' in the way that some other genuinely oppressed peoples are dilutes and devalues the term almost beyond recognition (Hennessey 2005).

In response it could be argued that even if being a minority group within a society does not *entail* oppression of that group, nor even necessarily make it more likely, it does make it *possible*; and where it is possible, there is no *guarantee* that rights will be respected and that equality and justice will be enjoyed by all. This response fails for at least two reasons. First, the mere possibility that a group *could* be oppressed is insufficient to ground a right to a political state, because that possibility exists for *any* group. Second, this argument would count equally in favour of maintaining partition, because Protestants in a reunited Ireland would necessarily (according to this logic) have their rights placed in jeopardy. Any principle that generates such a result can hardly justify the republican view.

Finally, if the fundamental moral concern at issue here is simply the oppression of the minority Catholic population in Northern Ireland, then there exists an obvious alternative to the abolition (or the radical reform) of the Northern Irish state that would, in a stroke, eliminate the oppression of these people. As Saul Similansky (2004) points out, any Catholic living in Northern Ireland could move south or west an hour's drive to live in an independent, flourishing, democratic Irish state that fully enables the right of the Irish nation (assuming that such a right exists) to self-determination, to full cultural and religious self-expression, and to unencumbered national identity free from sectarian oppression.

Republicans, it goes without saying, would balk at this suggestion for a variety of reasons depending on their degree of traditional orthodoxy. They might deny that the Republic is a legitimate political entity, the Free State having been 'artificially' created in 1921 by a British act of partition. They might deny that the Republic truly satisfies the Irish nation's aspiration to self-determination, to cultural and religious development, and to the unencumbered formation of Irish national identity, consisting as it does of only twenty-six of the thirty-two counties of Ireland. They might object that Catholics in Northern Ireland should not have to relocate in order to have their fundamental rights realised, and that a need to do so in order to secure their rights would simply confirm their assertion of the fundamental unreformability of the Northern Irish state. In short, Similansky's suggestion would be rejected by many republicans as anathema.

The problem with all such responses, however, is that they beg the question by presupposing one or more of the intrinsic arguments discussed above. Contrary to the Oppressed Minority Argument, there manifestly *is* a way for the Catholics living in Northern Ireland to escape from their minority status short of the abolition of the Northern Irish state, although it would require ceasing to be Catholics who live *in* that state. Republicans would vehemently reject this 'solution'. This simple observation highlights the fact that it is not the oppression per se of the Catholics living in Northern Ireland that is at issue for republicans, but rather the status of the Northern Irish state that renders Catholics a minority *in* that state. Rejection of Similansky's solution requires the introduction of political considerations that are independent of the oppressed status of the Catholics living in Northern Ireland. But if so, then the republican claim that the oppression of Catholics in Northern Ireland can *only* be ended by the ending of partition and by the political reunification of Ireland is quite simply false.

Social and Economic Equality

Peter Simpson suggests that any justifiable political settlement in Northern Ireland should enhance 'the promotion of the common good' (Simpson 1986, p. 80), which would arguably include, at a minimum, social and economic equality and the protection of civil rights. Likewise, Paul Gilbert argues that 'the grounds and limits of claims to statehood must be *ethical* ones. They concern the protection of a decent communal life for some, and the prevention of interference with such a life for others'. He aptly calls this 'the common good model'. According to this model, 'a nation is a group which enjoys a certain kind of desirable common life – one which would be protected by statehood, but which would not damage the life of others thereby' (Gilbert 1993, p. 519).

Republicans could thus argue that only in a united thirty-two-county Ireland can Catholics in the Six Counties achieve social and economic equality and have their civil rights ensured. According to the Sinn Féin policy document 'Freedom',

> inequality is the price which has had to be paid for a state founded on a system of political, social and economic privilege. That price will be demanded and paid for as long as that state exists . . . The inequities which the Six-County state has spawned are an inevitable consequence of its very existence. (http://sinnfein.org/)

In other words, because the state was *founded* on a system of political, social and economic privilege, inequality is guaranteed so long as that state exists. Thus, the only way to rectify that inequality is to dissolve or destroy (rather than reform) that state. Hence the necessity of an armed struggle.

This argument, if sound, would have considerably more force than the others we have so far examined, because it bears directly on what *is* relevant to the question of the moral justification of IRA violence, namely, the question of whether fundamental human rights can only be secured through a change in the political status of Northern Ireland. Unfortunately, like the Oppressed Minority Argument, the Social and Economic Equality Argument takes for granted that Northern Ireland is unreformable and therefore that only through its abolition can Catholics be assured of social and economic equality. But even if, as seems undeniable, Northern Ireland was founded on a system of political, social and economic privilege, unless some peculiar notion of causality is operative there is no reason to conclude that, necessarily, that state in its later stages *must* entail a system of inequality. This is not to deny that it will typically be difficult to reform a state which had inequalities inherent in its design. Indeed, structural inequalities between Catholics and Protestants persist in Northern Ireland, despite significant reform. But the conclusion that radical reform is *impossible*, and therefore that the only alternative for achieving true equality is destruction of the state, is offered without any supporting evidence. In addition, as argued in Chapter 1, if radical reform *seemed* impossible, this may have been in large measure an intended effect of the IRA's strategy of prolonged ideological resistance to accommodation. That the IRA had to *ensure* that Northern Ireland was unreformable suggests that the leadership of the IRA did not originally view it as such.

The Cultural Self-Realisation Argument

The Oppressed Minority and the Social and Economic Inequality arguments assert that having one's own self-governing state is necessary in order to overcome certain social ills. A different tack would be to argue that certain cultural *goods* are only available to ethnic groups that have their own self-governing state. Specifically, the free expression and celebration of one's cultural identity is a basic human right requiring a self-governing state configured along ethnic lines. In this view, a state of one's own becomes the ultimate means for a group to protect its identity and determine its own destiny (Knight 1985). Call this the 'Cultural Self-Realisation Argument'.

If sound, this argument would establish the right of Irish Catholics (qua distinct ethnic group) to their own self-governing state.

The argument is not sound, or at least not obviously so. Eagleton pinpoints the fundamental problem with this argument: 'People have a right
to affirm their ethnic identities; but there is no reason in principle to
suppose that they need to fashion their own political state in order to do
so' (Eagleton 1999, p. 45). National autonomy does not entail state sovereignty (Smith 2001). Ethnic cultural expression can, in principle,
flourish in a state configured along any of a number of lines other than
ethnic homogeneity. The United States, perhaps, provides a good example
of how this is possible. Politically, the US is configured around the principles contained in certain documents (for example, the Constitution, the
Bill of Rights, and so on), and embodied in certain institutions (the executive, legislative and judicial branches of the federal government, analogous institutions at the state and local level, and so on), rather than being
configured on the basis of ethnic homogeneity. The US as a whole is eth-
nically diverse, and it is the very fact that its political structures are *not*
fundamentally based on, or configured along, ethnic lines that permits
diverse ethnic cultural expressions to flourish. It follows, contrary to the
presupposition of the argument being considered, that significant cultural
goods are not necessarily only available to ethnic groups that have their
own self-governing state.

This is not to deny that ethnicity is important in other ways, or to deny
that ethnicity is ever relevant to the issue of political self-determination.
As Allen Buchanan notes,

> One cannot simply dismiss . . . the possibility that there can be circumstances
> under which a group living within the jurisdiction of the state may reasonably seek
> to achieve political autonomy . . . to be able to express and sustain values . . . such
> as a distinctive conception of community or a particular conception of the religious
> life'. (Buchanan 1991, p. 325)

For example, Tibetans' right to cultural self-expression may require
Tibetan political autonomy, since this may be, in fact, the only way such
cultural self-expression can be achieved, given the repressive nature of the
Chinese regime. In practice it may thus be difficult to distinguish between
the aspiration for cultural self-expression as a basic human right, and the
pursuit of political autonomy as a member of a particular ethnic group. The
important point, however, is that cultural self-realisation for members of a
particular ethnic group is only *contingently* related to a right to political
self-determination. Thus for any particular case, an independent argument

would have to be constructed showing that, given the facts of the matter, a community can only (or less stringently, can best) achieve cultural self-expression within its own self-governing state – a requirement whose satisfaction can only be judged on a detailed case-by-case basis.

Despite the aspirations of republicans for Ireland to be 'one nation – united, Gaelic and free', there is no reason to assume that Irish cultural self-realisation requires a self-governing Irish state co-extensive with the geographical boundaries of the island of Ireland. Ironically, if the Cultural Self-Realisation Argument were sound, it could just as easily be used to justify the continued existence of Northern Ireland as a Protestant state as it could the reunification of Ireland as a Catholic state, for reasons that have already been elaborated.

A right to cultural self-realisation does not entail a right to, or the need for, a distinct independent state. But for the sake of argument, suppose that it did. If the people of Ireland constitute a single cultural nation requiring a political state of their own in order to enjoy cultural self-realisation, it would follow (given the assumptions being granted) that they have a right to a political state of their own. What would *not* follow, however, is that they have a right to a political state co-extensive with the physical boundaries of the island of Ireland, rather than, say, with just the twenty-six counties of the Republic. From the mere fact that a people have a right to a political state of their own, nothing whatsoever follows concerning the *location* or *boundaries* of the physical embodiment of this state. The right to a state and the right to establish one's state *on a particular piece of real estate* are two distinct issues that could only be bridged by connecting the right to a specific territory in some way. Perhaps only the democratically expressed will of the people of that territory can do that.

PROCEDURAL ARGUMENTS FOR A RIGHT TO A UNITED INDEPENDENT THIRTY-TWO-COUNTY IRISH STATE

The modern conception of 'self-determination' owes much to Woodrow Wilson, who in the aftermath of World War I articulated the principle that 'every people has a right to choose the sovereignty under which they [sic] live' (Knight 1985, p. 254). By 'self-determination' he meant government by consent of the governed (Whelan 1994, p. 100). It might seem that all of the difficult substantive (and value-laden) issues just discussed could be by-passed simply by permitting presently existing democratic structures to operate unfettered. That is, the issue of statehood could be decided procedurally through the operation of a democratic decision process. Granted, in societies lacking effective democratic institutions, the distinctive minority communities of those societies might correctly conclude that the only way to achieve political self-determination is through the use of force. But in societies structured on effective democratic institutions the situation seems entirely different. After all, the United Kingdom and the Republic of Ireland are democratic societies, the vast majority of whose people are committed to the non-violent resolution of political issues. The majority of unionists and nationalists agree that the people of a nation are entitled to exercise a right of self-determination, expressed democratically through majority rule. Indeed, the Sinn Féin document 'Freedom' asserts that, 'When a people are [sic] divided in political allegiance, the democratic principle is that majority rights should prevail, the more so when such fundamentals as national rights are in question' (http://sinnfein.org/). But if so, why not simply adopt a voluntarist approach according to which it is the will of the people that determines the nature of their own governance?

The critical issue here is the identification of 'the people' for the purpose of democratic political self-determination. Republicans take for granted that the Northern Irish state is illegitimate, having been imposed upon the Irish people by force at the conclusion of the Anglo-Irish War, and that it is the Irish people as a whole who possess the right to self-determination. According to Gerry Adams, speaking on 12 August 1993, 'national self-determination is national self-determination . . . the Irish people who reside in this island have the right to national self-determination as a whole' (O'Brien 1999, p. 274). He previously dismissed the idea that unionists in Northern Ireland possess a similar right: 'To bestow the power of veto over national independence and sovereignty on a national minority is in direct contravention of the principle of self-determination' (Adams 1988, p. 41). The republican activist Danny Morrison expressed exasperation at the idea of a legitimate unionist veto: 'I'm tired of hearing about the democratic wishes of the people of Northern Ireland. It's the democratic wishes of the people of the whole of Ireland that matters' (Rees 2005, p. 182). Since (it is presumed) the majority of people in Ireland desire a united independent Ireland, it follows that the political association of Northern Ireland with Great Britain should be dissolved, and the Six Counties should be re-integrated into a thirty-two-county united independent Irish state. Call this the 'Republican Democratic Self-Determination Argument'.

Despite the apparent simplicity of this proposal, in practice it is fraught with difficulties. One problem concerns the republican assumption that a majority of the people of Ireland desire a united independent Ireland – an assumption that may well be false. As O'Mahony and Delanty (1998, p. 12) note, 'The population of the Irish Republic . . . on the whole do not regard nationalist political violence in Northern Ireland as legitimate, though a majority continue to hold an "aspiration" towards a united Ireland. The aspiration is a weak one.' Electoral support for Sinn Féin in the Republic typically amounts to only a few per cent, suggesting that Irish reunification (the most important item on Sinn Féin's political agenda) is not a matter of great concern for most Irish citizens. More surprisingly, even Catholics in Northern Ireland have been strongly divided on the issue of whether Irish reunification is desirable. In 1972, at the height of the IRA's campaign, only 53 per cent of Catholics in Northern Ireland said that they would vote for the reunification of Ireland. By 1998 that figure had risen to 55 per cent and by 2001 had risen to 59 per cent. By contrast, only 2 per cent of Protestants in Northern Ireland were prepared in 2001 to back a united Ireland (Mulholland 2002). The uncritical republican assumption that reunification would be democratically supported were the issue to be placed before the people of Ireland as whole is thus problematic.

A second problem concerns the argument's neglect of an important alternative perspective. Almost entirely absent from the republican world view for many years was the simple fact that most of the inhabitants of Northern Ireland embraced the 'Britishness' of Ulster. Unionists take for granted that the Northern Ireland state is legitimate and that it is the people of that state who have the right to exercise national self-determination for themselves. Since the majority of the people in that state desire continued inclusion in the UK, it follows that Northern Ireland should remain part of the UK. Call this the 'Unionist Democratic Self-Determination Argument'.

The fundamental problem with simply insisting upon 'national self-determination by majority rule' then becomes clear: 'the people cannot decide until someone decides who are the people' (Jennings 1956, pp. 55–6). As Woodrow Wilson's own Secretary of State, Robert Lansing complained, 'When the President talks about "self-determination", what has he in mind? . . . Without a definite unit which is practical, application of this principle is dangerous to peace and security' (Lansing 1921, p. 7). In (Northern) Ireland, the identification of the relevant majority is not simply an objective fact open to direct inspection. An appeal to democratic self-determination via majority rule cannot get off the ground in this case because the identity of the relevant 'majority' is precisely what is contested. Unionists correctly point out that they are a majority within Northern Ireland (which they view as a legitimate political entity), and conclude that the nationalist minority in their midst must bend to their democratically expressed will. Citizens of the Republic of Ireland, in this view, have no say at all in the matter, because they are not members of the relevant political community. Republicans insist that their political aspiration is shared by a majority within Ireland, both in the Republic and in the Six Counties (which together, they assert, constitutes the only legitimate political entity on the island), and conclude that the unionist minority in their midst should bend to the will of the majority of the people of Ireland. Clearly, appealing to the democratically expressed will of 'the people' in order to resolve the issue of national self-determination requires identification of the relevant population.

Such arguments, it should be noted, do not *have* to fail. Were a majority of the people of Great Britain, Northern Ireland and the Republic of Ireland to maintain that Northern Ireland should remain part of the UK (or be reunified with the Republic, or be established as a completely independent, sovereign state, with no political ties to either Great Britain or to the Republic of Ireland), that would democratically resolve the issue (although it probably would not end the conflict, since republicans would be unlikely to simply accept that verdict). Likewise, were a majority of the people of Northern Ireland and the Republic of Ireland to express a preference that Northern Ireland remain a part of the UK for so long as a majority of those living in Northern Ireland so desired, that would also democratically resolve the issue. This is precisely what the overwhelming approval of the Good Friday Agreement in 1998 indicated. It could therefore be argued that *if* there is a right to self-determination, it should include the right to choose *how* to exercise self-determination, even if this results in choosing political arrangements that fall short of complete sovereignty and independence (O'Brien 1999). Self-determination by majority rule is thus not *necessarily* doomed to failure. But it is also clear that it is not sufficient, given the current desires of people north and south of the border, to support the republican demand for an end to partition.

CONCLUSIONS

I have been concerned in this chapter to show that a range of republican arguments in support of a right of the Irish people to a united, independent, thirty-two-county Irish nation-state fail. Making the political boundaries of Ireland congruent with its geographical boundaries, or with a particular cultural nation, or aligned with the will of a particular sub-population of the island, are all inadequate grounds for asserting the necessity of reunification. However, I have not attempted the considerably more ambitious project of showing that the republican demand for a united, independent Irish nation-state *must* fail. Padraig O'Malley does attempt to do this by narrowing republican arguments down to one, and then showing that this singular argument fails. He quotes Daithi O'Connaill as stating: 'Fundamental to our philosophy is the principle of the sovereignty and integrity of the nation. As Republicans we have never accepted the right of any minority to opt out of the nation.' O'Malley then goes on to pose the following intriguing thought experiment: 'But what if Northern Ireland's population was entirely Protestant, wholly loyal in its allegiance to Britain and altogether opposed to unification? Would the concept of a thirty-two-county Irish nation-state make legal, political, or moral sense?' The correct answer, he thinks, is 'obviously not'. It follows, he continues, that 'the IRA's campaign owe[s] whatever legitimacy [it claims] *solely* to the presence of Catholics in Northern Ireland' (O'Malley 1983, p. 297; emphasis in original). The logic of the IRA's armed struggle is that the demands of a dissenting minority in the Six Counties validate the demands of a majority in Ireland as a whole. But this is fallacious: 'It is untenable when the minority are few in number, and therefore untenable even when the minority are many in number' (O'Malley 1983, p. 298).

O'Malley's argument appears to take for granted the unionist view that the right of political self-determination necessarily belongs to the population of Northern Ireland rather than to the population of Ireland as a whole. Why accept this assumption? O'Malley treats this claim as self-evidently true, but clearly someone like Daithi O'Connaill, in the quote above, would not consider it to be self-evident, and would in fact reject it as inconsistent with the fundamental principle of republican ideology and therefore as simply begging the question. In addition, the argument assumes, without justification, that the numbers of Catholics in Northern Ireland *in principle cannot* make any difference to the legitimacy of republican demands for a thirty-two-county Irish nation-state, so long as they constitute a minority in Northern Ireland. This is far from obvious. Consequently, if all but one argument for the republican demand for a united independent Ireland fails, and it has not been shown (for example, by O'Malley) that any republican argument for a united independent Ireland *must* fail, then in order to probe more deeply into the question of the moral justification of the IRA's armed struggle we must go on to examine in more depth the sole possible ground for such a moral justification.

The only legitimate grounds for the reunification of Ireland are *ethical*, namely, that doing so would end injustices against some of the people of Ireland and thereby help them to experience full, flourishing human lives, without in the process creating even greater injustices and diminished lives for others. This is a worthy political aspiration. Is politically motivated violence (including terrorism) ever a morally legitimate means to establish a political order in which such rights are honoured? Many would recoil from this question because it seems to open the door to the possibility of morally justified terrorism. But as Coady notes, 'The really interesting moral issue is . . . not whether terrorism is generally wrong, but whether it is nonetheless sometimes morally permissible' (Coady 2004, p. 58). This is one of the central questions that will occupy us in the next three chapters.

CHAPTER 4

Permission to Kill: Just War Theory and the IRA's Armed Struggle

War is an ugly thing, but not the ugliest of things: the decayed and degraded state
of moral and patriotic feeling which thinks nothing worth a war, is worse . . .
(John Stuart Mill 1868, p. 26)

INTRODUCTION

Detonating bombs that over the course of three decades injured, maimed
or killed hundreds of people certainly counts as causing harm to others, if
anything does, and would prima facie seem to be morally wrong, if anything is. Yet what is morally impermissible in ordinary circumstances may
be morally permissible in the extraordinary circumstances of *war*, which
by its very nature involves intentionally harming others. Just as clearly, not
everything done in war is morally justifiable. The fact that certain types of
actions are by international agreement classified as 'war crimes' suggests
that there are moral limits differentiating permissible from impermissible
wartime acts. Since at least the Middle Ages, philosophers have drawn a
distinction between just and unjust wars, and have attempted to identify
the conditions under which the resort *to* war, and sorts of actions undertaken *in* war, are morally justifiable (Evans 2005). 'Just War Theory' formalises these conditions.

From its beginning the Provisional IRA conceived of itself as an *army*
engaged in a morally justified armed struggle against the British occupation of Ireland. On occasion the IRA has asserted that its armed campaign
is justified according to the formal rules governing warfare. On 29
September 1979, Pope John Paul II delivered a homily to 250,000 faithful
at Drogheda in County Louth. The Pontiff declared that 'violence

destroys what it claims to defend – the dignity, the life, the freedom of human beings'. He appealed to 'the men of violence' to lay down their arms, to 'turn away from violence and to return to the ways of peace'. A few days later a spokesperson for the IRA responded by asking for 'clarification' on whether the Church's 'teaching on the right to resort to legitimate revolt and the right to engage in a just war has been changed', implying that the IRA's activities were justified according to just war doctrine, and moreover that the Holy Father had failed to recognise this important fact.[1]

Can the IRA's armed struggle be morally justified according to traditional just war principles? In order to answer this question, several preliminary questions must be answered. First, according to just war principles, under what conditions is the *resort* to war morally justified, and what are the conditions governing the morality of the *conduct* of war? Second, was the IRA's armed struggle accurately described as 'war'? Finally, to what extent can the IRA's campaign be morally justified according to the criteria of Just War Theory? My aim in this chapter is to provide reasoned answers to these and related questions. I will argue that although the IRA's armed struggle, at least in some of its phases, can reasonably be described as war, it fails to satisfy key conditions both for the just initiation of war and for the just conduct of war. Despite the IRA's claims to the contrary, its armed struggle was not justified according to the principles of Just War Theory.

JUST WAR THEORY

War might seem like the most brutal and uncivilised of human activities. Yet every culture capable of waging war has had implicit or explicit rules for the initiation and prosecution of violent actions against others – when it is right to wage war and how war once initiated should be conducted. Just War Theory formalises the conditions under which it is just to go to war (*jus ad bellum* conditions), and the conditions under which a war, once initiated, can be justly waged (*jus in bello* conditions).[2] As a *prescriptive* guide to when it is just to go to war and for how a war is to be justly conducted, Just War Theory is an attempt to mitigate the evils of war and to civilise, so far as possible, this destructive activity. *Ex post facto*, it is a tool for the moral *assessment* of wars. Since our concern here is with the moral assessment of the IRA's armed struggle from 1969 to 2005, it will be considered mainly in this latter capacity.

Jus ad Bellum Conditions

Just War theorists identify five (sometimes six) conditions, all of which must be satisfied in order for acts initiating war to be just. These conditions can be briefly described here before considering each more closely in the context of their application to the IRA's armed struggle.

Legitimate authority: The agent declaring war must be a legitimate authority. Typically, this will be a state. Private groups (or individuals) cannot (justly) declare war.

Just cause: War must be declared only as a defence against a real and serious attack on the common good, although this does not preclude conducting an offensive action in order to prevent an enemy attack that would compromise the common good were it allowed to proceed unimpeded. Offensive wars conducted simply for the sake of expanding borders or for economic growth would not satisfy this condition.

Right intention: It is not enough that the cause itself be just; the act of going to war must issue from right intentions. An intention to defend the common good of the community would be a right intention. An intention to use force out of hatred for one's enemy, or from a desire for political domination, would not satisfy this condition.

Probability of success: There must be a likelihood of success. War inevitably involves loss of life. To undertake war when the chances of success are slim is unjust.

Proportionality: The probable overall benefits of going to war must outweigh the probable overall costs of doing so. Not only must there be a likelihood of securing some good through war, but the good to be achieved must compensate for the costs likely to be incurred.

Last resort: War is perhaps the most serious human undertaking, with enormous stakes. According to some theorists, before resorting to war all other means of securing the good of the community must have been tried and found insufficient.

Jus in Bello Conditions

In order for the conduct of a war to be just, it must satisfy two *jus in bello* conditions.

Proportionality: A just war must be conducted in such a way that the overall benefits outweigh the overall costs. The use of force always

94

involves costs. Consequently, only as much force should be used as is necessary to secure the good being sought.

Discrimination: Violence must be directed only at legitimate targets. Although non-combatant casualties may be inevitable in war, they cannot be intentionally targeted.

Taken together, the *jus ad bellum* and *jus in bello* conditions provide a general framework for the moral evaluation of war. Given the abstract way in which these conditions are stated, a great deal of interpretation must accompany their application to specific situations. Applications to IRA violence have proven especially contentious, beginning with the fundamental question of whether the IRA's armed struggle should be considered 'war'.

Is the IRA's Armed Struggle Accurately Described as 'War'?

According to its own self-conception, the Provisional IRA has since its inception been engaged in a *war* to end British occupation in the Six Counties and to thereby secure Ireland's complete independence. 'A Scenario for Peace', for example, informs us that

> Sinn Féin seeks to create conditions which will lead to a permanent cessation of hostilities, an end to our long war and the development of a peaceful, united and independent Irish society. Such objectives will only be achieved when a British government adopts a strategy for decolonization. (http://sinnfein.org/)

Although this statement was issued by Sinn Féin, it is safe to say that it expressed the viewpoint of the republican movement's military wing as well. That the IRA was at war with the British was also presupposed in its insistence that republican prisoners be accorded prisoner of war status – a status that the British government at times appeared to accept. In June 1971 Reginald Maudling, the Conservative British Home Secretary, announced that the British government was now 'at war with the IRA' (Mulholland 2002, p. 92). Likewise, after internment in August 1971, Brian Faulkner, the Northern Ireland Prime Minister at the time, explained: 'I have taken this serious step solely for the protection of life and the security of property. We are, quite simply, at war with the terrorists and in a state of war many sacrifices have to be made' (O'Doherty 1998, p. 81).

At other times, however, the British government insisted that the Troubles in Northern Ireland were not a war at all, but simply a civil conflict between the legitimate authority of the state and a well-armed, fanatical gang of criminal terrorists. This was the major thrust of Britain's 'criminalisation' policy introduced in March 1976, according to which paramilitary prisoners should be incarcerated as criminals rather than as prisoners of war. Some journalists and scholars have adopted a similar view. Malachi O'Doherty treats the IRA's claims to be involved in a war in the early 1970s as simply republican propaganda: 'The IRA were playing at warfare, or acting out a semblance of warfare . . . they were presenting an image of exacerbated crisis to disgrace the government which had discarded normal legislative procedures to intern people without trial' (O'Doherty 1998, p. 81). He later calls the IRA's campaign a 'mock war' with the British army (p. 88) and an 'imitation war' (p. 96). Rogelio Alonso, likewise, suggests that the IRA was at best engaged in a 'fantasy war' (Alonso 2007, p. 91). He quotes a former IRA member who admitted, 'I don't believe for one minute that the IRA had a war. There was no war, it was a nasty little conflict where they shot this one, they shot that one. It's like an assassination campaign' (Alonso 2007, p. 91). J. Bowyer Bell's comments reflect the difficulty of classifying the IRA's armed struggle unambiguously as war. He describes the IRA's campaign as 'a real war in the middle of the United Kingdom' (Bell 1990, p. 19), as 'not war or not conventional war' (pp. 29–30), and finally concludes that the IRA 'wanted a war, planned for a war, and by 1971 . . . had a war' (p. 107).

Resolving this issue requires drawing some distinctions. 'War' is conventionally understood to be a state of armed conflict between different nations, states or armed groups. According to this conventional definition, some activities of the IRA can reasonably be considered as constituting war. For example, in 1971–2 when IRA units instigated street battles with the British army, the RUC and with Protestant paramilitary groups (seen as the instruments of foreign occupation), it was engaging in a species of warfare. It would not follow, of course, that *every* activity of the IRA is properly construed as war. Sectarian killings of Protestant civilians, reprisal killings of loyalist paramilitaries, punishment beatings of Catholics who collaborate with the security forces, 'knee-capping' suspected informants and criminal activities undertaken to raise money for weapons, do not qualify as acts of war, although they may occur in the course of prosecuting a war. Attacks on off-duty military or security personnel fall into a grey zone somewhere between guerrilla war and conventional war. The British government's policy of criminalisation was based more on judgements of political efficacy than on an attempt at objective classification, and hence cannot settle the question. Certainly the IRA's goal of ending British jurisdiction in the Six Counties through armed struggle makes its activities closer to war than to ordinary criminal activity, where the latter is usually undertaken solely for the criminal's own personal (for example, economic) benefit. Thus a reasonable case can be made that the IRA's armed struggle can be properly considered as war, albeit an unusually long one involving some unconventional tactics.

If significant aspects of the IRA's armed struggle can reasonably be described as war, what becomes of the common characterisation of some of its activities as involving the use of *terrorism*? Does the former exclude the latter? Rather than defining 'war' and 'terrorism' as mutually exclusive kinds of acts, they should instead be viewed as conceptually orthogonal to one another. War can assume a variety of different forms, from hit-and-run guerrilla tactics to large-scale invasions. Likewise, acts of terrorism can range from issuing threats of harm to acts that involve massive loss of life and property. Unless one insists on a priori grounds that war and terrorism are mutually exclusive, there is no reason to conclude that some acts cannot be both. The IRA's armed struggle as a whole is reasonably described as war *and* as involving the use of terrorism. Such a dual description by itself, however, leaves entirely unresolved the question of whether that armed struggle was morally justified, to which we now turn.

The IRA's Armed Struggle and the *Jus ad Bellum* Conditions of Just War Theory

Consider first the *jus ad bellum* criteria for when it is just to go to war.

Legitimate Authority

Was the Provisional IRA a legitimate authority for conducting war? Its leadership certainly thought so and offered a historical argument in defence of this view. The Provisionals traced their roots to the Irish Volunteers (*Óglaigh na hÉireann*) who staged the rebellion in Dublin during Easter Week, 1916. Moreover, they claimed the authority of the 1919 Sinn Féin government in Dublin that had sanctioned the Irish Republican Army as one of the 'moral foundation stones on which the republican movement rested' (Holland 1999, p. 213). As explained in the *Green Book*, the IRA's indoctrination manual for new recruits:

> The moral position of the Irish Republican Army, its right to engage in warfare, is based on: (a) the right to resist foreign aggression; (b) the right to revolt against tyranny and oppression; (c) the direct lineal succession with the Provisional Government of 1916, the first Dáil of 1919 and the second Dáil of 1921. (O'Brien 1999, p. 104)

Because the IRA split in 1969, it was important to the Provisional leadership that this authority be conferred on the Provisional IRA rather than on their rivals in the Officials. On 31 December 1969, Ruairí Ó'Brádaigh, representing the Provisional IRA Army Council, visited seventy-seven-year-old Tom Maguire at his home in Cross, County Mayo. Maguire, the sole surviving member of the Executive of the Second Dáil Éireann, and the sole surviving signatory of the 1938 proclamation that delegated the executive powers of government to the IRA Army Council, released a statement declaring that 'the governmental authority delegated in the Proclamation of 1938 now resides in the Provisional Army Council and its lawful successors'. The Provisional IRA was now the moral and legal heir of the government of the all-Ireland Republic (White 2006, pp. 153–4).[3]

This reasoning is rejected by George (2000), who argues that a sovereign Irish state did not come into existence until 1949, and even then it wasn't the authentic 'Irish Socialist Republic' proclaimed in the 1916 Proclamation – both because it wasn't socialist and because it included only twenty-six of the thirty-two counties of Ireland. Consequently, the 'Irish Republic proclaimed in 1916, reaffirmed in 1919 by the First Dáil Éireann and the object of allegiance of militant Republicans ever since, was, and is, a legal nonentity' (George 2000, pp. 85–6). He concludes that the Provisional IRA was entirely lacking the legitimate authority to wage war. Moreover, in George's view it is a necessary rather than a contingent fact that the IRA, qua terrorist group, failed to satisfy the condition of legitimate authority: 'This summary dismissal of the IRA's claims is easy because sovereignty is an attribute of the state . . . and so it is inevitably absent from any insurgent terrorist group like the IRA' (George 2000, pp. 86–7).

Membership in the IRA is illegal in both the UK and in the Republic of Ireland. George takes the illegality of the IRA to be decisive for dismissing it as a legitimate authority entitled to wage war. But there are good reasons for questioning the identification of moral legitimacy with legality, and with it the summary dismissal of the IRA's claim to possess the legitimate authority to wage war on behalf of its constituency.

First, to equate the legitimate authority to wage war with being a sovereign state necessarily renders unjust all revolutions in which all or part of a population wages war against a tyrannical regime. Such an identification would *necessarily* render unjust many wars of independence that seem, prima facie at least, to *possibly* be morally justified. George's position would make all of them *necessarily* morally illegitimate. To the extent that the moral legitimacy of such wars should be left open to critical debate, George's view is defective.

Second, equating legitimate authority with legal authority entails that only states can justly go to war, giving states a monopoly on the legitimate use of force. Arguably, being a state (for example, Nazi Germany) is not always a sufficient condition for being a legitimate moral authority. Perhaps it is not necessary, either. Valls (2000) argues that what matters for being a legitimate authority is that an organisation claims to act on behalf of a community, and that it be widely seen by that community as acting on its behalf. Such an organisation need not be associated with a state per se. If the Palestinian Authority, for example, claims to represent the interests of the Palestinian people, and is widely recognised by the Palestinian people as acting on their behalf, then the Palestinian Authority may be de facto a legitimate authority, regardless of the fact that there is (currently) no Palestinian state.

This suggests a different way of interpreting the condition of legitimate authority. Even if the IRA cannot be considered a de jure legitimate authority in virtue of being, or representing, a sovereign state, might it not be a de facto legitimate authority in virtue of representing 'the Irish people'? Unfortunately, problems arise here as well. As discussed in Chapter 3, the problem is that of identifying the correct referent of the term 'the Irish people'. Presumably, the people residing in Ireland should be considered 'the Irish people' if anyone should, yet the vast majority of them completely reject the IRA's claims to be representing them. What about Catholics in Northern Ireland? Could the IRA be considered a legitimate authority for that subset of the population of Ireland? According to the standard republican narrative, the Provisional IRA has always enjoyed widespread support in the Northern Irish Catholic community and this support validates its role as that community's defender and representative. The IRA, according to its own conception, is the voice of a community (O'Doherty 1998). Hence, Robert W. White opines that 'when the British negotiated the 1975 truce with the IRA, they essentially recognized the IRA as a legitimate representative of part of the Northern Nationalist community' (White 1993, p. 175).

This is surely an exaggeration. First, it is equally consistent with the British decision to talk with the IRA that they simply wanted to find a way to stop the bloodshed, and if talking with the IRA would help to bring about that result, they were willing to do it. Second, in 1978 a Northern Ireland Attitude Survey found that 39 per cent of Catholics in Northern Ireland would settle for a power-sharing devolved government within a UK framework. Subsequent surveys consistently indicated that a plurality of Catholics in Northern Ireland considered this type of solution to be acceptable. This hardly sounds like widespread community support for the IRA's armed campaign. Third, as Padraig O'Malley reported in 1983, most Northern Irish Catholics did not believe that they were being politically repressed to an extent that justified the IRA's campaign of violence to end it. 'On the contrary, the majority are more inclined to see themselves as victims of the IRA's actions, and thus they support a tougher policy toward the IRA on the parts of both the British and the Irish governments' (O'Malley 1983, p. 313). Certainly many of the numerous Catholics in Northern Ireland who have lost loved ones as a result of the IRA's armed struggle might be loath to acknowledge the IRA as representing their interests. It is true that in recent years Sinn Féin has surpassed the SDLP as the largest nationalist party in Northern Ireland and this could be taken as indicating increased support for the IRA. But caution is required in making such inferences. People may vote for Sinn Féin candidates for a range of reasons, including simply because the available alternatives do not look more attractive. Hence votes for Sinn Féin candidates cannot be taken as necessarily indicating support for the IRA, despite the close linkage between the two organisations. The claim that the IRA is a de facto legitimate authority is therefore dubious.

Just Cause

According to traditional Just War Theory, war must be declared only as a defence against a real and serious attack on the common good. Republicans make much of a handful of purely defensive actions undertaken by the IRA. When loyalists in June 1970 threatened to burn down St. Matthew's church and to kill the priests inside, the IRA took up arms to defend the church. In the ensuing gun battle, three Protestants were shot dead. Even if we assume that this account is accurate, however, it is unclear how it could be used to satisfy the 'just cause' condition of Just War Theory. First, this was a limited, isolated military engagement, not the beginning of a war. Second, this defensive action was (according to the standard republican account) in response to an attack by loyalists, against whom the IRA never declared a war. Third, the Provisional IRA had declared a war on the British army in Ireland *prior* to June 1970. When the Provisional IRA Army Council met in January 1970 to determine the new organisation's strategy, IRA Chief of Staff Seán MacStiofáin explained that the first priority was to protect Catholic neighbourhoods from loyalist attacks, a second phase would combine defensive and retaliatory action, and after a sufficient period of preparation the third phase would focus on 'launching an all out offensive against the British occupation system' (MacStiofáin 1975, p. 146). Thus the decision to wage a war against the British in Ireland was made prior to the events of June 1970. Throughout 1970 the IRA operated primarily in defensive and retaliatory modes. By March 1971, the Provisional IRA was in full-scale offensive mode, determined to force a British withdrawal as the precondition for Ireland's reunification. From that point on offence supplanted defence as the IRA's primary activity. Assassinating members of the royal family and setting off bombs in English pubs, among other activities, cannot plausibly be interpreted as essentially defensive in nature. The bulk of the IRA's activities had a different goal: the irredentist nationalist goal of establishing a united independent all-Ireland Republic.

Against this judgement it could be responded that this argument overlooks the fact that violence against a community need not be construed only in the narrow sense of the use of physical force. As Kai Nielsen points out, 'When [a state] has exceeded its legitimate authority and still exercises force on people, then that force is a form of violence' (Nielsen 1981, p. 438). Thus it could be argued that the IRA was in fact engaged in a morally justified *defensive war* against the British, because the British-supported Protestant domination of Northern Ireland constituted a kind of 'cultural violence' against the Irish Catholic nationalist minority in the Six Counties. The IRA declared a war in order to defend Catholics from this state-sanctioned cultural violence. Therefore the condition of 'just cause' has been satisfied.

The problem with this argument is that such 'cultural violence' would only justify resistance, not a resort to war. Even if discrimination against Catholics regarding public housing, jobs and electoral representation was as extensive as it appears to have been, such abuses of power require redress but do not justify going to *war* to rectify them. Significantly, egregious discrimination against Catholics was significantly reduced through reforms in the early 1970s, just when the IRA's bombing campaign escalated, suggesting that the defence of Catholics in Northern Ireland was not the primary motivation for the campaign.

Right Intention

According to the *jus ad bellum* condition of 'right intention', war can only be justly initiated from an intention to secure the common good, and not out of revenge, hate, desire for territorial expansion or other non-defensive motivations. It is difficult to see how the IRA's armed struggle could satisfy this condition. It is noteworthy that the leadership of the IRA has never announced that it would end the armed struggle when Catholics in the Six Counties achieve political, social and economic equality with Protestants. Even if these fundamental elements of the common good were secured, republicans would not be satisfied until Ireland as a whole is completely free from British control. Yet it is unclear how this would add anything to the common good. Republicans, of course, would reject this conclusion. They would maintain that the common good for the people of Ireland can only *truly* be achieved through reunification. Given the high costs of the armed struggle, however, the burden of proof is on republicans to provide convincing reasons to believe that this *is* the case, and not merely that it *might* be the case. Such reasons have so far not been provided.

Probability of Success

For a resort to war to be just, there must be a probability of success. Whether a group is likely to succeed in its aims depends on what those aims are, on the resources available for achieving those aims, and on the resources and resolve of its enemy. Even in seemingly ideal circumstances it will be extremely difficult to determine with precision the probability of success of a military campaign, since the success of such campaigns depends on so many factors that are not known, and cannot be known, at the time the action is initiated.[4] Still, in order for a resort to war to be just, those considering such campaigns must at least attempt to determine whether a resort to war in other similar situations proved to be successful.

The leadership of the IRA had some reason to believe that a guerrilla war against the British military presence in Ireland might be successful. It clearly understood that the British army could not be defeated through conventional military engagements. The British military was too strong, and the IRA's resources too meagre, for such a strategy to have been seriously considered. Instead, reviewing their limited resources and reflecting on other struggles against colonial oppression, the IRA embarked on a campaign of low-intensity, opportunistic attacks on personnel, installations and public targets designed to force the British government to the conclusion that its Irish colony had become prohibitively expensive to maintain, and therefore that severing its political connection with it was the only viable option. Such tactics had succeeded in the Irish War of Independence, resulting in the liberation of most of Ireland from British control. The Provisional IRA's war, however, would be confined to the more manageable area of Northern Ireland, where the IRA enjoyed a strong base of support in the Catholic population, and to occasional attacks in England in order to 'bring home' to the British people and their political representatives the seriousness of the Irish question. The IRA leadership could note that similar campaigns in Algeria and Kenya had succeeded in securing national liberation for the peoples in question, the latter involving the overthrow of *British* colonial domination. As late as 1979 the Provisional IRA declared that 'we believe that our prospects for victory are supported by the examples of other colonial struggles, and by the widespread support which we know we command and which our operations prove' (*An Phoblacht/Republican News*, 6 October 1979; in English 2003, p. 215).

It is also undeniable, however, that the IRA grossly underestimated the resolve of both the British government and of loyalists, especially failing to grasp ordinary Ulster Protestants' deep aversion to any weakening of their ties to Britain. Opinion surveys in Northern Ireland have consistently registered huge Protestant majorities in favour of remaining in the UK, as high as 91 per cent of the community, with one poll in the late 1970s revealing only 1.5 per cent Protestant support for a united Ireland. Had the British government simply withdrawn from Northern Ireland, it is likely that violence would have erupted on a scale that would make the violence associated with the Troubles look like a minor skirmish by comparison (Smith 1995), scuttling the dream of gliding smoothly into a united Ireland. This possibility seems to have been ignored or dismissed by the Provisional IRA's leadership, yet it was critical to a reasoned assessment of the probability of success of the IRA's campaign.

Ultimately, the IRA leadership did not know, and could not know, whether its campaign would be successful until it actually implemented it and assessed the results. An analyst looking back on the IRA's campaign with the benefit of hindsight might confidently assert that its prior probability of success was slight, but it is far from clear that such confidence would have been warranted in, say, 1972. But if so, then satisfaction of the 'probability of success' condition of Just War Theory must remain indeterminate.

Proportionality

For the initiation of a war to be just, there must be good reasons for judging that the overall benefits of going to war are likely to outweigh the overall costs. Given the impossibility of knowing beforehand the outcome of any war, this will be an extremely difficult judgement even in the best of situations, and might seem to disqualify any decision to go to war as satisfying the proportionality condition. However, the point of the condition is not to require certainty that overall benefits will exceed the overall costs of going to war, but rather that such factors receive careful consideration and that a reasonable judgement of proportionality is made prior to initiating a war in which considerable costs in suffering and death are assured. The condition, so understood, is far more easily satisfied.

Considerations of proportionality seem to have been absent both from the IRA's decision to go to war and from the prosecution of its war. The IRA's approach was characterised by the conviction that victory was inevitable, that the achievement of a united independent Ireland was an absolute good, and therefore that success in that endeavour would necessarily justify *any* costs of the campaign. At the height of the IRA's urban bombing campaign, Seán MacStiofáin, the IRA's Chief of Staff at the time, chillingly proclaimed: 'Let it be placed on record that the Army Council is determined to continue the armed struggle until total victory, regardless of the cost to ourselves or others' (*Republican News*, 10 November 1972; in Smith 1995, p. 115). Such statements are astonishing and indicate a total disregard for matters of proportionality. Rather than carefully attempting to weigh the benefits and costs of an armed campaign (fallible though such a process must be), it seems instead that the IRA leadership simply eschewed such considerations.

Last Resort

Some Just War theorists require that before a group initiates war, all other options must have been exhausted. It is easy to see why some might balk at this condition. Strictly speaking, it might be the case that all other options short of war are *never* truly exhausted. In order for a group representing an oppressed people, for example, to correctly claim that war is indeed its last resort, it must not only have tried everything else, but it must have done so for so long that it became clear that there was no possibility of any of these other efforts succeeding. It is difficult to see how the condition of last resort, understood in this stringent sense, could ever be satisfied. A strict application of this condition might render unjust *any* decision to go to war. Consequently, the condition of last resort, if it is to be applied at all, needs to be construed in some weaker sense, perhaps that of repeatedly deploying non-violent means to secure the rights of one's community, failing each time, and having good reason for concluding that subsequent efforts short of war would likewise be futile. Precisely when that judgement may be made is a question which does not admit of any a priori specification, yet presumably it will be clear that in some cases such a judgement was made prematurely.

In the standard republican narrative, the resumption of the IRA's armed struggle is presented as a last resort to achieve for Catholics their basic civil rights after all peaceful means to achieve reforms had been tried and had been brutally suppressed. Consider the following statement from Sinn Féin that comprised part of the Hume–Adams talks in 1988:

> Armed struggle is forced upon the IRA. Neither the IRA nor Sinn Féin want this war but the ineffectualness of all other forms of struggle, the conditions of repression that we have experienced and British attitudes, have made armed struggle inevitable. The deaths and injuries caused by the war are all tragedies, which have been forced upon the people by the British presence. (http://www.sinnfein.ie/peace/document/79)

Elsewhere Sinn Féin president Gerry Adams was even more explicit:

> We believe that [the] Irish people have the right to use armed struggle in the context of seeking Irish independence and in the conditions of British occupation in the six counties . . . The IRA says that armed struggle is a method of political struggle adopted reluctantly and as a last resort in the absence of any viable alternative . . . The onus is on those who claim that there is an alternative to the IRA's armed struggle to prove that this is the case. (15 November 1990; in O'Brien 1999, p. 212)

The claim that the IRA embraced an armed struggle as a last resort to alleviate the 'conditions of oppression' of Catholics in Northern Ireland, however, is questionable. First, the IRA's decision to resume the armed struggle predated the emergence of the civil rights movement, and therefore could not have been embraced as a last resort after the civil rights movement ended. Indeed, the available evidence suggests that the pre-split IRA saw in the civil rights movement an opportunity to mobilise its natural support base, the Catholic community, in preparation for resuming the armed struggle. Second, the achievement of basic civil rights for Catholics in Northern Ireland was not the aim of the IRA's armed struggle. Rather, its aim was the end of partition and the long sought-after united Irish republic. Third, by the early 1970s, peaceful agitation for civil rights had achieved substantial gains for Catholics and it was far from obvious that additional gains were impossible using the same methods. Certainly the IRA's opponents (including those in the SDLP) would disagree that republicans were driven to an armed struggle and that they had no alternative. Finally, given the high costs of the armed struggle, it would seem that the onus was on republicans, rather than on the advocates of peaceful methods, to show that an armed struggle was a last resort, all peaceful means to the end of improving the lot of Catholics in Northern Ireland having been already exhausted. Even if such an approach ultimately failed, the costs of such failure would still be preferable to the human costs associated with thirty years of IRA violence.

The IRA's armed struggle appears to fail some of the *jus ad bellum* conditions of traditional Just War Theory, *all* of which must be satisfied in order for the decision to go to war to be morally justified. This might seem to settle the question of the moral justification of the IRA's armed struggle according to Just War Theory. A war that is unjust in its *initiation* cannot be considered morally justified in terms of Just War Theory even if it satisfies all of the conditions for justice *in* war. But if so, what could be the point of going on to examine the IRA's armed struggle in light of the *jus in bello* conditions for the just *prosecution of* a war?

There are at least four reasons for proceeding further. First, it is *possible* that, despite the considerations discussed above, the IRA's armed struggle in some overlooked way does satisfy the various *jus ad bellum* conditions after all, in which case in order to determine whether that armed struggle was morally justified it would be essential to consider whether it satisfied the *jus in bello* conditions as well. Second, it could be argued that Just War Theory developed under specific historical circumstances, such that the

106

socio-cultural conditions of a later time require the relaxation of some of its conditions, including the ones that the IRA's armed struggle appears to violate. Third, one of the aims of this book is to consider the morality of terrorism in general, for which the IRA's armed struggle provides a rich case study. Terrorism is primarily a tactic deployed in the hope of achieving certain aims. Examining the IRA's armed struggle in light of the *jus in bello* conditions provides a way of morally assessing the use of terrorism in general as a strategic option in the pursuit of political, ideological, social or religious agendas. Finally, it is common to draw a moral distinction between terrorism and conventional warfare, in which the former is almost universally condemned whereas the latter is often condoned. A comparison of terrorist acts with acts that occur in conventional warfare is essential for determining whether the common moral distinction between terrorism and war is cogent. It is therefore worthwhile to examine the *jus in bello* conditions of Just War Theory in relation to the IRA's armed struggle as well.

THE IRA's ARMED STRUGGLE AND THE *JUS IN BELLO* CONDITIONS OF JUST WAR THEORY

Proportionality

For a group's prosecution of a war to be morally justified the tactics used by that group must not cause harm or suffering beyond what is necessary to achieve the war's morally justified goal. Precisely how much destruction is necessary in a war cannot be specified in advance and independently of particular circumstances. It will depend, in part, on the strategic goals to be achieved and the means available for achieving these goals. It will also depend on the nature of the enemy's threat to the common good. Despite these uncertainties, it will often be clear when the degree of force used by a group has exceeded that which is strictly necessary.

The *jus in bello* proportionality condition is meant to govern the use of force in war. Peter Simpson (writing in 1986) argued that the situation in Northern Ireland was not accurately described as war, or one of occupation and rule by an alien power, but was instead better described as a case of a tyrannical regime unjustly oppressing one of the communities under its control. Nonetheless, he interprets the proportionality condition as entailing that 'whatever is necessary to defend against the attempts of the regime to impose its rule, and whatever is necessary to create a political

107

arrangement that will better respond to the requirements of the common good, is in principle just' (Simpson 1986, p. 83). Thus, on the one hand, the IRA was justified in repelling by force army or police patrols entering nationalist neighbourhoods. It was also justified in attacking army barracks or police stations from which such patrols came. Moreover, alternative centres of control, such as no-go areas in places like Derry, could be established and defended with arms against the regime's attempts to recover them. On the other hand, certain activities were not morally justifiable. Assassinations of off-duty security personnel who posed no immediate threat to the community, tit-for-tat killings of paramilitaries and random sectarian killings were *illegitimate* because these were not cases of immediate self-defence against present attack. A fortiori this was true of acts such as detonating bombs in London, because such acts were not undertaken in the defence of one's community. Their only purpose was to cause sufficient havoc in the mainland UK that the British people would exert pressure on their parliament to withdraw from Northern Ireland. Finally, according to Simpson, the withdrawal of the British from Northern Ireland was not in itself a situation that sanctioned the use of such tactics.

Simpson's interpretation of the proportionality condition as applied to the IRA's actions is extraordinarily generous. First, it apparently overlooks the fact that the primary reason that army and police patrols felt it necessary to enter (hostile) nationalist neighbourhoods and no-go areas was because it was (correctly) believed that the existence of such areas permitted the IRA to recruit, organise, train and stage operations without interference from the security forces. Second, attacks on army barracks and police stations would only be necessary in order to impede the ability of the security forces to carry out counter-terrorist operations against the IRA. Third, the moral distinction between attacking army barracks or police stations, on the one hand, and assassinations of off-duty security personnel, on the other, is murky at best, because neither would appear to be justified in terms of self-defence against present and immediate attack.

Despite the generosity of Simpson's interpretation, a consequence of it is that the vast majority of IRA operations during the thirty years of the Troubles failed the proportionality condition. Repelling army or police patrols from nationalist neighbourhoods, attacking the barracks from which such patrols originated and defending no-go areas constituted a minute fraction of the IRA's activities over the course of its long campaign. The bulk of its operations focused on detonating bombs aimed at 'sickening the British' into a withdrawal from the Six Counties as the necessary precondition for the reunification of Ireland. Given the alternatives to an armed struggle for addressing the legitimate grievances of Catholics in Northern Ireland, any use of force by the IRA might be considered excessive in relation to securing the common good of the community it claimed to represent. But since the harm and suffering caused by the IRA's armed struggle was far in excess of anything necessary to secure the common good of Catholics in Northern Ireland, it fails the proportionality condition.

Discrimination

The *jus in bello* discrimination condition requires that a distinction be drawn between legitimate and illegitimate targets of military action, and that military force only be directed at the former. The most common way of drawing this distinction is to distinguish between *combatants* and *non-combatants*. However, the moral significance of this distinction needs to be made clear and its application to the IRA's armed struggle needs to be considered. Three questions concerning this distinction are relevant here. (1) What is the moral significance of distinguishing between combatants and non-combatants? (2) Given this moral significance, how should this distinction be drawn? (3) How should the IRA's armed struggle be judged in relation to the discrimination condition? We can consider each of these questions in turn.

What is the *moral significance* of distinguishing between combatants and non-combatants? Recall that one of the *jus ad bellum* conditions for engaging in war is that it must have as its goal protecting the common good of the community. The discrimination condition could therefore be understood as requiring that in order for military action to be morally legitimate, it must only target individuals who pose a threat to the community's common good. Consequently, military actions that target individuals who pose no threat to the community's common good fail the discrimination condition and are morally illegitimate.

This way of understanding the moral significance of the discrimination requirement helps us to see why a number of proposals for distinguishing between combatants and non-combatants are problematic. For example, a simple but manifestly inadequate way of making this distinction would be to say that those personnel wearing uniforms are combatants whereas those not wearing uniforms are non-combatants. Besides the problem of determining what counts as a 'uniform' (Do the black 'pyjamas' of the Viet Cong count as uniforms? What about US Special Forces soldiers wearing regional Afghan attire or Apache warriors going into battle in war paint?), this criterion would lead to the absurd conclusion that one's status as a legitimate target of attack could in some cases change simply by removing one's hat.

This consequence is not purely hypothetical. Consider, for instance, IRA attacks on off-duty security personnel in Northern Ireland. On 28 October 1976, the IRA killed Stanley Adams, at the time of his death a postman and an off-duty, part-time member of the Ulster Defence Regiment. Adams' killing was carefully planned. The IRA sent a letter to a remote farmhouse on Adams' postal delivery route near Pomeroy in County Tyrone. Patiently lying in wait, they shot him as he arrived to deliver the letter. On 19 October 1977, Tommy McKearney was arrested and charged with the murder of Adams. He was sentenced to twenty years in prison for the crime. While never admitting guilt, McKearney defended the killing of Adams on the grounds that, although killed in the course of delivering a letter as part of his job as a postman, Adams nevertheless remained a legitimate military target:

> An off-duty UDR man is a member of the British army. Now it is very naïve and stretching credulity to breaking point to suggest that a man delivering the milk, delivering the mail, or driving a school bus sets aside his role while delivering or driving; that he would ignore what he sees through the day, that he ceases to observe, that he ceases to record, that he ceases to report. Now, by anybody's standard, an intelligence officer for a regular army is carrying out a very necessary function without which the regular forces in uniform cannot and do not operate. It is a key pivotal point. (Taylor 1997, p. 206)

McKearney has a point. As Bell asks, 'In real war the B-52s don't wait until the target rises, puts on a uniform, and thus becomes a legitimate target. Why should the IRA in Tyrone or Knightsbridge?' (Bell 1990, p. 30). Wearing a uniform, by itself, is irrelevant.

Presumably a deeper way of making the distinction would be to distinguish between military and civilian personnel. But a moment's reflection shows that this criterion is inadequate as well. The men and women in the military may be only the leading edge of an enemy force that consists of all the support structures (including civilians who supply the military with weapons, food, clothing, medical treatment and so on) without which the military would be unable to carry out its activities. The civilian leaders of a country, in particular, are not part of the military, but targeting them could well be far more effective in securing the common good of one's community than would be the killing of any number of infantrymen on the front lines.

A more promising approach would be to distinguish between those *actively engaged* in the conflict and those *not actively engaged* in it. Those actively engaged in a conflict are part of a 'chain of agency' leading from specific decisions and actions ultimately to the application of force against enemy targets. Their removal would make a difference to the military's ability to prosecute the war. Those not actively engaged in a conflict would stand outside the chain of agency leading to the application of force against enemy targets. Their removal would make no difference to the military's ability to prosecute the war. Rather than focusing on superficial factors such as uniforms and membership in the military, this way of making the distinction focuses on what seems to matter, namely, on causal agency.

Although less arbitrary than the other proposals so far considered, this one also suffers from the defect that there can be no *sharp* demarcation between combatants and non-combatants along these lines. At best there will be a distinction between those who are clearly combatants (soldiers in uniform firing weapons), and those who are clearly non-combatants (young children, some but not all of the elderly, the seriously infirm, those in comas, and so on), as well as a vast range of people whose activities are in the 'grey zone': for example, those whose activities to a greater or lesser extent make the application of military force possible. There is a continuum between 'pure combatants' and 'pure non-combatants' in terms of their causal contributions to the application of force to the enemy. If so, then the scope of legitimate targets might include anyone who through his actions aids, abets or supports the enemy, and thereby contributes to the attacks upon the common good of one's community.

This way of thinking found expression in the IRA's rationale for considering some ordinary businessmen as legitimate targets. In the late 1970s, the IRA began targeting industrialists, building contractors and military suppliers. IRA Chief of Staff Seamus Twomey's explanation was that such people 'are exploiting the Irish working class . . . everyone directly connected with British imperialism are [sic] definite targets' (*An Phoblacht/ Republican News*, 19 February 1977; in Moloney 2002, p. 185). In this view, the industrialists, contractors and suppliers were not simply ordinary businessmen attempting to make a living and provide for their families. Rather, they were categorised as part of the British colonial system designed to oppress Catholics in Northern Ireland. The danger of this view is that the circle can keep expanding indefinitely in order to rationalise any acts of violence against anyone seen as even remotely providing support to one's enemy.

111

The distinction between combatants and non-combatants is sometimes thought to reflect a deeper moral distinction between *innocence* and *non-innocence*, such that whereas intentionally targeting the non-innocent can sometimes be morally permissible, intentionally targeting the innocent never is, for the simple reason that it is never morally legitimate to target innocents. Unfortunately, 'innocence', like causal agency, comes in degrees. Is the news-stand vendor who sells papers biased toward the government's analysis of the war innocent or non-innocent in relation to that specific war? Even if we judge him to be innocent, other problems remain. Classifying non-combatants as 'the innocent' may suggest that combatants, even those fighting a just war, are by contrast necessarily 'the guilty'. As Noam Zohar (2004, p. 737) notes, however, 'it is often far from clear that soldiers are morally blameworthy even if their country's going to war is morally dubious'. Additionally, many armies consist almost entirely of conscripts, some as young as twelve years old – child soldiers who find themselves in military service reluctantly and who have little choice but to fight. Are they innocent or non-innocent? Combatant/non-combatant and non-innocent/innocent are not obviously congruent distinctions.

Is there some principled way of circumventing these conceptual conundrums? Although the conceptual problems just discussed pose serious challenges for operationalising the discrimination condition, they do not rob that condition of its relevance or importance. From the fact that it is difficult to find an unproblematic way of making the combatant/non-combatant distinction, it does not follow that there aren't clear cases where the discrimination condition fails to be satisfied. There is no sense in which young children, for example, may be said to be a threat to a community's common good. If the discrimination condition is understood as requiring that in order for military action to be morally legitimate it must only target individuals who pose a threat to the community's common good, and that military actions that target individuals who pose no threat to the community's common good fail the discrimination condition, then even if we cannot always say when a military action unequivocally *satisfies* the discrimination condition, we can nonetheless sometimes identify military actions that clearly *fail* to satisfy this condition. In particular, any acts that intentionally target those who clearly pose no threat to a community's common good must be judged as violating the *jus in bello* discrimination condition.

How might this proposal apply to the IRA's armed struggle? Although the standard republican narrative emphasises the crucial defensive role of the IRA, it is difficult to identify unambiguous instances in which the IRA stepped in to prevent an assault on the Catholic community. Rather, early in the conflict as the IRA's operations shifted into a predominantly retaliatory and offensive mode, the discrimination condition was violated repeatedly. For example, on 'Bloody Friday', 21 July 1972, the IRA detonated some twenty-two bombs in Belfast, killing two soldiers but also killing seven civilians. The bomb that killed Lord Louis Mountbatten on 27 August 1979 also took the life of his daughter's mother-in-law, his fourteen-year-old grandson and a fifteen-year-old boat boy. Killing Mountbatten alone would have constituted the 'spectacular' the IRA was after. Killing his three companions was entirely gratuitous, even from the point of view of advancing the IRA's political agenda. These two examples are particularly infamous but they are not uncharacteristic of the IRA's operations. It would be easy (albeit depressing) to multiply such examples (cf. McKittrick et al. 2001). The vast majority of those killed by IRA bombs placed in crowded pubs or in busy commercial centres posed no threat to the common good of Catholics in Northern Ireland. Such bombings were undertaken in order to make the British presence in Northern Ireland costly in human terms and to draw attention to the republican cause. Even if some IRA operations did satisfy the discrimination condition, a vastly greater number clearly did not.

TERRORISM AND CONVENTIONAL WARFARE

The IRA's armed struggle appears to fail a number of the conditions of Just War Theory, both for the initiation of war and for the prosecution of war. If we suppose that Just War Theory correctly identifies the conditions that must be satisfied in order for a group's initiation of and participation in war to be morally justified, it follows that the IRA's armed struggle was not morally justified. This would seem to settle the matter. Yet the determined IRA apologist could argue that in fact nearly all conventional wars *also* fail one or more of Just War Theory's conditions, and therefore that nearly all conventional wars are likewise not morally justified – a conclusion that to all but pacifists might seem absurd. Consequently, it could be argued that what the discussion so far in this chapter has demonstrated is not that the IRA's armed struggle was morally unjustified, but rather the poverty of traditional Just War Theory.

This response is worth taking seriously. Andrew Valls (2000) points out that both in public and in scholarly assessments of political violence a double standard is often operative. Whereas violence targeting civilians by states is often assumed to be morally legitimate, politically motivated violence targeting civilians by non-state actors is presumed to be morally illegitimate. At the very least, a more lenient moral standard is frequently applied when evaluating the authorised wartime actions of states than the perhaps equally destructive operations of non-state actors. Nevertheless, 'from a philosophical point of view, this double standard cannot be maintained' because 'consistency requires that we apply the same standards to both kinds of political violence, state and nonstate' (Valls 2000, p. 66).

Is there some fundamental difference between conventional warfare carried out by a state and an armed struggle by non-state actors that may include the use of terrorist tactics, that would morally differentiate the former from the latter? Many people would hold that they *are* fundamentally morally different. Consider, for example, how the Principle of Double Effect is sometimes invoked in support of the claim that whereas the terrorist who detonates a bomb in a pub that kills a hundred civilians in order to advance his political agenda has committed a terrible wrong, the bomber pilot who during wartime kills a hundred civilians in the process of destroying an enemy munitions factory may be morally excused. In the latter case the death of those civilians is conceptualised as a *foreseen but unintended* consequence of accomplishing the strategic goal of destroying a munitions factory; the bomber pilot did not intentionally kill the people on the ground, and their deaths in no way contributed to the achievement of his strategic objective. Were he to learn that the destruction of the munitions factory would *not* result in harm to anyone, it would make no difference to the successful execution of his mission, which is simply to destroy the munitions factory by dropping bombs on it. But in the terrorism case the death of the hundred civilians is *itself* the intended consequence of the pub bombing and is essential to advancing the terrorist's political agenda. Were the terrorist to learn that detonating his bomb in the pub would result in no harm to anyone (or to anyone's property), his mission would have lost its essential point. For him, it makes all the difference in the world that the people he targets are harmed through his actions. Therefore, according to this argument, whereas the death of civilians is a foreseen *but unintended* consequence of the bomber pilot's mission, it is a foreseen *and intended* consequence of the terrorist's mission, making the former morally excusable, but rendering the latter deserving of moral condemnation.

Jonathan Bennett (1981, p. 27) rejects such arguments. He points out that it is true the bomber pilot would destroy the munitions factory without harming anyone if he could; but the terror bomber might *also* prefer to detonate his bombs without harming anyone if by doing so he could equally well advance his agenda. The difference in the two cases is merely that it is easier to imagine the bomber pilot achieving his goal without killing civilians than it is in the case of the terror bomber. But this is not a relevant *moral* difference. Both acts of detonating bombs result in the exact same number of casualties. He concludes that there is therefore no significant moral distinction between the two kinds of acts.

Judging solely by outcomes, Bennett has a point: the terror bomber's actions are no worse than the tactical bomber's actions if they both kill the same number of people. Such a perspective is useful for placing the significance of IRA terrorism into a broader moral context. By any reckoning the IRA is responsible for a large number of civilian deaths. Yet as Bell points out, 'War . . . always kills the innocent . . . The RAF in one night in Hamburg killed more German civilians than all the victims of the Republican movement since 1798' (Bell 1990, p. 42).

Looking at the bombing campaigns of both the RAF and the IRA from a broader perspective that acknowledges the importance of outcomes but also takes into account *intentions* as morally significant, a similar conclusion appears to follow. From 1941 until the end of World War II the vast majority of bombing raids against Germany consisted of 'area bombing' – the deliberate targeting of towns and other civilian areas, rather than of 'strategic bombing' – the precision targeting of military bases, factories, supply lines or other facilities directly connected with the enemy's war effort (Webster and Frankland 1961). It was no accident that the RAF's strategy of area bombing resulted in enormous numbers of civilian casualties. As Wallace notes, 'The death of these civilians was not incidental to the pursuit of some other strategic goal such as the destruction of factories or marshalling yards; the civilians themselves were the target' (Wallace 1989, p. 3). Area bombing of German cities was intended to weaken the morale of the German people and to thereby contribute to Germany's defeat. It had no other strategic purpose. Similarly, IRA bombs placed in British pubs in 1974 were intended to kill civilians and to contribute to the strategy of sickening the British populace who would presumably exert pressure on its leaders to withdraw British troops from Northern Ireland. But if so, can one consistently affirm the moral justifiability of the RAF's area bombing during World War II while denying the moral justifiability of the IRA's pub bombing campaign in 1974?

There are a number of possible responses to this question. One could conclude that because the RAF's area bombing of German cities and the IRA bombing of British pubs both involved the deliberate killing of innocent civilians, if the former is morally justifiable then so is the latter. Alternatively, one could conclude that the RAF's area bombing and the IRA's pub bombings were both morally wrong because both involved the intentional targeting of innocent civilians, which is always morally wrong. As a third possibility, one could conclude that although the RAF's area bombing of German cities in World War II and the IRA's pub bombing campaign both involved the deliberate targeting of innocent civilians, there are features of the former that make it morally justified that are lacking in the latter. It would then be incumbent on one to spell out these differences. Finally, one could conclude that although the RAF's area bombing of German cities in World War II and the IRA's pub bombings both involved the deliberate targeting of innocent civilians, there are features of the latter that make it morally justified that are lacking in the former. Again, this would require the identification of some morally significant difference between the two kinds of actions. What are the prospects for discovering such a difference?

It could be argued that the most important difference between the two campaigns concerned what was at stake should they fail to achieve their objectives. For the IRA failure meant the continued British administration of Northern Ireland and consequently the (perhaps temporary) frustration of the republican dream of a united independent Irish Republic – in other words, a continuation of the situation that already existed in Ireland. Contrast this with the situation the British faced in 1940–1.[5] Hitler's aim was nothing less than to establish Nazi control over all of Europe. Rapid early victories suggested that this goal might be attainable. France had suffered total military collapse. Other, smaller countries had offered little or no resistance. The Luftwaffe was conducting nightly bombing raids on English cities such as London, Coventry, Hull, Birmingham, Liverpool and Southampton, intentionally targeting civilian population centres. The United States was on the sidelines, reluctant to enter the European war. In the Atlantic, German U-boats were taking a heavy toll on food and military supply lines. With its navy on the defensive, its army withdrawn from mainland Europe, the rest of Europe under Nazi control, America on the sidelines, its supply lines in jeopardy and a full-scale German invasion simply a matter of time, Britain's very existence hung in the balance. The decision to engage in area bombing, therefore, was the result of facing a severely limited range of military options in a situation of grave peril – a 'supreme emergency', in Prime Minister Winston Churchill's words. If Britain was to avoid the fate that befell the countries already overrun by the Nazis, the RAF was its only hope.

The RAF, however, was limited in its capacity to inflict damage on German military targets. In daylight British bombers were easy targets for German fighters. At night, thanks to inadequacies in navigation and bomb-aiming systems, British bombers were almost completely ineffectual in placing bombs on their targets. Many bombers never made it to within five miles of their targets, and those that did failed to inflict any damage on the intended targets. If British bombers were to do any significant damage to the German war effort, they would have to take aim at very large targets, namely, major cities. The decision to engage in area bombing was truly a last resort in desperate circumstances (Wallace 1989).

This relatively simple picture is complicated by the fact that British area bombing continued long after the 'supreme emergency' Churchill invoked had passed. After German defeats at El Alamein (6 November 1942) and at Stalingrad (2 February 1943), other military options (for example daylight raids on strategic targets) were available (Garrett 1993). Consequently, even if it is supposed that a 'supreme emergency' morally justified the intentional targeting of civilians, this would not apply to the bulk of the British area bombing of Germany. Walzer (2000, p. 261), therefore, does not hesitate to call this 'terror bombing' and to conclude that, 'the greater number by far of the German civilians killed by [the RAF's] terror bombing were killed without moral (and probably also without military) reason.'

What this indicates is that it is possible to draw a distinction between wars which (for the most part) do and wars which (for the most part) do not satisfy the conditions for initiating a just war, and to draw a further distinction between those operations during a war which (for the most part) do and those which (for the most part) do not satisfy the conditions for the morally justified prosecution of a war. In other words, different decisions to go to war, and different operations within war, may satisfy the conditions of traditional Just War Theory to different degrees. This is hardly surprising. But it does mean that unqualified claims that a given military campaign is 'just' or is 'unjust' need to be looked at with some scepticism. There is no alternative to careful analysis before issuing a sweeping judgement.

CONCLUSIONS

Intentionally harming others would seem to be morally wrong if any-thing is, yet, according to a widely embraced view, what is morally imper-missible in ordinary circumstances may be morally permissible in the extraordinary circumstances of *war*, which by its very nature involves intentionally harming others. But this does not mean that there are no principles governing the moral use of force in war. Just War Theory attempts to articulate and formalise the conditions that must be satisfied in order for it to be just to go to war, and in order for the prosecution of a war to be just. From its beginning in December 1969 the Provisional IRA conceived of itself as an *army* engaged in a morally justified war, and on occasion asserted that its armed struggle was justified according to tradi-tional just war doctrine. The truth of this claim is not obvious and requires considerable analysis to evaluate. Although at least some aspects of the IRA's armed struggle can reasonably be described as war, the Provisionals' campaign as a whole failed to satisfy key conditions both for the just ini-tiation of war and for the just conduct of war. Consequently, despite the IRA's claims to the contrary, its armed struggle was not justified according to the principles of Just War Theory.

It does not follow, of course, that the IRA's armed struggle was morally unjustified *tout court*, because one might reject the principles of traditional Just War Theory as being too restrictive, perhaps as evidenced by the fact they would render many (or perhaps almost all) conventional wars unjust as well. Additionally, the Provisional IRA's armed struggle might be morally justified according to one or more alternative moral theories – for example, according to a moral theory that focuses exclusively on the net benefits and costs of the Provisional IRA's armed struggle. It is to this pos-sibility that we turn next.

CHAPTER 5

'Pointless Heartbreak Unrepaid': Consequentialism and the IRA's Armed Struggle

Violence, being instrumental by nature, is rational to the extent that it is effective in reaching the end that must justify it.

(Hannah Arendt 1970, p. 79)

INTRODUCTION

Attempts to morally justify the IRA's armed struggle in terms of Just War Theory encounter a number of serious problems. It does not follow, of course, that the IRA's armed struggle was morally unjustified, because it might be morally justified according to the standards of *other* moral theories. Some scholars have concluded that if terrorist campaigns such as the IRA's can be morally justified at all, it will be in terms of their overall beneficial consequences. It is therefore worthwhile to examine the morality of terrorism in general and of the IRA's armed struggle in particular, in relation to consequentialist moral considerations. An adequate exposition and evaluation of consequentialism itself is beyond the scope of this chapter.[1] My aim is more modest, namely, to understand how consequentialist considerations could be used to morally justify at least some terrorist acts, and then to determine whether any of the IRA's acts of terrorism should be judged as among those so justified. The prospects for such a defence, I will argue, are slim.

CONSEQUENTIALISM

Consequentialism is the moral theory that maintains that the moral status of any action is solely a function of the net positive and negative consequences of that action. Classical utilitarianism is the best-known version of consequentialism. First propounded by Jeremy Bentham (1748–1832) and later popularised and extended by John Stuart Mill (1806–73), it asserts that acts are right to the extent that they result in the greatest total balance of pleasure over pain – that is, in the greatest *utility*. Classical utilitarianism came in for considerable criticism from the very beginning, but doubts about its cogency do not entail rejection of consequentialism per se. Many consequentialists reject classical utilitarianism's exclusive focus on pleasure as the only good, and recognise other sorts of goods in addition to, or as ranking above, pleasure, such as knowledge, freedom, rights, satisfaction of preferences, happiness, minimising suffering, security, safety, family, health and creativity. In principle, consequentialists could take the maximisation of any of these or other goods singly or in combination as the standard of moral rightness. This gives contemporary consequentialists considerably more flexibility in responding to objections than was possible for classical utilitarians. It would take us too far afield to consider each of the many different contemporary versions of consequentialism. Here it is enough to understand consequentialism as the moral theory that takes the consequences (however 'consequences' are to be cashed out) of an act as the sole criterion of moral rightness, and to ask whether any acts of terrorism in general, and any acts of IRA terrorism in particular, can be plausibly judged to be morally justified in consequentialist terms.

CONSEQUENTIALISM AND TERRORISM

An act of violence, including an act of violent terrorism, is morally justified in consequentialist terms to the extent that it is effective in bringing about sufficiently good consequences. For example, if the total amount of suffering produced by a terrorist act is small in relation to the total amount of suffering alleviated as a result of that act, then that act would be morally justified despite the fact that it caused suffering. As Kai Nielsen notes, the basic consequentialist approach to the morality of violence is straightforward:

> If, on the one hand, only more suffering all round would result from such violence, then resort to violence is wrong; if, on the other hand, such acts of violence would likely lessen the sum total of human suffering and not put an unfair burden on some already cruelly exploited people, then such violence is justified. (Nielsen 1981, p. 440)

Plate 1   Ireland in bondage (the manacle is inscribed 'Made in Britain'), but the spirit of the 1916 Easter Rising (represented by the Easter lily) lives on. The burning GPO and rising phoenix appear at the top, along with the shields of the four historic provinces of Ireland. Note the 'RPG Avenue' street sign. Beechmount Avenue, Belfast. (© Timothy Shanahan)

Plate 2   The prophetic words of the 1916 Easter Rising poet-martyr Patrick Pearse. Falls Road, Belfast. (© Timothy Shanahan)

Plate 3   Defiance. The black ribbon commemorates the twentieth anniversary of the 1981 hunger strikes. In the background, a nationalist mural depicting 'the Battle of the Bogside'. Derry. (© Timothy Shanahan)

Plate 4   A British soldier leaving blood-soaked footprints on the Northern Ireland civil rights movement on Bloody Sunday, 30 January 1972. The Bogside, Derry. (© Timothy Shanahan)

Plate 5　H-Block hunger strike memorial. Pictured is Martin Hurson (1956–81), a Provisional IRA volunteer who died after 46 days without food. The Bogside, Derry. (© Timothy Shanahan)

Plate 6　The ten 1981 Republican hunger strikers/martyrs, immortalised in a nationalist mural. Falls Road, Belfast. (© Timothy Shanahan)

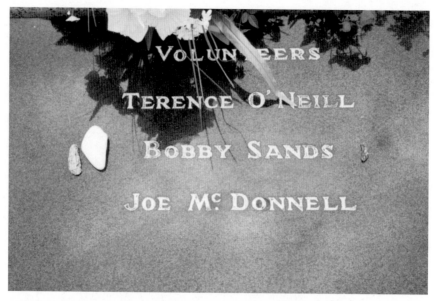

Plate 7   The graves of Provisional IRA volunteer Terence O'Neill, and republican hunger strikers Bobby Sands and Joe McDonnell. Republican plot, Milltown Cemetery, Belfast. (© Timothy Shanahan)

Plate 8   Republican icon Bobby Sands smiles down beneficently from the side of the old Sinn Féin office. Falls Road, Belfast. (© Timothy Shanahan)

Plate 9 The grave of Dan McCann. Republican plot, Milltown Cemetery, Belfast. (© Timothy Shanahan)

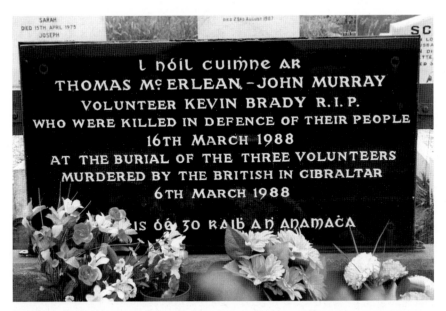

Plate 10 Violence in Northern Ireland had a tendency to spawn more of the same. The grave of three mourners killed by loyalist Michael Stone in the 'Milltown Massacre'. Republican plot, Milltown Cemetery, Belfast. (© Timothy Shanahan)

Plate 11 Members of the Ulster Volunteer Force use a 'skeleton key' (i.e. a sledgehammer) to pay someone a surprise visit. Loyalist paramilitary mural, Shankill Road, Belfast. (© Timothy Shanahan)

Plate 12 Members of the Ulster Freedom Fighters show off the tools of their trade. Loyalist paramilitary mural, Shankill Road, Belfast. (© Timothy Shanahan)

Plate 13   Overwhelming public approval of the Good Friday Agreement in 1998 was only the first step toward peace. Full implementation proved more difficult. Dromara Street, Belfast. (© Timothy Shanahan)

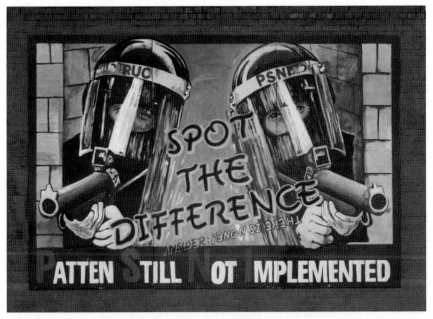

Plate 14   In 2002 the Royal Ulster Constabulary (RUC) was replaced by the Police Service of Northern Ireland (PSNI). Many nationalists viewed it as merely a cosmetic change. Belfast. (© Timothy Shanahan)

Plate 15   From revolutionary to peacemaker. The author with Provisional Sinn Féin President Gerry Adams, June 2001, Dublin. (© Timothy Shanahan)

Plate 16   The Provisional IRA's campaign may be over, but the struggle continues by other means. Republican mural, Falls Road, Belfast. (© Timothy Shanahan)

He then characterises the plight of these 'cruelly exploited people' in more detail:

> Suppose that the members of a small, impoverished, ill-educated ethnic minority in some democratic society are treated as second-class citizens. They are grossly discriminated against in educational opportunities and jobs, segregated in specific and undesirable parts of the country . . . For years they have pleaded and argued their case but to no avail. Moreover, working through the courts has always been a dead end, and their desperate and despairing turn to nonviolent civil disobedience has been tolerated . . . but utterly ignored . . . And finally suppose that this small, weak, desperately impoverished minority has no effective way of emigrating. In such a circumstance, is it at all evident that they should not act violently in an attempt to attain what are in effect their human rights? (Nielsen 1981, p. 440)

In such a desperate situation, is there any good reason why the oppressed people should not employ violence in order to improve their lot? As a consequentialist, Nielsen thinks not:

> There is no principled reason as to why they should refrain from certain acts of violence . . . If there were good reason to think that human welfare . . . would be enhanced by their acts of violence, then they would be justified in so acting. (Nielsen 1981, p. 440)

What about violence that takes the form of terrorism? Can it ever be morally justified? According to Nielsen it can. Like all other acts, acts of terrorism are justified solely by their consequences. Specifically, acts of terrorism are morally justified

> when, everything considered, there are sound reasons for believing that, by the use of that type of violence rather than no violence at all or violence of some other type, there will be less injustice, suffering, and degradation in the world than would otherwise have been the case. (Nielsen 1981, p. 446)

Nielsen is not alone in maintaining that under certain circumstances terrorism can be morally justified in virtue of its consequences. According to J. Angelo Corlett, for example,

> morally justified instances of terrorism, when or if they do obtain, have the role of helping victims of significant forms of injustice to revolt against their oppressors, thereby enabling the group to establish or re-establish itself as a free and equal society . . . violence does not *always* beget violence only, but sometimes peace, solidarity, democracy and justice. (Corlett 1996, p. 175; 2003, p. 134)[2]

Likewise, Robert Young acknowledges the possibility that acts of terrorism can be morally justified under certain conditions when committed by the powerless against the powerful: 'it may . . . be that limited forms of terrorism can be justified, even where some of the features of democracy are present, if getting a fair hearing for serious grievances would otherwise be impossible' (Young 2004, p. 59). On consequentialist grounds, therefore, some acts of terrorism are morally justified if they bring about better consequences than any alternative available actions would have. A world with such terrorism in it would thus be a better world than one sans that terrorism.

OBJECTIONS AND REPLIES

Not everyone has been convinced by such arguments. Nicholas Fotion objects to principled consequentialist justifications of terrorism on the grounds that even if *some* forms of terrorism are morally justifiable (for example, when used in war against an enemy who is himself committing acts of terrorism), 'there are nevertheless other forms, especially those in which the terrorist directs his acts against innocent people, that should *always* be condemned' (Fotion 1981, p. 463; emphasis added). He advances two arguments in support of this claim.

The 'Burden of Proof' Argument

A necessary condition for a terrorist act to be morally justified in consequentialist terms is that the act produce better overall consequences than would have been produced by any alternative act available to the agent in question. Some of the harms resulting from an act of terrorism will be immediate, whereas others will only become evident later. To provide a convincing consequentialist justification of an act of terrorism, therefore, there must be a convincing argument that the eventual overall beneficial consequences resulting from an act of terrorism *at least* outweigh the *immediate* harms produced, to say nothing of whatever unforeseen harms may later result from the act. In other words, given the fact that acts of terrorism typically or always bring about suffering as their immediate effect, the burden of proof rests squarely on the defender of such acts to demonstrate, rather than simply to assert, that such acts produce greater overall benefits than harms. If terrorists assert that they find it 'necessary' to sacrifice innocent human beings for the greater good, then they owe us some explicit, detailed calculation of how they arrived at this conclusion. 'Minimally what would be required is a careful set of calculations showing us just how much value was placed on their victims and just how they made the calculations that resulted in their victims' losing out to the greater good' (Fotion 1981, p. 465). Such calculations are never produced by the defenders of terrorism. In the absence of such calculations, Fotion argues, there is no reason whatsoever to accept the claim that the obvious immediate harms caused by acts of terrorism are eventually justified.

In response, it could be argued that Fotion sets the requirements for a consequentialist moral justification too high. It is never possible to produce precise calculations of the benefits and harms resulting from *any* act, terrorist or otherwise; and yet often we do, reasonably it seems, prospectively justify a course of action by comparing the expected positive and negative consequences of that action, and retrospectively justify a course of action by comparing the actual positive and negative consequences of that action. Fotion's requirement would render impossible a consequentialist justification of *any* act. In other words, his criticism essentially amounts to a blanket rejection of consequentialism. In addition, his argument would appear to rule out any act aimed at a greater good that produces harm as its *immediate* effect. As Burton Leiser notes,

> Fotion takes terrorists to task for their willingness to sacrifice their victims for some allegedly higher good. But are their acts significantly different from those of governments that send their military forces into battle, knowing that many of them will never return? (Leiser 1981, p. 472)

Leiser implies that the answer to this rhetorical question is 'No', and that Fotion's argument fails by proving too much.

With regard to the first criticism of Fotion's argument, it could be responded that, even if he does set the standard for a consequentialist justification too high by requiring that terrorists produce a detailed calculation of how they arrived at their conclusion that terrorism is morally justified, it does not follow that he was wrong in placing the *burden of proof* on apologists for terrorism to provide an adequate justification for such acts. Any harm-producing act is prima facie morally wrong from a consequentialist perspective because, by definition, it produces a cost, but without any guarantee of benefits, greater or otherwise. For a consequentialist justification of harm-producing acts to be plausible it must be the case, so far as we can tell, that the overall benefits outweigh the overall harms. It follows that with regard to harm-inflicting acts, the burden of proof is on the consequentialist to justify such acts by providing a convincing argument, with or without detailed calculations, showing that the overall benefits resulting from such acts are likely to outweigh at least the immediate costs. If apologists for terrorism fail to meet even this *minimal standard*, then they fail to provide a convincing consequentialist moral justification for terrorist acts.

With regard to the second criticism of Fotion's argument, Fotion could agree that some acts of terrorism are not significantly different from those of governments that send their military forces into battle, knowing that many of them will never return, but could conclude from this that a convincing argument is needed in *both* cases to show that it is reasonable to conclude that the overall benefits of the acts exceed at least the immediate costs. If such arguments can be produced, then such acts can be morally justified on consequentialist grounds. If such arguments cannot be produced, then such acts are as yet unjustified on consequentialist grounds. The burden of proof, in *both* cases, rests squarely on the defender of such acts to generate a convincing consequentialist justification.

The 'Other Alternatives' Argument

Fotion advances a second argument against consequentialist moral justifications of terrorism. Recall that it is not enough for a consequentialist defence of terrorism merely to show that the use of terrorism in some situation resulted in greater benefits than harms. That condition is necessary but not sufficient to show that an act is morally justified. There must also be good grounds for concluding that no other *alternative* act in that context would have resulted in a *greater* balance of benefits over harms. As Fotion notes, this condition will not be easy to satisfy: 'The terrorist case is unconvincing, not just because the moral burden of attacking innocent people is so heavy, but also because it is very difficult to show convincingly that there is no other way to get the revolutionary job done' (Fotion 1981, p. 467). Given the harms to innocent people typically resulting from terrorist acts, it is incumbent upon the apologist for such acts to provide a convincing argument that there was no other way to achieve a greater balance of benefits over harms. It is not clear that the apologist for terrorism can ever satisfy this condition.

Again, not everyone has been persuaded. Igor Primoratz criticises this argument on the grounds that while it is true that terrorists always have other options, for example, the option of attacking military rather than civilian targets, it does not follow that they can thereby achieve their objectives. According to Primoratz, it is the achievement of the objective that, for a consequentialist, constitutes the moral justification of terrorism . . . It is entirely possible that in certain particular cases it will turn out that there is no effective alternative to terrorism, that is, that terrorism *is* necessary if the objective is to be achieved (Primoratz 1997, p. 223).

In such cases a consequentialist will draw the conclusion that terrorism is necessary and thus morally justified.

The cogency of Primoratz's criticism turns on what is meant by 'the objective'. What constitutes moral justification for any act, according to the consequentialist, is *not* whether some particular objective (for example, driving out an oppressor) has been achieved, but rather whether the act in question produced a greater balance of benefits over harms compared to any other act that had been available to the agent. It is true that *the terrorist* may judge the morality of his own actions by considering the consequences of his actions in light of a narrowly conceived strategic objective; but consequentialism as a *moral theory* judges the morality of actions in relation to their overall effects, not just in relation to some proximate goal that the agent believes has importance. Even if terrorism has proven to be an effective tactic for achieving proximate goals in certain historical contexts, it does not follow that it is morally justified on consequentialist grounds in those contexts, because this begs the further question of whether the achievement of these goals itself produces greater benefits than harms than would have been produced by any alternative acts available to the agents in those situations. That remains an open question.

CONSEQUENTIALISM AND THE IRA's ARMED STRUGGLE

The question of whether acts of terrorism can ever, in principle, be morally justified in consequentialist terms is distinct from the question of whether any *specific* act of terrorism *is*, in fact, justified in consequentialist terms. Specifically, were any acts of Provisional IRA terrorism morally justified in consequentialist terms?

Interestingly, in the mid-1970s Gerry Adams seems to have embraced a consequentialist justification, of sorts, of IRA violence. In an article written to commemorate the sixtieth anniversary of the 1916 Easter Rising, he wrote:

Rightly or wrongly, I am an IRA Volunteer, and rightly or wrongly, I take a course of action as a means to bringing about a situation in which I believe the people of my country will prosper ... The course I take involves the use of physical force, but only if I achieve the situation where my people can genuinely prosper can my course of action be seen, by me, to have been justified. (Taylor 1997, p. 201)

The interesting philosophical question here is not whether this amounts to an admission of membership in the IRA (Adams has always vehemently denied that he was ever a member of the IRA), nor even whether *Gerry Adams* considered the IRA's armed struggle to be morally justified, but rather whether the IRA's armed struggle, including its use of terrorism, *was* morally justified on consequentialist grounds. Frey and Morris frame the issue in exactly the right way:

Is the reunification of Ireland worth all the suffering and loss the IRA inflicts? Is this a goal worth, not only members of the IRA's dying for, but also their making other people die for? For consequentialists, it typically will not be enough that members of the IRA think so; those affected by the acts of the IRA cannot be ignored. (Frey and Morris 1991, p. 5)

'The question', as Padraig O'Malley correctly notes, 'is basically a moral one: are Northern Ireland's Catholics being politically repressed to an extent that justifies a campaign of violence to end it?' (O'Malley 1983, p. 312).

It is worthwhile to distinguish two closely related issues and to treat them separately. Although the consequences of actions can only be evaluated (if at all) after they have occurred, in moral decision-making consequentialists are forced to anticipate the beneficial and harmful consequences of their actions and to make prospective consequentialist moral assessments on that basis. After at least some of the consequences of an action become known they are then in a position to make a retrospective assessment of these actual consequences. Decision-making prospective and consequence-assessing retrospective judgements form the two parts of a consequentialist perspective on morality. Given this distinction, we can then ask, first, was the IRA prospectively morally justified in consequentialist terms in undertaking, and for three decades sustaining, an armed struggle in Northern Ireland involving the use of terrorism; and second, in retrospect, given what it actually accomplished, can the IRA's armed struggle involving the use of terrorism be reasonably judged on consequentialist grounds to have been morally justified? Each of these questions is addressed in turn.

A Prospective Consequentialist Evaluation of the IRA's Armed Struggle

Burleigh Wilkins articulates the essential consideration for a prospective consequentialist judgement about the use of terrorism:

> From a strictly consequentialist point of view it would seem that where human suffering is concerned the additional suffering caused by terrorism might be but a drop in the bucket, a drop which would seem justifiable if there were any chance at all that it might alleviate the wider human suffering to which it is a reaction. (Wilkins 1992, p. 58)

This abstract perspective can be given more concrete form. Recall Kai Nielsen's description of a small, impoverished, ethnic minority in a democratic society whose members are treated as second-class citizens. They are discriminated against in educational opportunities and jobs. They are forced to live in less desirable areas. For years they have voiced their grievances and pleaded for equal treatment, but to no avail. Working through the courts has been a dead end, because the courts are controlled by powers intent on maintaining their oppression. Attempts at non-violent civil disobedience have been ignored (or rewarded with police brutality). Emigrating to a more just society is not possible for most members of this impoverished group. In short, all attempts to improve the basic conditions of their lives through purely non-violent means have proven unsuccessful. 'In such a circumstance', Nielsen asks, 'is it at all evident that they should not act violently in an attempt to attain what are in effect their human rights?' (Nielsen 1981, p. 440).

Apart from the characterisation of the group in question as 'small', such a description might well describe the plight of Catholics in Northern Ireland until at least the early 1970s. Add to this list of oppressive conditions the fact that their dire situation is the result of a political settlement to which they were opposed, and that they are completely lacking the means to mount a conventional military campaign to throw off the yoke of their oppressor, and recourse to a terrorist campaign of liberation begins to appear morally justified and perhaps even morally obligatory.

To be prospectively morally justified in consequentialist terms in undertaking and sustaining such a campaign, the IRA leadership would need to have had reasonable grounds for believing that such a campaign would produce a greater balance of benefits over harms than would any alternative possible course of action. Haig Khatchadourian pinpoints the critical difficulty the IRA leadership faced in making such an assessment:

127

How can we possibly measure the expected good resulting from the creation of . . . an independent Catholic Northern Ireland or a Catholic Northern Ireland united with the Irish Republic, and compare it with the overall evil likely to be the lot of the Ulster Protestants in such an eventuality or on different scenarios of their eventual fate – then add the latter evil to the evils consisting in and consequent upon all the acts of terrorism that are supposed to help realise the desired good end? I see no possible way in which these factors can be quantified, hence added and subtracted (Khatchadourian 1998, p. 27).

Despite the fact that Khatchadourian misunderstands the nature of the republican struggle (the creation of a 'Catholic Northern Ireland', independent or otherwise, has never been part of the republican agenda), his criticism nevertheless identifies an important point, one already discussed briefly in connection with Nicholas Fotion's arguments. Precise quantification of the benefits and harms reasonably expected to result from a terrorist campaign appears to exceed anyone's epistemic power. There are simply too many uncertainties to permit such calculations. Normally this epistemic limitation does not prevent us from acting in ways that we believe will bring about good consequences. But when the acts being contemplated involve the *certainty* of inflicting serious harm on others, the requirements for moral justification rise precipitously. There is no guarantee that all of our actions, even those that emanate from the noblest of motives, will result in beneficial consequences. On the contrary, there is substantial evidence suggesting that the consequences of our actions are frequently quite different from what we might have anticipated or desired – a truth enshrined in the aptly dubbed 'Law of Unintended Consequences' (Gillon 2000; Tenner 1997).

This law is strikingly illustrated by Shane Paul O'Doherty. As a young IRA operative in London in 1973, O'Doherty was responsible for sending a series of parcel bombs to prominent British officials, many of which exploded in the hands of secretaries or other administrative assistants rather than in the hands of the intended victims. Already as a sixteen-year-old IRA Volunteer in Derry in 1971, the Law of Unintended Consequences was well-known to him. Stepping out from behind a building, he fired a rocket at a British army observation post high on the historic walls of the city. The rocket missed the post by a matter of inches, and exploded instead somewhere off in the distance, followed by the sound of gunfire. O'Doherty beat a hasty retreat before he could be shot or captured. The action had been a failure – the intended target was missed. Or had it? In fact the rocket had fortuitously landed on *another* British army post, at Bishop's Gate – a direct hit. However, the British soldiers at that post, not knowing where the projectile had originated, responded by firing on a car that just happened to be passing by at the moment, assuming that was its source. Inside the car was a mother with her two children, who were badly injured. O'Doherty's later response to his commanding officer (who was livid over the gaffe and its horrific consequences) was an attempt to deflect personal responsibility: 'I fired the rocket. It soared over the observation post and exploded somewhere else, and I heard some shots after that. That's as far as I'm responsible. Don't try to make me responsible for a British army shooting' (O'Doherty 1993, p. 107). But of course assigning responsibility is never as simple as that. Every action creates a ripple of effects. Once the action has been performed, it immediately ceases to be under one's direct control, and the consequences that ensue often cannot be contained or circumscribed. As O'Doherty sagaciously summed up the lesson of this and similar incidents, 'Violence, just or otherwise, escapes every known restraint. The innocent are continually injured or killed by stray bullets or bombs . . . Violence is guaranteed to injure or kill the innocent' (O'Doherty 1993, p. 214).

Such examples can easily be multiplied. Each year the IRA in Derry organised a parade to honour those killed in the 1972 Bloody Sunday shootings, to focus protest against British rule in Ireland, and to rally its supporters. Each year British security forces established a surveillance position on a specific point on Derry's seventeenth-century city walls to monitor the demonstrators in the Bogside two hundred feet below. Prior to the start of the 1990 commemoration, the IRA concealed explosives in the city wall close to where they knew that the security forces would be gathering. When the security forces assembled at their usual location on 28 January, the IRA detonated the explosives by remote control. Rather than blasting up from the wall to kill the soldiers and police, however, it blasted out toward the demonstrators below. Whereas the security forces experienced only minor injuries, a piece of rock from the wall was hurled three hundred yards over the top of a block of flats and struck seventeen-year-old Charles Love, a Sinn Féin supporter, in the head, killing him instantly. Kevin Toolis notes the manifest irony: 'The IRA had murdered one of their [sic] supporters at a rally organized by Republicans to commemorate republican suffering' (Toolis 1996, p. 229).

The killing of Charles Love was a direct but unforeseen consequence of an action intended to have a completely different effect. And yet, it was certainly not an inconceivable consequence of deploying a weapon as crude as a bomb concealed in a centuries-old wall, detonated within a few hundred yards of a large assembly of people. As Virginia Held notes, 'It may in fact be almost impossible to predict whether an act of terrorism will in fact have its intended effect of hastening some political goal sought by the terrorists, or whether it will in fact do the terrorists' cause more harm than good' (Held 1991, p. 71). If this is true of individual acts of terrorism, then it would seem to be true a fortiori of a thirty-six-year terrorist campaign. Such reflections, it could be argued, ought to at least moderate the 'utopian terrorism' (Hutchinson 1996, p. 108) characteristic of the IRA.

Two different responses to this objection are possible. First, it could be noted that this objection would count equally against the attempt to prospectively morally justify *any* course of action in consequentialist terms, because one is *never* in a position to quantify precisely the benefits and harms resulting from *any* course of action. But if so, is there something special about acts of violence which makes them different from other acts where judgements about consequences are concerned? Aren't the consequences of *any* action ultimately unknown? For example, when I decide that I should take my sick child to the doctor, I cannot calculate with precision all of the benefits and harms that might result from such an action, but I am still morally justified in taking my child to the doctor, given what I understand about the probable consequences of the courses of action available to me. Or, to consider an example closer to that of Ireland, it would not have been unreasonable to conclude that violence deployed to topple the system of apartheid in South Africa, despite the harms certain to result from such violence, nonetheless might result in greater benefits – not for every person, but for those most in need. Had the IRA's campaign succeeded in 1970 or 1971, it may well have produced greater benefits than harms. Whether such a judgement was still reasonable in 1977, 1983 or 1994, after the consequences of terrorist tactics were abundantly evident, is another matter. Because acts of violence are by their nature intended to harm, whereas other kinds of acts can have causing harm among their consequences but don't necessarily have that as their explicit aim, the prospective moral evaluation of the former is special. Where the intended effects include harm to others, the standards should be correspondingly high.

Second, it could be argued that it is possible to construct a prospective consequentialist moral justification of the IRA's armed struggle without the need for detailed calculations of benefits and harms by treating the good to be achieved through that struggle as an *absolute good*, that is, as a good so valuable that it automatically warrants *any* means employed toward its realisation and justifies *any* collateral harms produced en route to its realisation. If the end justifies the means, then an absolutely good end justifies any and every means to its attainment. Consequently, no matter how much harm results from the IRA's armed struggle, it will *necessarily* pale in comparison with the absolute good to be brought into being by it. Such a response is suggested in the frequently enunciated republican conviction that the attainment of a united independent Ireland would be worth all the 'sacrifices' required to attain it. As Jack Holland observes, 'The moral basis for [the IRA's] vision was a semimystical incantation of sacrifice and martyrdom where absolutes reigned: the absolute right of . . . the 'Irish people', to an independent united Ireland, and the IRA's absolute right to use violence to achieve it' (Holland 1999, p. 37). Writing in 1993, Séamus Murphy observed that Catholic support for the IRA 'is partly rationalized by the delusion that Irish unity is good in itself, detachable from the means used to achieve it, and that somehow this abstract . . . "goodness" will compensate for the slaughter, misery and terror which purchased it' (Murphy 1993, p. 284).

The main problem with this line of argument is that it presupposes, rather than establishes, that there are such things as 'absolute goods', much less that the reunification of Ireland is (or is a necessary precondition for attaining) such a thing. Certainly few outside the republican movement would consider the reunification of Ireland to be an *absolute* good. Such a view might help to explain IRA Volunteers' dedication to their armed struggle (signalled, perhaps, by Gerry Adams' inclusion of the words 'to me' in his claim that the use of physical force is justified in terms of its ultimate results), but it would do little to provide a convincing moral justification to anyone else.

Even if it is granted, for the sake of argument, that the political reunification of Ireland is an absolute good meriting any means to this end, it would still make sense to ask about better and worse *means* for achieving this end. A significant sector of the republican movement chose violence, claiming that it was the only way to achieve its goal. What would have happened if these republicans had devoted the same time, money and effort that they poured into the armed struggle instead to persuading Protestants that a united Ireland would be in their interest, *and to reshaping their part of the world so that this was actually true?* Alternatively, or in conjunction with this, republicans could have embraced the principle enunciated by UK Home Secretary Reginald Maudling in August 1970, later embodied in the Good Friday Agreement, that 'Northern Ireland will not cease to be part of the United Kingdom without the consent of [a majority] of the people of Northern Ireland' (English 2003, p. 363). Making demographics rather than an armed struggle the cutting edge of their campaign for a united independent Ireland, republicans could have encouraged Catholics to have as many children as possible, and worked tirelessly to ensure that economic conditions in the Six Counties were conducive to raising large families with a decent standard of living. With an absolute majority in a few generations, nationalists could simply vote themselves out of the UK and (assuming that a majority in the Republic still aspired to Irish unity) into a united Ireland. The absolute good being sought – a united independent Ireland – would have been the same, but the method would have been entirely different: a baby boom rather than the sort of 'boom' associated with car bombs. From a consequentialist perspective such an approach would almost certainly have had greater moral justification than an armed struggle, with all the suffering that entails. It might have been thought that it would take longer than a military campaign, but was there any reason to think that it had to be less effective?

A Retrospective Consequentialist Evaluation of the IRA's Armed Struggle

According to Robert W. White, writing in 1993, 'Irish republicans have good reason to perceive that their violence is effective', and this for two reasons. First, 'the implementation of direct rule in 1972 . . . [was] the result of IRA bombs'. Second,

> the Northern Nationalist community in general has benefited indirectly from IRA violence. The British, in searching for a solution to the violence, now accept that at least moderate Nationalists must have a political voice in the politics of Northern Ireland . . . Since 1974, the British have sought to include the SDLP in any political initiative related to Northern Ireland'. (White 1993, p. 172)

Such a positive assessment is rather implausible. Rendering Northern Ireland ungovernable may well have resulted in the imposition of direct rule, but despite the IRA's decades-long armed struggle, Northern Ireland remains a part of the United Kingdom. The British army has not disengaged from Northern Ireland, although it has dismantled its fortress-like military installations and dramatically reduced troop numbers. The 'holy grail' of Irish republicanism, the reunification of Ireland, has not been achieved. To put it mildly, not many republicans would consider the fact that the British have sought to include the SDLP in any political initiative related to Northern Ireland as a great victory. As Anthony McIntyre, a former IRA volunteer who spent eighteen years in prison, poignantly put the issue in the mid-1990s,

> We went to jail, our people hunger striked, we suffered in protest, we died, and we killed an awful, awful lot of people in the process – we killed British soldiers, we killed an awful lot of RUC, we lost an awful lot of our own lives, and we blew up London, we blew up Belfast, we wrecked the place. Now we're back to where we started. (Stevenson 1996, p. 1)

Elsewhere he summed up the critical consequentialist moral issue in one short, heart-wrenching question: 'And so much horror, what for?' (Alonso 2001, p. 132).

The IRA's armed struggle failed to achieve its stated goal. Nonetheless it might be possible to argue that the armed struggle was critical in *advancing* the republican agenda and therefore that it was morally justified in virtue of playing this necessary *preliminary* role in securing Ireland's ultimate liberation. Gerry Adams, in his 6 April 2005 'plea' to the IRA to end its armed struggle, suggested something like this: 'Many of your comrades made the ultimate sacrifice. Your determination, selflessness and courage have brought the freedom struggle towards its fulfilment. That struggle can now be taken forward by other means' (http://www.sinnfein.ie/news/detail/9106).

Adams' statement admits of both a stronger and a weaker reading. According to the stronger reading, he might be suggesting that even if the IRA did not achieve its ultimate goal, perhaps its armed struggle was *necessary* to lay the groundwork for peaceful means to achieve this goal. In the spirit of Michael Collins, it could be suggested that the IRA's armed struggle was necessary to achieve 'not the ultimate freedom that all Nations desire and develop to, but freedom to achieve freedom' (O'Connor 1996, pp. 191–2). Unfortunately, it is very difficult to see why the IRA's armed struggle, including its use of terrorism, should be thought *necessary* for the success of subsequent peaceful efforts to secure its political goal. It is neither an analytic truth that successful political means *must* be preceded by prolonged violence, nor is this a well-established general principle based on empirical evidence. Thus the burden of proof for such a counter-intuitive claim is clearly on its proponent. Certainly neither Gerry Adams nor any other republican spokesperson has provided such a justification.

A weaker reading of Adams' statement would interpret him as claiming, not that the IRA's armed struggle was strictly *necessary* for the success of peaceful political means to achieve the goal of a united independent

Ireland, but rather that an armed struggle of the sort that the IRA waged was a more effective strategy for ensuring the success of a peaceful political achievement of its goal than was any other course of action available to it. That is, three decades of armed struggle was a more effective path to achieving a peaceful political achievement of a united independent Ireland than would have been a strategy based on peaceful political persuasion from the beginning. Perhaps, by analogy with the familiar strategy of police interrogators who employ a carefully choreographed 'bad cop/ good cop' routine to first scare a detainee before making nice, the republican movement cleverly disguised a three-decades-long armed struggle as ostensibly aimed at achieving its goal through coercion, whereas in fact it was all merely a propaedeutic to a peaceful political agenda. If so, however, it is plain that such a strategy did not, in fact, achieve its goal. Rather than smoothing the path for a republican political agenda to succeed in Northern Ireland, it created a nearly insurmountable obstacle to such success by engendering deep antipathy and distrust among those it most needed to persuade, namely, Ulster Protestants. Ironically, it also seems to have made the people of the Republic of Ireland equivocal about the value of reunification. As R. F. Foster (2007, p. 146) observes, 'The unintended achievement of thirty years of Republican strategy was to entrench the border more deeply than ever before'. It is thus more accurate to say that republicans have made great political gains in recent years *in spite of*, rather than because of, the violence long associated with the republican movement.

Neither the stronger nor the weaker reading of Adams' statement provides any good reason to conclude that it is true. The most plausible reading of Adams' statement, however, provides a reason to doubt its truth, because it depends on the problematic metaphysical view of causation examined in Chapter 2. The republican movement attempted to achieve its goal of a united independent Ireland through armed struggle. As Adams notes, many IRA volunteers courageously sacrificed themselves for this goal. Because such self-sacrifice has had no *observable* positive effect on advancing the republican agenda, and also cannot plausibly be regarded *empirically* as either necessary or effective in paving the way for the peaceful political achievement of the republican goal, then if (as is assumed) it has been effective in advancing the republican cause at all, it can only have done so by its positive effects on some other, perhaps transcendental spiritual plane, with practical observable effects in the empirical world only becoming manifest at some later time. While no doubt mildly reassuring for those looking for some compensation for the enormous sacrifices made on behalf of the republican cause, it will only appeal to those who choose not to think more deeply about the problematic metaphysical views on which Adams' claim crucially depends.

An even more implausible consequentialist justification of IRA violence was offered in 2003 by Joe McDonnell – a British Labour MP, no less – who declared:

> It is about time we started honouring those people involved in the armed struggle. It was the bombs and bullets and sacrifice made by the likes of Bobby Sands that brought Britain to the negotiating table. The peace we now have is due to the action of the IRA. (Alonso 2007, p. 191)

In a trivial sense, of course, McDonnell is absolutely correct. Without the bombs and bullets and sacrifices (especially of those killed by the IRA) there would be no *need* to negotiate a settlement to bring an end to three decades of violence. Likewise, it is truism that 'the peace we now have' is due to the action of the IRA, because it is a peace that was *made necessary* by three decades of IRA bombs, bullets and bloodshed. It is absurd, however, to insist as McDonnell did that 'without the armed struggle of the IRA over the past 30 years . . . the legitimacy of the aspirations of many Irish people for a united Ireland' would not have been recognised. In fact, the legitimacy of such an aspiration had been publicly affirmed by the British government since the early 1970s. Ironically, the IRA's campaign of violence did much to harden opposition to this aspiration, even among its strongest potential supporters.

The IRA's armed struggle cannot be judged as successful *in its own terms* as bringing about a united independent Ireland, nor (except in a trivial sense) as being necessary for a peaceful resolution of the conflict. But what matters for a retrospective consequentialist moral evaluation is not that this or that group's goals are achieved, but rather that an act bring about a greater total balance of benefits over harms than any alternative course of action would have produced. Might not the IRA's armed struggle be judged as morally justified because it produced a greater balance of benefits over harms than any alternative course of action would have achieved? Although this is theoretically possible, given its observable effects to date it seems highly unlikely. To understand how costly this failure has been, it is important to put into perspective, even if imperfectly, the violence that has characterised this conflict.

It is difficult to provide a meaningful metric for assessing the human cost of this or any other conflict. Suffering per se is an intensely private experience that cannot be quantified. Simply counting casualties is at best a crude method of measuring the losses suffered by victims and their loved ones, and at worst risks treating unique individual human beings as mere data. Nonetheless, a quantitative audit of the violence committed by the various actors in the Northern Ireland conflict gives some general indication of the contours of the conflict in terms of both its protagonists and its victims.

Summarising the total number of fatalities provides only the crudest accounting of the effects of the violence in the conflict. According to some estimates, over 33,000 people have suffered serious Troubles-related injuries since 1968 (O'Leary and McGarry 1996, p. 40). Injuries and maimings resulting from explosions, car bombs, non-fatal shootings associated with armed robberies (an important source of funds for paramilitary organisations), use of rubber and plastic bullets by security forces, kidnappings, house take-overs, torture under interrogation, incarcerations, intimidations (for example, death-threats), 'knee-capping' (firing bullets at point-blank range through the back of a suspected informant's knees), 'crucifixions' (shattering both the elbows and knees of a suspected informant), using kidnapping victims as components of bomb delivery systems, and so on, including the mental anguish caused by all of the above, significantly increase the total amount of suffering endured by the people of Northern Ireland.

A more precise accounting is also possible. Malcolm Sutton has provided an invaluable service by documenting every known Troubles-related death from 14 July 1969 to 31 December 2001 (http://cain.ulst.ac.uk/sutton/book/index.html). Others have added to his database to record subsequent Troubles-related deaths. A summary of the principal agents and victims will help to put the respective roles of the various parties to the conflict into perspective.

Republican paramilitary groups (including the Provisionals, the Official IRA, the INLA, the Real IRA and the Continuity IRA) have been responsible for 2,055 (58% of the) deaths, loyalist paramilitary groups for 1,020 (29% of the) deaths and security forces (army and police) for 363 (10% of the) deaths. The greatest annual death toll (1,863 deaths) occurred from 1971 to 1976. Of the killings by republican groups, the vast majority (1,821 out of 2,055 total) are attributable to the Provisional IRA. Of those killed by the Provisional IRA, 1,013 (56%) were security forces (British military, UDR, RUC and prison officers). Significantly, 151 victims of Provisional IRA violence were 'unintended targets', including 51 Catholic civilians.

Sutton's quantitative data provide the basis for drawing a number of conclusions about the conflict in Northern Ireland. But for our purposes the fact that stands out most clearly is that the Provisional IRA is responsible for more Troubles-related deaths than any other single organisation. Of the 3,523 Troubles-related deaths from 1969 to 2001 that can be attributed to specific organisations, 1,706 (48%) can be attributed to the Provisional IRA, compared with 426 (12%) to the UVF, 297 (8%) to the British army, 147 (4%) to the UFF and 113 (3%) to the INLA. The common perception that the Provisional IRA has been the organisation most directly responsible for the greatest number of deaths in the conflict is accurate.

Although it is impossible to accurately and with absolute precision calculate all of the benefits and harms resulting from the IRA's campaign, a meaningful accounting is still possible, especially in light of the fact that the IRA's campaign officially came to an end and hence reached closure on 28 July 2005. Restricting the costs just to the IRA's campaign from 1969 to 1994, George (2000) points out that there were 3,593 fatalities. Of these fatalities, 1,900 or 54 per cent were suffered by civilians. Nearly half (1,684) of the fatalities were the direct result of Provisional IRA terrorism. Injuries totalling 37,451 were reported for 1971–96; 68 per cent of these were suffered by civilians. Add to this the other forms of violence the people of Northern Ireland have endured: political murders, sectarian assassinations, tit-for-tat shootings, car-bombings, petrol-bombings, human bombs, armed robberies, knee-cappings, and so on, by paramilitary organisations, as well as various forms of state-supported violence, including internment and detention without trial, torture of prisoners, the shooting of unarmed civil rights demonstrators, and 'shoot-to-kill' activities on the part of some security forces. It is true that the Provisional IRA did not commit all of the violence associated with these figures. Nonetheless, it seems undeniable that the vast majority of these acts of violence would not have occurred had the Provisional IRA not embarked on its armed struggle in the particular ways that it did. According to a retrospective consequentialist moral analysis, what matters are the consequences of acts, even if many of these consequences came about indirectly and were not intended.

In addition to deaths, maimings and injuries directly or indirectly attributable to the Provisional IRA, its armed struggle was a crucial (but not, of course, the only) factor responsible for increased economic hardship for the people of Northern Ireland, but perhaps especially for the already economically disadvantaged Catholic community. As Murray and Tonge (2005, p. 167) note, 'IRA violence played [sic] a major contribution to the lack of economic investment in Northern Ireland, and consequently to high unemployment within the very community the IRA was claiming to represent'. In light of the discussion in Chapter 1, it is interesting to speculate about the extent to which such an effect was intentional. High unemployment among working-class Catholics would perpetuate the very grievances that the Provisional IRA claimed only the departure of the British could rectify, thus creating a self-sustaining justification for the armed struggle. As a bonus, a steady supply of disaffected jobless young men would be available for recruitment into the IRA.

A retrospective consequentialist reckoning of the IRA's armed struggle must take into account benefits as well as costs. Were there any benefits? George is blunt in his assessment:

> The benefits of IRA terrorism are easy to calculate. After some eighty years of terrorism, the IRA has failed to achieve its goal of an united Ireland within the socialist Republic proclaimed in 1916 or its precondition, the end of U.K. jurisdiction in Ireland . . . Thus, the benefits of an united Ireland to date amount to nil. IRA terrorism is inefficacious in relation to the kind of outcomes needed to achieve those benefits that might exceed the huge costs of its terrorism, namely, the realization of its ultimate ends. (George 2000, p. 96)

This assessment is in danger of conflating the attainment of the IRA's ultimate goal (a united independent Ireland) with benefits per se. What matters for the moral rightness of the IRA's armed struggle is not whether that armed struggle achieved its goal of a united independent Ireland, but rather whether the total benefits of the armed struggle exceeded the total costs, and if so, whether that armed struggle maximised the balance of benefits over harms compared to all of the possible alternatives. Still, George has a point. Despite the tremendous suffering which can be traced directly or indirectly to the Provisional IRA's armed struggle, there have been few or no benefits produced that could even begin to balance the costs. On any reasonable retrospective consequentialist weighing up of the benefits and costs, the IRA's armed struggle cannot be judged to have been morally justified.

It is true that in the years since 1968, the situation of Catholics *as a group* in Northern Ireland has improved tremendously. (This is consistent, of course, with the situations of some or all Protestants, and of some individual Catholics, becoming considerably worse.) From the founding of the Northern Irish state in 1921 to 1968, Catholics in the Six Counties suffered egregious discrimination in housing allocations, jobs, voting rights and civil rights. Their situation at present, although perhaps still not ideal, is hardly comparable to that of 1966. It could be argued that Catholics would not have made such gains without the leverage exerted by the IRA's armed struggle against the Protestant-dominated British government. According to Tom Hayden, for example, 'The military struggle appears to have been necessary to force the institutions of state and police away from their policy of "criminalization" towards one of political acceptance of Irish nationalism' (Hayden 2001, p. 260). Another author has argued that IRA violence and the continued threat of IRA violence has been an effective means for the republican movement to secure major political concessions from its adversaries (Lennon 2004). The Stormont government that had ruled Northern Ireland for fifty years was abolished. The Anglo-Irish Agreement and the Downing Street Declaration affirmed a formal role of influence for the Dublin government. Sinn Féin has made electoral gains in the North. Although all this may be true, why these should be considered *gains* from anything other than a republican perspective (which would beg the question) is unclear.

Whether these positive developments can be credited to the Provisional IRA's armed struggle is another matter. Discrimination against Catholics in terms of housing allocations, jobs and so on was largely (although not entirely) eliminated through reforms in the early 1970s, just when the IRA's bombing campaign began to escalate. Yet the IRA's campaign continued for another thirty years, long after a justification in terms of attempting to improve the lot of Catholics in the Six Counties (or of defending them from Protestant mobs) could be taken seriously. The relationship between the armed struggle and the improvement of the basic conditions of the Catholic minority in Northern Ireland was always tenuous at best. The IRA has never publicly declared that a condition for the cessation of its armed struggle was the attainment of social and economic equality between Catholics and Protestants in the Six Counties. Although republicans tried to co-opt social and economic concerns to their campaign, it was never really about that. The ultimate goal of the IRA's war was the establishment of a united independent Irish republic. One of the tasks of Sinn Féin was to make sure that the masses thought of themselves as exploited and that they came to view their own well-being as ineluctably linked with the success of the armed struggle. Convincing the working-class masses that their social and economic liberation was contingent upon the establishment of such a united Ireland (because

Northern Ireland was supposedly 'unreformable') was simply a means to the end of achieving a united independent Ireland.

Some authors have suggested that the IRA's long campaign was useful, at least in the eyes of the republican movement's core constituency, because it had played an indispensable role in bringing about a culture of equality in Northern Ireland. Thus, Murray and Tonge (2005, p. 266) write that, 'for the Republican mainstream . . . the IRA had served its purpose in removing the sectarian essence of the Northern state, helping nationalists to become part of an "Ireland of Equals", even if that Ireland remained partitioned'.

Suppose it is true that Northern Irish nationalists enjoyed greater political equality by the end of the IRA's armed struggle than they did at its beginning. This correlation leaves entirely open the question of the causal relationship between the IRA's armed struggle and that political gain. This correlation is consistent with the IRA's armed struggle (1) being a necessary condition for this gain, (2) being a non-necessary condition for this gain, but nonetheless making a greater positive contribution toward this gain than any alternative strategy would have, (3) being completely unrelated to this gain, or (4) retarding other nationalist efforts explicitly aimed directly at achieving this gain, perhaps by years or even decades. Given the centrality of IRA violence in the politics of Northern Ireland during the period in question, the third possibility is a priori extremely unlikely. The first possibility presupposes that no alternative (for example, nonviolent) strategies, taken singly or in combination, over a period of thirty years, could have generated that political gain. Clearly the burden of proof for such an exclusivist claim rests on its proponents. The second possibility requires almost as much faith to accept, because it suggests that an armed struggle whose goal was to force a foreign power to sever ties with its oldest colonial possession, and whose consistently observable effect was to heighten and exacerbate sectarian tensions, fortuitously had the beneficial effect of removing the sectarian essence of the Northern state without achieving the condition (the end of partition) that its advocates consistently claimed was the *sine qua non* of achieving such equality. This leaves the fourth possibility. The fact that proposals very much like 1998's Good Friday Agreement had been on offer for years before the Provisional IRA finally called off its armed struggle, but proved impossible to implement due (among other factors) to the republican movement's rejection of any such accommodationist compromises, strongly suggests that significant movement toward an 'Ireland of Equals' could have been achieved years sooner were it not for the IRA's obsession with Irish political reunification and its use of violence to achieve this goal. In the end, what the republican leadership eventually settled for in 1998 had been on offer from the British government since 1975. As Brendan Hughes, who proceeded Bobby Sands as OC (Officer Commanding) of republican prisoners in the Maze Prison (and who in 1980 led an abortive hunger strike), noted in 2000, 'Think of all the lives that could have been saved had we accepted the 1975 truce. That alone would have justified acceptance. We fought on and for what? What we rejected in 1975' (McIntyre 2000).

Even if at least *some* of the gains made by Catholics in Northern Ireland were due to the IRA's armed struggle, in a retrospective consequentialist analysis the losses incurred by this same community must also be taken into account. From 1968 to 2001, 1,522 Catholics in Northern Ireland lost their lives to Troubles-related violence. According to some estimates, up to 25 per cent of those killed in Provisional IRA bombing operations were Catholics, the very people the IRA was ostensibly working to benefit. Given the tremendous personal losses among Catholics in Northern Ireland that can be traced *directly* to the IRA's campaign, it seems likely that the IRA's campaign decreased, rather than increased, the well being of Catholics in Northern Ireland. The conclusion seems inescapable: not only did the IRA not achieve its goal of a united independent Ireland, but the IRA's campaign cannot be retrospectively judged as morally justified on other consequentialist grounds either.

One last avenue for a retrospective consequentialist justification of the IRA's armed struggle is open to its determined apologist. In 1997, Francis Molloy, speaking on behalf of Sinn Féin, referred to the IRA in the *Irish News* as 'the defenders of our people for the last twenty-five or thirty years' (English 2003, p. 339). As was argued in Chapter 1, such an assertion strains credibility if interpreted literally. And yet there is no reason to think either that Molloy was intentionally speaking ironically, or that he was deliberately distorting the truth for political purposes. Nor, for that matter, is there any reason to suppose that many of those reading the *Irish News* for 2 April 1997 would consider his claim to be manifestly absurd. In what sense, then, might Molloy and many in his intended audience sincerely believe that for over a quarter of a century the volunteers of the IRA had been their loyal defenders? The answer goes a long way to understanding what drove the IRA's armed struggle with such tenacity, against such overwhelming odds, at such a cost, for so long.

Despite failing to achieve its primary stated goal of a united independent Ireland, and despite imposing huge human costs on the Catholic community of Northern Ireland, what the IRA could with some justification claim to have given to its community was a sense of communal pride and self-respect engendered through symbolic acts of defiance, 'resistance' and retaliation for real and imagined wrongs committed against Catholics in the Six Counties. On an occasion where a final summation of the IRA's achievements would be expected, and where every word would be carefully scrutinised by the rank and file of the IRA, Gerry Adams gave clear expression to this conviction in his 6 April 2005 'plea' to the IRA to end its armed struggle: 'For over 30 years, the IRA showed that the British government could not rule Ireland on its own terms. You asserted the legitimacy of the right of the people of this island to freedom and independence' (http://www.sinnfein.ie/news/detail/9106). It was this, more than anything else, that the IRA could claim to have achieved. In other words, after it had become clear that a conventional military victory, or a more complex military-political victory, was unlikely for the republican movement, and (at least to some) that the most urgent defensive need of the Catholic community was protection from its own self-appointed defenders, the IRA continued to serve a vital emotional and psychological function for the nationalist community by supporting a 'culture of resistance' as an end worthy in itself. As Martin McGuinness explained in June 1984, 'Without the IRA we are on our knees. Without the IRA we are slaves. For fifteen years this generation of republicans have [sic] been off their knees. We will never be slaves again' (English 2003, p. 343). The psychological value of such symbolic resistance should not be minimised. To be dominated by those seen as 'other' without recourse to even symbolic acts of defiance is to be humiliated and rendered utterly impotent. Symbolic acts of resistance, where more efficacious actions are unavailable, at least create a space in which communal self-respect can survive.

And yet in the absence of other identifiable benefits of the IRA's armed struggle, in order for such psychological benefits to ground a consequentialist justification of the IRA's armed struggle they would have to exceed the overall costs of that struggle. Although no objective metric exists for comparing such benefits and gains, a rough guide might be to put the following question to a random sample of members of the nationalist community who lived through the 1970s and 1980s in the Six Counties: In your judgement, did the pride and self-respect you gained from the IRA's acts of defiance, resistance and retaliation regarding British rule in

Northern Ireland more than compensate for the human costs resulting from the IRA's three-decade-long armed struggle? Were anyone bold enough to conduct such a survey, perhaps more interesting than the answers such a question might generate would be the perplexed expressions on the faces of those polled. Many would probably find the question either offensive or incomprehensible. Jonathan Stevenson (1996, p. 258) perhaps sums up the legacy of the IRA's campaign of violence best with words as utterly simple as they are emotionally devastating: 'pointless heartbreak unrepaid'.

CONCLUSIONS

Some philosophers maintain that if terrorism is to be morally justified at all, it can only be judged as morally justified by way of a consequentialist moral theory. Indeed, there is no reason in principle why terrorist acts, in some situations, cannot produce a greater balance of benefits over harms than any alternative possible course of action, and hence be as morally justified. The problem for a consequentialist moral justification of terrorism comes in the application to *specific* terrorist acts and to specific terrorist campaigns. Even if such acts and campaigns can be morally justified in principle, in practice the prospects for such justification are slim. This is true both for the IRA's use of terrorism and for terrorism more generally. The weight of the evidence and arguments considered in this chapter point strongly to the conclusion that from a consequentialist moral perspective the IRA's armed struggle, including its use of terrorism, was morally unjustified. Of course, consequences are typically not the only morally relevant consideration when considering the morality of harm-producing acts. Other considerations are often thought to matter as well – human rights, for example.

CHAPTER 6

Violating the Inviolable: Human Rights and the IRA's Armed Struggle

Terrorism cannot necessarily be ruled out as unjustifiable on a rights-based analysis, any more than it can on a consequentialist one.

(Virginia Held 1991, p. 81)

INTRODUCTION

According to some philosophers, acts of terrorism are *necessarily* morally wrong because they always violate fundamental human rights. If this claim could be shown to be correct, it would decisively settle the question of the morality of terrorism in general and of the IRA's armed struggle in particular, insofar as the latter involved the use of terrorism. But not all philosophers agree that taking rights as centrally important shows that acts of terrorism are necessarily morally wrong. Virginia Held (1991) examines situations in which serious rights violations are already occurring and considers the moral justifiability of the limited use of terrorism in such situations in pursuit of a more just society. She argues that in some of these situations acts of terrorism are (or at least could be) morally justified when considered from a moral perspective that takes rights as fundamental to moral evaluation. Whether she is right, and whether IRA terrorism can be morally justified on this basis, are further questions.

My contention is that Held is correct that a rights-based justification of some acts of terrorism is possible, but her discussion of the conditions that must be satisfied for such acts to be morally justifiable merits greater elaboration. I articulate and defend the additional conditions that must be satisfied for acts of terrorism to be morally justified from a non-consequentialist

144

rights-based moral perspective, and then consider the extent to which the IRA's armed struggle satisfies these conditions. I will argue that the IRA's campaign failed to consistently satisfy a number of these conditions. The IRA's armed struggle, therefore, was not morally justified from a perspective that takes human rights seriously.

A Rights-Based Argument against Terrorism

That acts of terrorism are necessarily morally wrong because they violate fundamental human rights is probably the default position among philosophers and non-philosophers alike. Haig Khatchadourian provides an especially clear statement of this position. He supports the claim that 'terrorism, in all its types and forms, is always wrong' on the grounds that 'all forms of terrorism . . . seriously violate their immediate victims' and the sufferers' human rights', and that 'an act cannot be morally right if it violates anyone's human rights . . .' It follows in this view that 'acts of terrorism that cause the immediate or delayed death of their victims . . . are morally wrong' (Khatchadourian 1988, pp. 131–9).[1] In order to assess this argument, three questions must be addressed: (1) What are 'human rights'? (2) Are all acts that violate human rights *necessarily* morally wrong? (3) Under what conditions, if any, could acts of terrorism that violate human rights be morally justified?

What are 'Human Rights'?

Human rights have been described as 'basic moral guarantees that people in all countries and cultures allegedly have simply because they are people' (Nickel 1987, p. 561). People may recognise and protect human rights, or they may fail to do so, but the rights themselves are not dependent upon societies or on laws for their reality. Human rights, in this 'objectivist' view, are grounded in objective features of the world, making their existence independent of contingent social and historical conditions.[2] Although the existence of such rights is often taken for granted, it is worth asking what the basis for such fundamental rights might be. Historically, at least two distinct sorts of foundations have been asserted for human rights.

The 'classical objectivist view' locates the foundation of rights in the most basic substantive human goods – that is, in the fundamental requirements for human flourishing. The elements of this view can be traced back at least as far as Plato, Aristotle and the Stoics. They were further developed in the medieval period by natural law theorists such as St Thomas Aquinas, and received their classic formulation in the seventeenth century by John Locke. According to Locke, natural rights – to life, liberty and property – flow from natural law, which in turn originates in the will of God. Human rights, in this view, ultimately have a divine sanction. A stronger foundation for human rights is hard to imagine.

By contrast, the 'Enlightenment objectivist view' (whose basic ideas can be traced back to the eighteenth-century German philosopher Immanuel Kant) locates the foundation of human rights in the moral worth of each person as a rational agent. In this view, human rights originate in the human capacity for rationality, yet are universal and necessary because they are based upon formal principles expressing the moral autonomy, equality and *dignity* of all persons. To say that persons have 'dignity' is to say that they have incomparable worth. Unlike things which have a 'price' (that is, a market value), persons are understood to be beings whose value does not depend on their comparison with something else. They are intrinsically, rather than instrumentally, valuable. It follows that one can never morally violate a person's dignity for the sake of something with mere 'price', no matter how great the value of that thing. Accordingly, only those actions that treat human beings as *ends-in-themselves* and not simply as *means* can be morally permissible. 'Treating a person as an end' means respecting the conditions necessary for their effective functioning as a moral agent.

Although determining whether an objectivist view of human rights, in either of the senses outlined above, is *true* is obviously beyond the scope of this chapter, determining *what would follow from such a view it if it were true* is not. That is, given an objectivist view of human rights, what *follows* about the morality of acts that violate human rights?

ARE ACTS THAT VIOLATE HUMAN RIGHTS NECESSARILY MORALLY WRONG?

Appeals to human rights typically presuppose that identifying something *as* a right entails that it would always be morally wrong for anyone to violate that right. If rights are understood to be necessarily inviolable because they place exceptionless moral constraints on how persons may be treated, then obviously rights violations are never morally justified. The question at issue here, however, is whether human rights *ought* to be considered as morally inviolable. More precisely, the key question here concerns whether it is ever morally permissible *from a non-consequentialist rights-based perspective* to violate someone's rights. A non-consequentialist rights-based moral justification for rights violations need not completely ignore consequences; but to be a non-consequentialist view it would need to appeal to moral considerations *other than* or *in addition to* consequences, and such moral considerations would have to play a significant role in justifying the rights violation. To be 'rights-based' a concern with rights would have to be central. What might such a justification look like?

A Rights-Based Justification for Rights Violations

One class of situations in which it might be morally permissible from a non-consequentialist rights-based perspective to violate human rights is when violating a person's rights is the only way to prevent even more (or more serious) rights violations. Robert Nozick (1974) calls the intentional violation of a right in order to prevent more numerous or more severe violations of rights 'rights violation minimization'. If rights violation minimisation is ever morally justified, then the violation of some rights, in some circumstances, can be morally justified on the basis of respect for rights.

It is easy to construct imaginary examples of apparently morally justified rights violation minimisation scenarios (Williams 1973, p. 98, provides a much-discussed example). Uncontroversial historical examples of morally justified rights violation minimisation are harder to come by, but some plausible candidates exist. Consider, for example, a dilemma facing Winston Churchill during World War II. In 1940 the German Luftwaffe was conducting devastating nightly bombing raids on English cities such as London, Coventry, Hull, Birmingham, Liverpool and Southampton. British intelligence was desperate to decipher German military codes in order to anticipate the German attacks. A team of brilliant mathematicians, chess masters, linguists and academics were recruited from all over Great Britain and assembled at Bletchley Park, forty miles outside London, to work on cracking the German codes. On 14 November 1940 the British received a lucky break. Thanks to previous code-breaking efforts and a serious mistake made by a German code operator, it was learned that the Germans intended to conduct an air raid on Coventry that night. The information was relayed to Prime Minister Winston

Churchill, who then faced a terrible dilemma. If he ordered an immediate evacuation of Coventry, the people of that city might be spared (that night, at least), but the Germans would realise that their codes had been broken, and would immediately change them, thus denying the British access in the future to this vital source of information. If Churchill did nothing, the people of Coventry would be sitting ducks for the German air raid, but he would gain an invaluable weapon in the fight against Hitler and the Nazi menace. Churchill decided to put the city's emergency services on alert and to take no further action. Coventry was bombed, the Germans never suspected that their code had been compromised, and the British were able to use their ability to decipher German coded communications to good tactical advantage, almost certainly resulting in many more British lives saved and providing much-needed assistance in the British war effort.

Although there has been some dispute about whether the events unfolded precisely as just described, suppose that this account is a tolerably accurate facsimile of what happened. Suppose as well that civilian noncombatants being deliberately targeted and killed by military personnel under the command of a madman bent on world domination constitutes a serious violation of their human rights. Finally, and more controversially, suppose that Churchill's difficult decision to sacrifice the people of Coventry was made in order to prevent even more British citizens from having their human rights violated by a German victory in World War II. That is, suppose that Churchill's positive decision to not evacuate Coventry was an act that violated the rights of the people of that city in order to prevent even greater human rights violations, and was therefore a real-life example of rights violation minimisation. Given the enormous stakes involved, surely his difficult decision was morally justified, it seems, despite the fact that he willingly permitted people's rights to be violated.

Thomas Nagel would argue that Churchill's decision, understood in this way, was *not* morally justified, because it is *never* right to violate someone's rights. According to Nagel,

> Rights essentially set limits to what any individual may do to any other, even in the service of good ends – and those good ends include even the prevention of transgressions of those same limits by others. If there is a general right not to be murdered, for example, then it is impermissible to murder one person even to prevent the murders of two others . . . Rights tell us in the first instance what not to *do* to other people, rather than what to *prevent from happening to them*. (Nagel 1995, pp. 87–8; emphasis in original)

In this view, the very nature of rights would morally preclude one from violating the rights of one person even if doing so was the only way to prevent the more serious rights violation of that same person, or of many others. If Nagel is correct, then rights violation minimisation is never morally permissible.

Nagel's blanket prohibition of all rights violations is problematic for at least two reasons. First, the assertion that rights violations are never morally justified simply begs the question of the moral permissibility of rights violation minimisation. If rights violation minimisation *is* sometimes morally permissible, then it *is* sometimes morally permissible to intentionally violate someone's rights. The inviolability of rights cannot simply be assumed in an argument intended to show that it is never morally permissible to violate rights.

Second, Nagel's claim presupposes the Enlightenment objectivist conception of human rights according to which

> rights are a nonderivative and fundamental element of morality. They embody a form of recognition of each individual's value which . . . differs in kind from the form that leads us to value the overall increase of human happiness and the eradication of misery. (Nagel 1995, p. 87)

But even if rights violation minimisation were morally prohibited in this conception of rights (a claim considered in more detail below), it would not follow that rights violation minimisation is prohibited *tout court*. As Nagel himself notes, according to the classical objectivist conception of rights, human rights are understood to be derivative from fundamental human goods, for example, 'the goods of happiness, self-realization, knowledge, and freedom, and the evils of misery, ignorance, oppression, and cruelty' (Nagel 1995, p. 86). In this view, rights are perhaps of vital instrumental importance in the service of fostering human goods and of preventing human evils, 'but are not themselves fundamental either in the structure of moral theory or in the order of moral explanation' (Nagel 1995, p. 86). Nagel summarily dismisses the classical objectivist conception of rights, but acknowledging this alternative view of rights leaves open the possibility that rights may be justifiably violated when their nonviolation is incompatible with securing basic human goods or with preventing basic human evils.

In response, it could be conceded that some acts that violate rights could be morally permissible from a classical objectivist conception of rights, but that this admission has no bearing on the question of the moral permissibility of acts of *terrorism* that violate someone's rights. Presumably Churchill decided to permit the Germans to bomb Coventry on 14 November 1940 because had he evacuated the city in advance of the air raid planned for that night, the Germans would have realised that their codes had been broken, would have called off the air raid on Coventry, would have devised new codes, and would have then proceeded to bomb Coventry and other English cities on subsequent nights. In cases of this sort, if one does not violate (or permit the violation of) persons' rights, *they will be violated anyway.* Cases of terrorism, however, are cases in which persons' rights are violated, which rights would *not* otherwise be violated. In other words, were it not for the acts of terrorism, the rights in question would not have been violated. The question at issue, then, is whether acts that violate someone's rights which would not otherwise be violated can ever be morally justified from a moral perspective that takes a concern with rights seriously.

A RIGHTS-BASED JUSTIFICATION FOR TERRORISM

Virginia Held believes that they can. She describes a hypothetical scenario in which

> achieving effective respect for the fundamental human rights of the members of one group, which rights ought to be respected, requires the violation of the fundamental human rights of the members of another group, which are also rights that seemingly ought to be respected. (Held 1991, p. 75)

Consider two situations, S1 and S2, and two groups in each situation, group A and group B. In both situations both groups have a human right to *x*, but in S1 members of group A enjoy effective respect for this right whereas the members of group B do not. By contrast, in situation S2 the members of both groups enjoy effective respect for this right. From a perspective that values effective respect for rights, S2 is clearly morally preferable to S1. Suppose that non-violent means cannot effect a transition from S1 to S2, but that acts of terrorism *would* be effective in moving a society from S1 to S2. Given that it will involve rights violations, Held (1991, p. 78) asks, 'Can it be better to violate rights through terrorism than to avoid this violation?'

She concludes that it can: 'On grounds of justice, it is better to equalize rights violations in a transition to bring an end to rights violations than it is to subject a given group that has already suffered extensive rights violations to continued such violations' (Held 1991, p. 79). There are,

150

however, certain conditions. First, there must be a 'reasonable likelihood that limited terrorism will significantly contribute to bringing about . . . effective respect' for the rights of those who have already suffered extensive rights violations (Held 1991, p. 76). How reasonable the likelihood must be is not specified; presumably situational factors would play an important role in making such a determination.

Second, rights violations are not to be undertaken lightly. The intentional violation of anyone's rights can only be morally justified in situations in which 'no other effective means are available' for rectifying the rights violations in question (Held 1991, p. 76). This condition will presumably preclude the moral justifiability of rights violations in a vast number of situations, but not in all.

Third, the 'seriousness' of the respective rights violations matters:

> There would be a *prima facie* judgement against serious violations, such as those of rights to life, to bring about respect for less serious rights, such as those to more equitable distributions of property above what is necessary for the satisfaction of basic needs. (Held 1991, p. 80)

This restriction could be overridden if a serious rights violation against the members of one group would be effective in rectifying a large enough number of lesser rights violations against the members of another group – for example, if the violation of the right to life of a person in one group were effective in bringing about effective respect for the right to an equitable distribution of property among a very large number of people in another group. How large the set of lesser rights violations to be rectified would have to be in order to warrant the limited but more serious rights violation is not specified. Nonetheless, in situations of this sort it would be morally justifiable to violate the rights of the members of one group in order to achieve effective respect for the rights of members of another group, if engaging in such rights violations is the only way to effect a transition to a system in which rights violations are either eliminated or significantly reduced. Some rights violation minimising acts of terrorism may be among such acts that are morally justifiable from a rights-based moral perspective.

OBJECTIONS AND RESPONSES

Rights Violation Minimisation is Self-Contradictory

Held's view is controversial and not everyone has been persuaded that her argument in support of rights violation minimisation is cogent. Frances

Kamm articulates perhaps the most basic reason to reject the morality of rights violation minimisation, namely, that 'it would be simply self-contradictory for it to be morally permissible to minimize violations of the [right] itself for the sake of showing concern for *it*' (Kamm 1992, p. 384).[3] If rights specify the 'basic moral guarantees that people in all countries and cultures allegedly have simply because they are people', then permitting the violation of such basic moral guarantees seems to invalidate the essential *point* of human rights. Indeed, Held herself acknowledges the danger of opening the door to recognising morally justifiable rights violations: 'If we permit violations, we risk undermining the moral worth of the very rights for which we are striving to achieve respect' (Held 1991, p. 73). Is the very idea of violating some rights for the sake of achieving effective respect for those same or other rights simply incoherent?

It would be premature to draw such a conclusion. The cogency of Kamm's argument depends on the assumption that, necessarily, to show respect for rights, rights must be considered inviolable. It is worthwhile to reflect on this assumption. Why should rights be thought of as necessarily inviolable? One could simply *define* rights as necessarily inviolable, thereby stipulating that rights can never justifiably be violated. But such a move simply begs the question. Kamm's answer, by contrast, attempts to ground the inviolability of rights in a particular conception of persons: 'If we are inviolable in a certain way, we are more important creatures than violable ones . . . The world is, in a sense, a better place, as it has more important creatures in it . . .' (Kamm 1992, p. 386). On the other hand, if we permit rights violations, as Held would counsel us to do, we are in danger of making the world a worse rather than a better place, 'because we would have to live believing in a less sublime and elevated conception of ourselves. We might save more people, but they would, in a sense, be less worth saving in our eyes'. The reason is that 'individuals whose rights stand as a barrier to action are more potent individuals than they would be otherwise' (Kamm 1989, p. 254).

It could be argued in response that Kamm's argument risks treating a particular *conception of persons* – a conception enjoyed by those capable of alleviating great suffering – as more important than the alleviation of the *actual suffering* of those enduring human rights violations. One could imagine those suffering from human rights violations informing those who are capable of alleviating their suffering, but who refrain from doing so in order to preserve a 'sublime and elevated' conception of personhood, that their highly refined moral priorities are exactly backwards. What good is a 'sublime and elevated' conception of personhood if the cost of maintaining that grand conception is a refusal to do precisely what is required in order to alleviate the suffering of actual flesh and blood persons?

Kamm could counter that preserving a conception of persons according to which rights are *necessarily* inviolable is essential for achieving a world that is a 'better place'. But it is at least debatable that a world in which rights are thought of as necessarily inviolable would be a better world than one in which rights are thought of as inviolable *except in certain highly specified contexts* (for example, contexts in which rights violation minimisation is possible). If one's concern is to bring into existence the best possible world, then a world in which rights violations are nonexistent or few would presumably be a better world than one in which egregious rights violations exist. Yet, as Held argues, achieving a transition from the latter sort of world to the former sort of world might in some circumstances require that human rights be violated. This might simply be part of the cost of achieving that better world.

Alternatively, Kamm could counter that the inviolability of human *rights* is entailed by the inviolability of human *persons*. That is, 'it should not be permissible to minimize the violation of rights by violating a comparable right, for persons are, at least to some degree, inviolable, and are ends-in-themselves' (Kamm 1992, p. 355). To the extent that violating someone's rights for the sake of minimising other rights violations requires treating that person as a mere means, it would be morally prohibited by the inviolability of personhood.

In response, one could question this assumption by noting that even if *persons* are ends in themselves, and as such have a high degree of inviolability, expressed by rights to non-violation,

> it does not immediately follow . . . that *rights* should have an equally high degree of inviolability . . . The primary objects of our respect and concern are *persons*, not rights, so there is neither futility nor contradiction in violating the rights of persons if that is what circumstances demand to treat them as ends in themselves. (Applbaum 1998, p. 346; emphases added)

Rights, in this view, might be considered as analogous to laws. Laws are highly inviolable, in the sense that in general there are very few good reasons for violating laws. Yet laws exist to safeguard property, to provide security and the like, and one can easily imagine situations in which safeguarding someone's property requires violating a law (for example, it is against the law to break into someone's home, yet it might be necessary to do so in order to put out a fire that might otherwise destroy an entire neighbourhood). Laws can be thought of as highly inviolable, yet with exceptions in cases in which violating a law is the only way to prevent some great harm. So, too, rights can be thought of as existing for the sake of persons, such that even if *persons* are necessarily inviolable, it would not follow that *rights* are similarly inviolable. But if rights inviolability is not entailed by person inviolability, then morally permissible rights violation minimisation of the sort envisioned in Held's argument is not clearly self-contradictory in the way that Kamm's objection contends.

Rights Violation Minimisation Treats Persons as Mere Means

The determined opponent of rights violation minimisation need not concede defeat. He or she could respond that even if rights inviolability does not follow from person inviolability, acts of terrorism performed for the sake of rights violation minimisation necessarily treat persons *instrumentally* as mere *means* to the achievement of eliminating or reducing rights violations in a society. Because such acts fail to respect persons as ends in themselves, having intrinsic worth, they are never morally permissible. Thus, thinking in particular about the use of terrorism undertaken to minimise rights violations, Igor Primoratz argues that

> faced with the prospect of being killed or maimed on the grounds of this . . . justification, might I not . . . say that I am a person in my own right, that my life is the only life I have and all I have, and that nobody may take it away, nor ruin it by making me a cripple, for the sake of a more just distribution of, and subsequently more general respect for, the right to life and bodily security within a group of people? (Primoratz 1997, p. 231)

Rights violation minimisation, in this view, fails to respect persons as ends in themselves, and therefore is never morally permissible.

Responding to Primoratz's argument, Held counters that

> to fail to achieve a more just distribution of violations of rights (through the use of terrorism if that is the only means available) is to fail to recognize that the individual whose rights are already not fairly respected is [*also*] a person in his or her own right,

whose rights cannot be ignored (Held 2004, p. 77). She apparently takes this as negating Primoratz's point but, as with some of the arguments against her position, her response is in danger of merely begging the question. The opponent of rights violation minimisation can freely acknowledge that refraining from acts of terrorism that intentionally violate

154

persons entails that others will continue to have their rights violated, but nevertheless insist that this recognition does not justify treating individuals as mere means for achieving greater effective respect for rights. This is, indeed, the point of treating persons as inviolable.

A more powerful response would be to question the presumed connection between conceiving of persons as ends in themselves and persons as *necessarily* inviolable. Perhaps implicit in Primoratz's objection, voiced in the first-person singular, is that the person who morally may not be violated for the sake of rights violation minimisation is one who is in no way *responsible* for the rights violations whose rectification is at issue. Were we to learn that Primoratz was himself deeply responsible for the rights violations whose rectification is at issue, his defence that 'no one may take away his life for the sake of a more just distribution of and general respect for rights within a group of people' might begin to ring hollow. Being a person who is responsible for serious rights violations may have a bearing on whether one is, necessarily, inviolable as a person. I will return to this issue in the final section of this chapter where I sketch the conditions that must be satisfied for acts of terrorism to be morally justified within a non-consequentialist rights-based moral perspective.

Is Held's Argument Consequentialist after All?

As discussed in Chapter 5, although from a consequentialist moral perspective it is difficult to show that that an act of terrorism was, *in fact*, morally justified, understanding how an act of terrorism *could* be morally justified on this basis is relatively unproblematic. An act of terrorism would be morally justified from a consequentialist perspective if it produced a greater balance of positive over negative consequences (however these are defined) than any other alternative act available to the agent in that situation would have produced. Philosophers may disagree about whether the conditions for justifying terrorism on consequentialist grounds are ever, in fact, satisfied, as well as on the sorts of consequences that ought to be considered, but there is little disagreement that such a justification is, in principle at least, *possible*.

Held's argument is philosophically interesting precisely because it purports to offer a *non-consequentialist* rights-based moral justification of at least some acts of terrorism. But some critics have charged that the argument smuggles in consequentialist considerations and thus is not what it seems. Uwe Steinhoff, for example, asserts that Held cannot consistently justify rights violations 'with an appeal to a better end result' because 'this would be a utilitarian or consequentialist argument' rather than one based on 'distributive justice' (Steinhoff 2004, p. 102). That is, if Held judges that it is *better* that rights violations in a society be distributed equitably than it is for them to be distributed inequitably, then this requires appeal to an informal judgement about human flourishing and the sorts of actions necessary to achieve it, which in turn introduces calculations of harms and benefits into moral deliberation. But if so, Steinhoff argues, then Held's argument ultimately reduces to a consequentialist argument, rather than being a bona fide rights-based argument, for the moral justifiability of some acts of terrorism. In this case it would not, contrary to appearances, be a non-consequentialist rights-based argument that morally justifies some acts of terrorism.

The critical issue here can easily be stated. Is Held's argument fundamentally a consequentialist one? Some of her remarks suggest that she wishes to take both rights *and* consequences into consideration in judging the morality of terrorism: 'an adequate moral appraisal [of terrorism] will have to take violations of rights into account along with any calculation of benefits and harms produced' (Held 1991, p. 72). Yet, she says, her proposal does not require 'a consequentialist calculation' (Held 1991, p. 74). Is this a coherent position?

A more precise understanding of the difference between consequentialist and non-consequentialist moral theories suggests that it is. Consequentialism is the moral theory (more precisely, that class of moral theories) that maintains that the morality of any act is correctly judged *solely* on the basis of the consequences resulting from that act relative to the consequences that would result from any alternative possible act in that situation. Non-consequentialism, by contrast, is the view that consequences do not *exhaust* the factors that are relevant to the moral evaluation of acts. Thus, merely including a consideration of consequences in a moral analysis is not sufficient to make that analysis a consequentialist one. But if so, then Held's argument is not a consequentialist argument. Considerations of respect for rights and for justice, rather than of substantive benefits and harms produced, drives 'the major argument' of her essay, namely, that 'on grounds of justice, it is better to equalize rights violations in a transition to bring an end to rights violations than it is to subject a given group that has already suffered extensive rights violations to continued such violations' (Held 1991, pp. 79–80). 'Justice itself', she observes, 'often requires a concern for how rights violations are distributed . . . We can recognize that some distributions are unfair, and seek to

156

make them less so' (Held 1991, pp. 80–1). To do so is to act for the sake of justice. To be sure, to act *for the sake of justice* is to act *for* a consequence, but it is not to judge the morality of the actions in question in terms of the consequences *actually produced*. But if so, then Held's argument is not, as Steinhoff contends, a consequentialist one.

CONDITIONS FOR A NON-CONSEQUENTIALIST RIGHTS-BASED MORAL JUSTIFICATION OF TERRORISM

If Held's argument is sound, it follows that 'terrorism cannot necessarily be ruled out as unjustifiable on a rights-based analysis, any more than it can on a consequentialist one' (Held 1991, p. 81). It remains to spell out more precisely the conditions that must be satisfied for an act of terrorism to be morally justifiable from a moral perspective that takes rights seriously.

In Held's view, the most promising situation for a non-consequentialist rights-based moral justification of terrorism is one in which the fundamental rights of the members of one group are being violated by the members of another group, there is a 'reasonable likelihood' that the use of terrorism would help to rectify this situation, and 'no other effective means are available' for rectifying the rights violations in question. In addition, although there is a 'prima facie judgement' against committing serious rights violations for the sake of rectifying less serious rights violations, she permits such violations if a serious rights violation against one group would be effective in rectifying a large enough number of lesser rights violations against another group.

The specification of these conditions is essential for judging the morality of specific acts of terrorism, but would benefit from greater elaboration. I propose that in order for acts of terrorism to be morally justified from a non-consequentialist view that takes rights seriously, all of the following conditions must be satisfied:

1. Members of a distinct group in a society have for a considerable time suffered serious rights violations by another distinct group, whose members can be reliably identified as such.

2. All means of reducing or eliminating the rights violations that are less harm-producing than terrorism have been tried and have failed.

3. There is convincing evidence that the use of terrorism would be effective in bringing about a situation in which the rights violations at issue are significantly reduced or eliminated.

4. The aim of the terrorism would be to effect a transition to a society in which rights violations are significantly reduced or eliminated.

5. That the purpose of the acts of terrorism is to effect a transition to a society in which rights violations are significantly reduced or eliminated, and that the realisation of such a society is a sufficient condition for cessation of the acts of terrorism, is clearly communicated to the group responsible for the rights violations.

6. Acts of terrorism are initially directed only against the property of members of the group known to be responsible for the rights violations, and care is taken to ensure that persons themselves are not injured, maimed or killed by such acts.

7. The acts of terrorism are intended to inflict only as much harm as is necessary in order to bring about a situation in which rights violations are significantly reduced or eliminated; care is taken to ensure that the acts of terrorism do not inflict more harm on the target group than is necessary, and that other persons are not injured, maimed or killed by such acts.

8. The magnitude of the rights violations resulting from the acts of terrorism for any individual is not greater than the magnitude of any of the rights violations the rectification of which is the motivation for the acts of terrorism.

My suggestion is that if any acts of terrorism *are* morally justified from a non-consequentialist rights-based perspective, they must satisfy all of these conditions. Although more precise than the conditions Held presents, these conditions still leave plenty of room for interpretation. Rather than further explication of these conditions in the abstract, however, I will explain them more fully in relation to the question of the morality of the IRA's armed struggle, so that their further explication and application are combined. Each of the conditions above is identified in the discussion below by its corresponding number.

RIGHTS, TERRORISM AND THE IRA's ARMED STRUGGLE

1. That there must be distinct groups in a society whose members are reliably identifiable as such is implicit in the definition of 'terrorism' (T) proposed in the Prologue. In order for an act to be an act of terrorism, it must be the case that the harm or threat of harm is directed indiscriminately to members of a distinct group, rather than either indiscriminately to anyone whatsoever regardless of group membership, or to specifically targeted

individuals such that, because of their unique positions, attacks upon them are not generally seen by anyone else as having relevance either for the other members of the groups to which these individuals belong or for an audience group. In order for members of a distinct group in a society to have suffered serious rights violations for a considerable time at the hands of members of another distinct group, it is not necessary that all members of the rights-violated group suffer from rights violations, nor that all members of the rights violating group be equally responsible. It is enough that there be a clear pattern of rights violating and rights violation associated with the two groups.

It does not require extensive argumentation to show that this condition was satisfied in Northern Ireland. From the arrival of Scottish and English planters in Ulster in the seventeenth century to the present, that province has been home to two distinct, more or less homogeneous communities. Especially since partition in 1921, Catholics have tended overwhelmingly to be nationalists who consider themselves citizens of Ireland, a country that had been illegitimately divided by a foreign power. A common response of Catholics has been to cling to activities and symbols integral to their cultural identity, such as going to mass, watching and playing Gaelic (rather than English) sports, and sending their children to private Catholic schools. Protestants have tended overwhelmingly to be unionists who consider themselves loyal citizens of Great Britain. They have been devoted to their own symbols of cultural identification as British: attending Protestant churches, following English sports, sending their children to state schools and, at least among those who consider themselves the most 'loyal' subjects of the British Crown, flying the Union Jack, painting its colours on curb-stones and marching in parades each summer to celebrate the triumphs of Protestantism. This basic fact about Northern Ireland is not invalidated by observing that there are exceptions as well as degrees of commitment to one's community among both Catholics and Protestants. Catholics and Protestants constitute two distinct groups whose members are, by and large, reliably identified as such.

Partition bestowed majority status on Protestants in Northern Ireland, a status that allowed them to impose their will with relative impunity on the Catholic minority in their midst. From 1921 until at least the early 1970s, as a whole (despite local variations) Catholics were treated as second-class citizens, with priority for jobs, public housing and opportunities for political representation given to Protestants. Despite denials by some that discrimination against Catholics was as extensive as the data suggest, or even that there was discrimination at all, statistics support the claim of extensive discrimination against Catholics in employment, housing and civil service appointments. Although these systemic abuses were largely rectified by 1972, other forms of discrimination against Catholics were still pervasive. For example, Catholics had good reasons to believe that the state's security forces did not enforce the law in a completely even-handed fashion with respect to the two communities. Despite significant reforms, Catholics were justified in believing that they were still effectively second-class citizens, denied by the Protestant-dominated apparatus of the state respect for their human rights. To the extent that their perception of the situation was accurate, it can be said that Catholics in Northern Ireland for a considerable time suffered serious rights violations at the hands of the Protestant majority.

2. Because of the harm associated with acts of terrorism, the use of such acts should come, if at all, only after other less-harm-producing alternatives have been tried and have been determined to be ineffective in reducing or eliminating the rights violations. Although it will usually be obvious when non-terroristic methods have *not* been given an adequate opportunity to bring about the desired effect (for example, when they haven't even been tried), typically it will *not* be obvious when (if ever) the point has been reached such that it can be said with absolute confidence that 'all non-terroristic means of rectifying the situation have been tried'. But this sort of problem is hardly unique to discussions of terrorism and need not undermine reasonable (albeit fallible) judgements here any more than it does elsewhere.

The civil rights movement of 1967–9 was intended to publicise the inequalities in Northern Irish society in order to exert pressure on the Stormont government to bring about effective respect for the rights of all, but especially for Catholics who were the primary victims of rights violations. Among the demands insisted on by NICRA were the repeal of the Special Powers Acts of 1922, 1933 and 1943, the disbandment of the B Specials paramilitary police force, an end to the gerrymandering of local electoral districts, an end to discrimination in the awarding of public housing and in government employment, and full voting equality. The movement collapsed amidst loyalist and police violence against demonstrators and the perception on the part of some that the effectiveness of such non-violent activities in the face of state-supported violence was futile. The end of the civil rights movement coincided with the appearance of a revitalised IRA committed to a more radical solution to the problems of Catholics in the Six Counties. From that point forward, peaceful agitation for a more just society was overshadowed by gunfire, explosions and funerals.

It is far from clear, however, that all non-terroristic means of rectifying the inequalities in Northern Irish society had been exhausted at the time that the civil rights movement was abandoned and the Provisional IRA emerged to resume the armed struggle. It is conceivable that had the civil rights movement endured in the face of the considerable obstacles it encountered, it might eventually have been even more successful than it was. It is worth noting that the American civil rights campaign of Martin Luther King Jr, on which the Northern Ireland civil rights movement was modelled, overcame significant obstacles and succeeded in securing significant advances in effective respect for the rights of blacks in the US – without the use of terrorism. It therefore seems premature to judge with confidence that all means other than terrorism of rectifying the injustices in Northern Ireland were tried and were shown to be incapable of success. The fact that by 1972 Catholics had secured most of the rights for which the civil rights movement had agitated suggests that the use of terrorism was not necessary to secure basic human rights, and indeed was directed toward other goals.

3. Even if all non-terroristic means of reducing or eliminating the rights violations have been tried and have failed, however, it does not follow that the use of terrorism is morally justified, because the use of terrorism might *also* be ineffective in reducing or eliminating the rights violations at issue. For the use of terrorism to be justified from a moral perspective that takes rights seriously, there must be convincing evidence that the use of terrorism would be effective in bringing about a situation in which the rights violations at issue are significantly reduced or eliminated. Did the IRA have such evidence?

Sadly, it did not. First, it is not clear that anyone in a leadership position in the Provisional IRA made a reasoned assessment of the probable effectiveness of a terrorist campaign vis-à-vis other available strategies for securing effective respect for basic human rights for Catholics in the Six Counties. Although it was taken for granted that securing for the Irish people their birthright to a united independent Ireland, free from British control, would (somehow) usher in a (more) just society, and that an armed struggle was necessary to achieve this goal, there is no evidence that serious thought was given to the relative effectiveness of this strategy compared with others for achieving this goal.

Second, by the time the IRA's campaign was going full throttle (1971–2), the most serious rights violations at issue had been addressed and significant reforms had been achieved through non-violent agitation. Rather than lamenting the demise of the civil rights movement as a defeat for the quest for a more just society, some republicans saw in its destruction an opportunity to resurrect the quest to remove the British influence in Ireland, and attempted to convince others that (nearly) every ill in Irish society was attributable to the British occupation. Rather than pausing to analyse what role non-violent political agitation and acts of terrorism, respectively, had played in securing basic rights for Catholics in Northern Ireland, the IRA intensified its terrorist campaign.

Third, the leadership of the IRA grossly underestimated the resolve of both the British authorities and of Ulster loyalists, especially failing to grasp ordinary Ulster Protestants' deep aversion to any weakening of their ties to Britain. The IRA leadership nevertheless carried out a campaign of terrorism for three decades in the absence of convincing evidence that the use of terrorism would be effective in bringing about the beneficial effects they assumed it would yield. Indeed, as the conflict wore on there was increasing evidence that, far from enhancing respect for the rights of Catholics in Northern Ireland, the Provisional IRA's acts of terrorism were instrumental in the curtailment of such rights. House searches, vehicle checkpoints, detention in interrogation centres, injuries and deaths from plastic bullets, and all the rest, were a direct consequence of the IRA's campaign. To the extent that such activities violated persons' rights, the Provisional IRA's campaign could be judged to have decreased rather than enhanced effective respect for human rights.

4. In order for acts of terrorism to be morally justified from a perspective that takes rights seriously, it is not sufficient merely that the particular rights violations whose rectification is the rationale for the acts of terrorism be reduced or eliminated, because this is consistent with aiming at a society in which other rights, or the rights of the members of other groups, are systematically violated. The society being aimed at must be one in which, overall, rights violations are reduced or eliminated relative to the society that currently exists.

That the primary aim of the terrorism unleashed by the IRA in 1970 was not to effect a transition to a society in which the particular rights violations emphasised by the civil rights movement were significantly reduced or eliminated has already been established. But it is also worth pointing out that it was also not obviously aimed at effecting a transition to a society in which rights violations were significantly reduced or eliminated overall. To the extent that republicans believed that the rights of Catholics could only be guaranteed in a united independent Ireland, to that same extent it would appear to follow that the rights of Protestants (who constituted a greater proportion of Northern Irish society) could only be guaranteed in a Northern Ireland that remained within the UK. Yet this implication was either dismissed by republicans as being a function of 'Protestant paranoia', attributed to confusion on the part of Protestants concerning their 'real' identity as Irish, or else disregarded as being of little moral importance. By its own reasoning, had the IRA succeeded in achieving its political goals, more than half of the people of Northern Ireland would simply have traded places with the previous minority. But if so, then the IRA's campaign cannot be judged to have had as its aim the transition to a society in which rights violations are significantly reduced or eliminated overall.

5. Terrorism is a strategy intended to influence an audience group in ways believed to be conducive to the advancement of some agenda. For the acts of terrorism to achieve this effect, the audience group must be in a position to respond in such a way that the acts of terrorism cease, and this in turn requires that the condition for their cessation be clearly communicated to the audience group that the acts are intended to influence. This condition does not require that the audience group respond appropriately. Rather, this requirement is important because it permits the *possibility* of the audience group responding appropriately.

In the context of the IRA's armed struggle what matters for the satisfaction of this condition is not that the IRA was correct in its view of rights violations, but only that the relationship between its acts of terrorism and its view of rights violations was clearly communicated to the target audience for these acts. This condition was satisfied. Unlike terrorist organisations whose motivations remain obscure and whose acts of terrorism are unaccompanied by specific demands, the IRA was exceptionally forthright in its public declarations that the purpose of the armed struggle was to end British control of the Six Counties as a necessary precondition for the political reunification of Ireland. The IRA made it equally clear that the attainment of its political goal was a sufficient condition for the cessation of the armed struggle. That the IRA abandoned the armed struggle without securing its political goal shows only that the attainment of its goal was not, its pronouncements to the contrary notwithstanding, in fact a *necessary* condition for cessation of the armed struggle.

6. Although attacks on property indirectly harm persons, the harm to persons resulting from such attacks is typically less severe and more easily transcended than are direct attacks on persons. By requiring that acts of terrorism be initially directed only against the property of the individuals belonging to the group known to be responsible for the rights violations, with care taken to ensure that persons themselves are not injured, maimed or killed by such acts, those responsible for the rights violations are given an opportunity to respond appropriately before more harm-inflicting acts of terrorism are committed. If additional acts of terrorism are morally justified, they will be so only if directed at members of the group responsible for the rights violations. This condition is required to ensure that the acts of terrorism are directed against individuals that collectively cannot be considered innocent of the rights violations the rectification of which is their stated purpose.

Although many of the IRA's acts of terrorism directly targeted property rather than persons and some (usually inadequate) precautions were taken to ensure that persons were not injured, maimed or killed by such acts, it is nonetheless fair to say that a carefully graduated campaign in which property was always attacked before persons, and when property was targeted care was taken to preclude human casualties, was haphazard at best and frequently involved a casual disregard for the possibility (and in many cases the probability) of human loss of life and limb. Moreover, it is implausible to suggest that the IRA's acts of terrorism were directed only against the property of the individuals belonging to the group(s) known to be responsible for the rights violations against Catholics. Had the IRA exclusively attacked the property of Unionist politicians, or of ministers of state sent from London, this condition might have been more nearly satisfied. But attacking the property of ordinary Protestants as if they were all, indiscriminately, responsible for rights violations against Catholics, would be no different than the practice (condemned by republicans) of some loyalist paramilitaries of equating all Catholics with members of the IRA, and hence as legitimate targets for attack.

7. Terrorism is here being considered as a strategy employed in order to achieve the rectification of rights violations. As such, acts of terrorism potentially constitute the means toward certain noble ends. It may be an analytic moral truth that harm in excess of what is necessary in order to achieve some good is to be avoided. It follows that acts of terrorism undertaken in order to bring about a situation in which rights violations are significantly reduced or eliminated should be undertaken, if at all, only in

such a way as to cause the minimum amount of harm necessary in order to achieve the morally superior situation. Care must be taken in methods and target selection to produce the minimal amount of harm consistent with the attainment of the moral objective.

The IRA's armed struggle had as its political aim the withdrawal of all British troops from the Six Counties as a precondition for the establishment of a united independent Irish republic, rather than the more modest aim of rectifying the rights violations with which the civil rights movement was concerned. Counterfactually, had the IRA adopted an armed approach to securing effective respect for the rights that were the concern of the civil rights movement, then – because those rights could be and in fact were secured without a prolonged terrorist campaign – it would be obvious that its acts of terrorism inflicted far more harm than was necessary in order to bring about a situation in which *those* rights violations were significantly reduced or eliminated. John Hume spoke for many moderate nationalists when he declared that there is no injustice in Northern Ireland that would justify killing a single person (Murphy 1993). If so, then even if the IRA's killing *had* been for the sake of civil rights, the condition here being considered would not have been satisfied.

8. Requiring that the magnitude of the rights violations for any individual resulting from an act of terrorism not be greater than the magnitude of any of the rights violations the rectification of which is the motivation for the act of terrorism is important to ensure that particular individuals do not suffer disproportionately for the rights violations attributed to the group to which they belong. Being denied equal access to affordable public housing, and being dismembered by a bomb because one belongs to a group responsible for inequitable public housing policies, may both be a violation of one's rights. But the latter rights violation so far surpasses the former rights violation that an act of terrorism intended to rectify the inequitable housing situation by blowing up individuals belonging to the rights violating group would be grossly disproportionate. Although the seriousness of various rights violations will not always be so easily compared, it will still be the case that some rights violations are so clearly of different orders of magnitude that such a comparison becomes both possible and necessary (Murphy 1993). This condition imposes a limit.

Virginia Held notes, 'In a defective society . . . where rights are not in fact being respected, we should be able to make comparative judgments about which and whose rights violations are least justifiable' (Held 1991, p. 73). By any reasonable standard, Northern Ireland, with its unequal treatment of Catholics and Protestants in terms of housing, employment, voting rights and so on, constituted just such a defective society for at least half of the twentieth century. These rights violations needed to be rectified. Yet it is equally clear that the magnitude of the rights violations resulting from the IRA's acts of terrorism was considerably greater for many individual persons than was the magnitude of any of the rights violations afflicting Catholics in the Six Counties. The importance of being denied the right to adequate housing, to equal access to jobs and to participation in democratic institutions is not to be minimised, as denial of such rights seriously compromises individuals' access to the best possible lives for themselves. Yet denial of such rights is not commensurate with being injured, maimed or killed by bombs detonated in crowded pubs or in cars on busy streets. A fortiori, the denial of the right to a united independent Ireland is not commensurate with rights violations resulting from the IRA's thirty-year armed struggle. The rights violations resulting from IRA bombing operations were of a much greater magnitude than the rectification of the rights violations which were the ultimate rationale for such operations in the first place. As such, these bombing operations were not justified according to a moral perspective that takes rights seriously.

CONCLUSIONS

According to some philosophers, acts of terrorism are *necessarily* morally wrong because they always violate fundamental human rights. If this claim could be shown to be correct, it would decisively settle the question of the morality of terrorism in general and of the IRA's armed struggle in particular, insofar as the latter involved the use of terrorism. But not all philosophers agree that taking rights as centrally important shows that acts of terrorism are necessarily morally wrong. Some have argued that in cases where serious rights violations are already occurring, the limited use of terrorism in pursuit of a more just society may be morally justified. I have argued that this latter claim is correct, but that the conditions that must be satisfied for such rights violations to be morally justified need to be elaborated in greater detail. When they are, it becomes clear that only a very narrow range of acts of terrorism can satisfy these conditions. Although it is possible to imagine acts of terrorism that would be justified on the basis of a concern for rights, the IRA's armed struggle as a whole, which relied heavily on acts of terrorism to accomplish its goals, was not morally justified on this basis. Indeed, it must be judged to have been morally unjustified from a perspective that takes rights seriously. This is a view that many would no doubt embrace without feeling the need to work through the difficult issues and detailed arguments in this chapter. The point of this chapter, however, has been to firmly establish this conclusion and, equally important, to show *why* this conclusion is warranted.

CHAPTER 7

'Crime is Crime is Crime': British Counter-Terrorism in Northern Ireland

> The struggle to govern Ireland may fairly be regarded as Britain's longest counterinsurgency campaign.
>
> (Charles Townshend 1986, p. 45)

INTRODUCTION

It is a truism that counter-terrorism activities can cause harm as great or greater than the terrorism they are intended to combat; yet such activities frequently proceed without their agents engaging in detailed reflection on the morality of the policies or practices pursued. This is true both in general and with regard to the conflict in Northern Ireland in particular. Thus an examination of the morality of IRA terrorism ideally should include an examination of the morality of British counter-terrorism as well. My aims in this chapter are thus twofold. First, I want to survey British counter-terrorism policies and practices in Northern Ireland, distinguishing among activities authorised by counter-terrorism legislation (for example, internment without trial), those that clearly go beyond anything authorised in legislation (for example, alleged shoot-to-kill executions) and those that exist in the grey area in between (for example, methods of interrogation alleged to involve torture). Second, recalling that the domains of the legal and of the moral typically overlap but are not coextensive, I want to provide at least the beginning of a moral evaluation of a subset of these activities. Absent will be any detailed discussion of the covert intelligence war waged against the IRA which became increasingly important as the conflict wore on (Jackson 2007). Although some attention will be paid to the relative effectiveness

168

of various counter-terrorism efforts, my main focus will be on the moral evaluation of such efforts. Effectiveness and morality are not unrelated, but there is no reason to suppose that they must always or even usually coincide.

COUNTER-TERRORISM LEGISLATION

Because British civil liberties are based on tradition and common law, rather than in formal legislation (as, for example, in the US Bill of Rights), in times of perceived crisis Parliament can enact emergency powers legislation as it deems necessary without being constrained by legally or constitutionally protected liberties. Legislatively, Northern Ireland has been in a state of emergency since its formation. A year after partition, Parliament passed the Civil Authorities (Special Powers) Act of 1922. This and subsequent emergency legislation were superseded by the Northern Ireland (Emergency Provisions) Acts of 1973, 1978 and 1987, and the Prevention of Terrorism (Temporary Provisions) Acts of 1974 and 1989. Michael Freeman (2003) relates the introduction of emergency powers legislation to four phases in British counter-terrorism efforts in Northern Ireland: internment without trial, Diplock courts, criminalisation and the supergrass system. The policies associated with each essentially extended a de facto separate legal system created for dealing with individuals accused of terrorist offences, often with unforeseen and unwanted effects.

Internment without Trial

Internment without trial, authorised by the Civil Authorities (Special Powers) Act of 1922, had been used effectively in Northern Ireland by the British in dealing with internal security threats in 1922–6 (following partition and the Irish Civil War), 1939–44 (World War II), and 1956–62 (the IRA's Border Campaign; O'Boyle 1977). In each of these cases it was applied almost exclusively against Catholics. Internment without trial was re-introduced on 9 August 1971 in an effort to remove suspected IRA volunteers from circulation. By the end of 1971, over 900 Catholic men were being held without trial. Internment without trial ended with the release of the last prisoner on 5 December 1975. During this time, 1,981 people had been interned: 1,874 were Catholic, only 107 were Protestant. Of the 1,590 people interned between 9 August and 15 December 1971, only 18 were eventually charged with criminal offences (Neumann 2003). Tactically, internment was ineffectual in diminishing IRA activity. As quickly as suspected IRA members were taken off the street, additional volunteers took their places. Indeed, shortly after the introduction of internment, *Republican News* (9 October 1971) carried an article in which the Provisionals gloated over this fact: 'The Republican movement in Belfast extends to her Majesty's forces their [*sic*] heartfelt thanks for the magnificent recruiting drive that they have held on our behalf'. Politically, internment was a disaster for the British and a boon to the republican movement.[1] Because of the perceived sectarian nature of internment, it further alienated the entire nationalist community from the state and its security forces, and in the process garnered support in Catholic neighbourhoods for the IRA. As Ó Dochartaigh (2005, p. 231) notes, 'The comprehensive alienation of huge sections of the Catholic community from the state had the effect of transforming the Republican movement from a small, marginal and conspiratorial group of individuals . . . into a major force within the Catholic community'. Its indirect effects were also far-reaching. It was in the context of a NICRA march against internment on 30 January 1972 that British troops killed over a dozen unarmed demonstrators. Because of Bloody Sunday, in turn, the IRA's ranks swelled with willing volunteers, some of them reasoning 'you were going to be shot anyway so you might as well be shot for something as for nothing' (Ó Dochartaigh 2005, p. 247).

Diplock Courts

In light of the deteriorating security situation in Northern Ireland following Bloody Sunday, Parliament commissioned Lord (William John Kenneth) Diplock to issue recommendations concerning more effective ways of combating IRA terrorism. An important issue concerned trials of individuals accused of offences against the state. Aware that Protestant and Catholic juries were prone to render sectarian verdicts, and that ordinary jurors were vulnerable to intimidation by paramilitaries, he recommended that trial by jury be suspended in favour of hearings before a tribunal of judges who would render verdicts and assign prison sentences. This recommendation was formalised in the Northern Ireland (Emergency Provisions) Act of 1973, which also granted the security forces wide powers of arrest and detention. Individuals could be arrested even when no specific crime was suspected, and could be held for extended periods of time for 'in-depth' interrogation. It also relaxed the requirements for the admissibility of evidence to allow confessions obtained during interrogation. If indicted, the prosecution could give as evidence, and the accused could be convicted on the basis of, any statement made by the accused while in detention – an apparent necessity in a context in which witnesses might be reluctant to testify in court, but also a policy that seemed tailor-made for widespread abuse by the security forces. Complaints that confessions were obtained through the use of torture were common and often corroborated by compelling evidence (Taylor 1980). By the mid 1980s, over 300 cases had been heard in Diplock courts. Conviction rates in Diplock courts were not appreciably higher than convictions in jury trials in the regular court system (Nelson 1991). The conviction rate for Diplock courts in the years 1984–6 averaged 51 per cent by comparison with 49 per cent for jury trials in Northern Ireland and 50 per cent for jury trials in England and Wales during that same period. Nonetheless, by 1986 up to 90 per cent of the convictions in terrorist trials to that point had relied wholly or primarily on confessions made to the police (Nelson 1991).

Criminalisation

In June 1972 the British government introduced special category status for paramilitary prisoners, thereby acknowledging the political nature of their offences. Such prisoners were permitted to wear their own clothes, to associate with other prisoners and were exempt from the work required of prisoners incarcerated for criminal offences. In March 1976 their special category status was withdrawn as the British government introduced its related policies of 'Ulsterisation' and 'criminalisation'. Ulsterisation meant giving the locally recruited RUC (rather than the British army) the day-to-day responsibility for security in Northern Ireland. This amounted to an important shift in counter-terrorism strategy. Formerly the situation in Northern Ireland was conceptualised as an insurgency requiring a military response. The essential problem with this, according to some analysts, was that in the context of Northern Ireland the British military was unable to implement the full arsenal of counterinsurgency measures that had worked in other colonial contexts. To put it bluntly,

> if South Armagh were a province in Malaya many of its Catholic inhabitants would have had their homes burned down and have been either forcibly resettled in heavily policed 'new villages' or deported across the border. Obviously such

draconian measures were not politically possible in the context of contemporary Britain. (Newsinger 2002, p. 164)

'The result', Newsinger notes, 'was that the army did enough to alienate the Catholic working class, but not enough to successfully intimidate them' (Newsinger 2002, p. 179). With the introduction of Ulsterisation the conflict would henceforth be conceptualised as an internal security problem to be dealt with by law enforcement agencies. The RUC was given additional men and equipment, whereas the army was relegated (officially, at least) to its original role of merely assisting the civil authorities.

Criminalisation meant ending special category status for paramilitary prisoners. Henceforth they would be treated as ordinary criminals. As Margaret Thatcher later explained, 'We are not prepared to consider special category status for certain groups of people serving sentences for crime. Crime is crime is crime. It is not political, it is crime.' To the extent that paramilitary prisoners were incarcerated for their violent *deeds* rather than for their political *beliefs*, she had a point. But her insistence that 'there is no such thing as political murder, political bombing or political violence. There is only criminal murder, criminal bombing and criminal violence' conveniently overlooked the fact that the hunger strikers had been arrested and convicted under legislation stemming from the Prevention of Terrorism Act (1974) that had defined terrorism as 'the use of violence for political ends' (Neumann 2003, pp. 110–11). In addition, it was in response to the withdrawal of special category status that the blanket protest, dirty protest and hunger strikes were undertaken by republican prisoners (both Provisional IRA and INLA) in the first place, suggesting that much republican paramilitary violence was indeed politically motivated.

Supergrass Trials

By the early 1980s, nationalist outrage following negative publicity connected with the interrogation procedures used on suspected terrorists convinced British authorities of the need for a different method of obtaining convictions. If confessions from suspected terrorists could not be obtained through coercive means, then security forces would find other suspects who would implicate their former associates in exchange for reduced prison sentences or immunity from prosecution. Beginning in 1981, British authorities staged 'supergrass' trials in Diplock courts. ('Grasshopper' was British slang for an informer. A particularly well-placed informer was a 'supergrass'.) In addition to circumventing new restrictions on the use of confessions obtained during interrogation, the use of supergrasses was intended to mitigate the problems of collecting evidence in areas where security forces might be at high risk of ambush, or where crime scenes might be booby-trapped. In 1981, supergrass Christopher Black gave statements which led to thirty-eight arrests. Based on his testimony, twenty-two members of the Provisional IRA were convicted and sentenced collectively to over 4,000 years in prison. (Eighteen of these convictions were overturned on appeal in 1986.) In April 1983, fourteen members of the UVF were imprisoned on testimony given by Joseph Bennett. In December 1984 all of these convictions were overturned. The last supergrass trial concluded in December 1985. Twenty-five members of the INLA were imprisoned on the word of Harry Kirkpatrick. All but one of these convictions was overturned a year later. By the time it ended, some 500 persons had been charged on the word of twenty-seven supergrasses (Bonner 1988). Because many of the informers were of questionable credibility, and their testimony was usually uncorroborated, supergrass trials turned out to have questionable judicial value. Of the 217 defendants in the first ten supergrass trials, 120 were found guilty. Of these, sixty-seven convictions were overturned on appeal (Freeman 2003). Although in the short-term they succeeded in taking (suspected) terrorists out of circulation, they also had the long-term effect of further eroding confidence in the judicial system among ordinary citizens (Soule 1989).

MISCARRIAGES OF JUSTICE

Internment without trial, Diplock courts, criminalisation and supergrass trials were intended to assist the authorities in the aggressive prosecution of suspected terrorists. In this they succeeded brilliantly. Their effectiveness in *combating terrorism*, however, was considerably less obvious. Thanks to the well-publicised abuses associated with each, their main effect seems to have been to damage the credibility of the British legal system. By the early 1990s, three highly publicised cases involving miscarriages of justice confirmed what many in the nationalist community already believed – that the British authorities were more zealous in seeking convictions for terrorist offences than in protecting the innocent or serving justice.

The Guildford Four

In the autumn of 1974 the IRA pursued a major bombing campaign on the British mainland. On 5 October 1974 at 8:30 p.m. an IRA bomb exploded without warning in the Horse and Groom pub in Guildford, England, killing five people and injuring sixty-five more. Thirty minutes later a second bomb exploded in the nearby Seven Stars pub, which had been evacuated after word spread of the first explosion. The pubs were selected by the IRA because they were popular with army personnel, and indeed four of those killed in the Horse and Groom were young army recruits. A month after the Guildford bombs, at 10:00 p.m. on 7 November 1974, a bomb containing nuts and bolts packed around plastic explosive was thrown into the King's Arms pub in Woolwich. Two people were killed in the blast and many more were injured. On 29 November (within hours of the Prevention of Terrorism Act becoming law) the police arrested Paul Hill in Southampton. The following day police arrested Gerry Conlon at his home in Belfast. He was taken first to the Springfield Road police station and then flown to the Guildford police station in England. The Guildford police obtained confessions from Hill and Conlon, along with the names of relatives and friends said to be involved in bomb-making activities. Among these were Patrick Armstrong and his English girlfriend, Carole Richardson, who were both then arrested.

Although in their October 1975 trials they claimed that they had been tortured by the police until they agreed to sign confessions, the Guildford Four, as they came to be known, were convicted and given life sentences for the Guildford bombings. (Hill and Conlon were also convicted for the Woolwich bombing.) Despite a number of appeals over several years, the four remained in prison, protesting their innocence. However, in 1989 a detective re-examining the case discovered typed notes from the police interrogation of Patrick Armstrong. It was clear that the notes had been heavily edited; deletions and additions had been made, and the notes had been rearranged. These notes matched hand-written notes presented at the trial as having been taken down *during* the interrogation, suggesting that the hand-written notes were in fact composed *after* the interviews had been conducted. A further appeal was made on the basis of this new evidence. The judge in the appeal case concluded on the basis of this new evidence that the police had manipulated the notes in order to incriminate Armstrong. In 1989 the convictions of the Guildford Four were overturned. Gerry Conlon, Paul Hill, Patrick Armstrong and Carole

Richardson were released after spending fifteen years in prison for crimes they did not commit. Although three policemen were charged with crimes in connection with the Guildford Four's interrogation and prosecution, each was acquitted of any wrongdoing.

The Birmingham Six

On 14 November 1974, an IRA man named James McDade died when a bomb he was planting outside the Coventry telephone exchange exploded prematurely. On 21 November 1974, the day McDade's remains were being flown back to Belfast, at 8:25 p.m. and 8:27 p.m. bombs exploded in the Mulberry Bush and the Tavern in the Town, two popular pubs in Birmingham. The first bomb killed ten people; the second bomb killed eleven. In total 182 people were injured. That evening five men from Northern Ireland travelling from England to Belfast for McDade's funeral were detained by police and taken in for questioning: Gerry Hunter, Dick McIlkenny, Paddy Hill, William Power and John Walker. A sixth man, Hugh Callaghan, was brought in the following evening. After forensic tests and routine questioning, the men were transferred to the West Midlands Serious Crime Squad police unit, where for three days they were interrogated by officers of the Birmingham Criminal Investigation Department. Each eventually signed a confession admitting involvement in the bombings. When they appeared in court on 28 November, all had bruises and manifested other signs of maltreatment. On 12 May 1975, the six men were charged with murder and conspiracy to cause explosions. Their trial began on 9 June 1975. Their signed statements admitting guilt were deemed admissible as evidence, despite the fact that the men repudiated the confessions as having been signed under duress. Other evidence brought against them was circumstantial at best. Nonetheless, the jury found the six men guilty of murder. On 15 August 1975 they were sentenced to life terms. The judge presiding in the case expressed regret that capital punishment was no longer an option in the British legal system.

Despite several appeals over the next few years, the convictions of the Birmingham Six were upheld. In explaining his rejection of one of the appeals, a judge explained with impeccable logic that should the prisoners' appeal succeed based on the charge that their confessions were beaten out of them, it would mean that the police were guilty of perjury as well as of violence and threats, that the confessions were involuntary and hence improperly admitted in evidence, and consequently that the convictions were erroneous. Since they would then have to be pardoned, the appeal process could not be permitted to proceed any further. However, during the late 1980s, books, newspaper articles and television documentaries brought forward new evidence questioning the convictions, while groups in Britain, Ireland, Europe and the US campaigned for the men's release. On 14 March 1991, after they had spent sixteen years in prison, new information demonstrating that police had fabricated evidence led to their convictions being overturned. In a dramatic understatement, the judge at the appeal declared laconically of the police witnesses at the original trial: 'they must have lied'. None of those policemen has ever been prosecuted.

The Maguire Seven

In December 1974, police followed Patrick 'Giuseppe' Conlon from Belfast to the home of Patrick and Anne Maguire in London. He had travelled to London to meet with solicitors who were defending his son, Gerry, who was under arrest on suspicion of carrying out the Guildford pub bombings. Police already had their eyes on the Maguire home, because under interrogation Gerry Conlon had identified the home of his aunt, Anne Maguire, as a bomb-making facility. In a raid on the Maguire home, no bombs or bomb-making materials were found. Nonetheless, in 1975 Giuseppe Conlon, Patrick and Anne Maguire, their two younger sons, Vincent and Patrick, Mrs. Maguire's brother, Sean Smyth, and a family friend, Patrick O'Neill, were arrested, tried and convicted of running a bomb-making factory for the IRA. Throughout their six-week trial all protested their innocence. Patrick and Anne Maguire were each sentenced to fourteen years in prison for possessing explosives. Vincent, seventeen, and Patrick, fourteen, were sentenced to five and four years in prison, respectively. Sean Smyth, Giuseppe Conlon and Patrick O'Neill were each sentenced to twelve years, although Giuseppe Conlon would die in incarceration from a long-standing lung ailment, exacerbated by conditions in the prison. Tellingly, after the verdicts were announced, Chief Constable Peter Matthews of the Surrey police, who led the investigation, remarked: 'We are delighted with the verdicts. These are the people we were after. We have cut off a major supply pipeline to the terrorist. We are only sorry we did not find the bombs.' The convictions of the Maguire Seven were overturned in 1991 when it was established that confessions had been obtained from some of them after they had been beaten by members of the London Metropolitan Police, and that police had withheld evidence that would have cleared them of the charges. No police officers involved have ever charged in connection with the case.

Security versus Individual Rights

The Guildford, Birmingham and Maguire convictions were significant not merely because they constitute tragic miscarriages of justice, but because together with other similar cases they signified a troubling pattern in the British judicial system concerning the prosecution of individuals suspected of terrorist offences. Woffinden (1987), writing before these cases had been legally resolved, came to the conclusion that innocent persons were convicted because of the desire of authorities to appear tough on terrorism and to demonstrate effectiveness in combating it. The cases suggested that in the dilemma between maintaining security and safeguarding rights, the former took priority to such an extent that the latter was frequently completely disregarded. Acceptance of the risk of such miscarriages of justice was rationalised in the Gardiner Report, published in January 1975 in the immediate aftermath of the IRA's autumn 1974 mainland bombing campaign:

> When times are relatively normal, the needs of an ordered society may be met by the criminal courts functioning with a high regard for the Common law's presumption of innocence and a strict observance of the rules of evidence and the standards of proof. But when normal conditions give way to disorder and lawlessness, with extensive terrorism causing widespread loss of life and limb and the wholesale destruction of property . . . the very safeguards of the law then become the means by which it may be circumvented. (O'Boyle 1977, p. 675)

The Gardiner Report noted that the situation had changed considerably since 1972 when the Diplock Commission had issued its recommendations for combating terrorism. The most effective protection against terrorism, it stated,

> lies . . . in the recognition by government that it must act with speed to demonstrate its determination to sustain its authority . . . Terrorism and subversion in Northern Ireland can only be defeated, or guarded against, by the energetic pursuit of measures against them by the Government . . . (http://cain.ulst.ac.uk/hmso/gardiner.htm)

That representatives of the British government acted with speed, determination and energy in their pursuit of terrorists is clearly illustrated in the three cases just discussed. Whether they also acted with due regard for individual rights is another matter. Against those who had argued that such emergency provisions as detention without trial, arrest on the mere suspicion of terrorist activity without supporting evidence, and trial without jury 'are so inherently objectionable that they must be abolished on the grounds that they constitute a basic violation of human rights', the Gardiner Report countered that

> while the liberty of the subject is a human right to be preserved under all possible conditions, it is not, and cannot be, an absolute right, because one man may use his liberty to take away the liberty of another and must be restrained from doing so. Where freedoms conflict, the state has a duty to protect those in need of protection. (http://cain.ulst.ac.uk/hmso/gardiner.htm)

But of course those (rightly or wrongly) accused of terrorist offences are also individuals whose freedoms the state has a duty to protect. The application of emergency terrorism legislation in Britain during the height of the Troubles tragically illustrates the dangers involved in seeking to enhance security at the expense of respect for individual rights. Woffinden (1987) quotes Cyril Connolly, writing in the *Sunday Times* of 15 January 1961: 'The test of a country's justice is not the blunders which are sometimes made but the zeal with which they are put right'. 'Zeal' is probably not the first word that comes to mind in considering the British government's attempts to put right the cases just discussed.

BRITISH COUNTER-TERRORISM METHODS AND OPERATIONS

Torture Interrogation

Internment without trial was used extensively from August 1971 to December 1975. Toward the beginning of this period, internees who were considered especially valuable potential sources of information were subjected to 'interrogation in depth' utilising 'the five techniques': covering the detainee's head with a black hood; exposure to continuous, monotonous, loud noise; sleep deprivation; severely restricted food and water; and requiring the detainee (through the forceful application of a baton) to stand against a wall, legs apart, with hands raised overhead and against the wall, for four to six hours at a time – all over a period of several days. Here is how Tommy Gorman, interned in 1971, described the experience:

> [It] was bad . . . They brought us into the cell, in this place, had blankets hanging up everywhere and there were eye-holes in the blankets . . . you could see the eyes at these holes in the blanket and we walked in [and they said], 'That's him, that's

178

him' . . . we were battered, just battered for three days. There was no subtlety to it. It was just, you were hauled out of bed at two o'clock in the morning and brought in and questioned, battered up against the wall, stuff like that . . . It was just sheer brutality. (English 2003, p. 142)

As an officially sanctioned method for breaking down the resistance of those being interrogated, the five techniques had an impressive track-record. They had been found effective in previous colonial counterin-surgency operations in Palestine, Malaya, Kenya, Cyprus, the British Cameroons, Brunei, British Guiana, Aden, Borneo/Malaysia and the Persian Gulf (Brownlie 1972; Hennessey 2007; O'Boyle 1977). Although a committee led by Sir Edmund Compton was formed to look into allegations of brutality against those arrested in the internment sweep on 9 August 1971, it ruled that the five techniques constituted ill treatment but not torture nor even 'physical brutality': 'We consider that brutality is an inhuman or savage form of cruelty, and that cruelty implies a disposition to inflict suffering, coupled with indifference to, or pleasure in, the victim's pain. We do not think that happened here' (Brownlie 1972, p. 502). In other words, so long as it is supposed that those applying the five techniques did not expressly enjoy doing so, application of these techniques did not constitute brutality, much less torture.

Disquiet over the conclusions of the Compton Report led to the formation of a second committee, chaired by Lord Parker, who concluded that 'there is no reason to rule out these techniques on moral grounds' and that 'it is possible to operate them in a manner consistent with the highest standards of our society' (Brownie 1972, p. 505). However, Lord Gardiner wrote as a minority opinion on the committee:

I do not believe that, whether in peace time or for the purpose of obtaining information . . . in emergency terrorist conditions, or even in a war against a ruthless enemy, such procedures are morally justifiable against those suspected of having information of importance to the police or army, even in the light of any marginal advantages which may therefore be obtained. (Taylor 1980, p. 15)

The European Commission on Human Rights later judged that the five techniques constituted a practice of inhuman treatment *and torture* in violation of Article 3 of the European Convention on Human Rights, which states unequivocally that 'no one shall be subjected to torture or to inhuman or degrading treatment or punishment' (http://www.hri.org/docs/ECHR50.html). Following unfavourable publicity, authorised use of the five techniques was discontinued on 2 March 1972.

The European Convention on Human Rights condemns torture but does not define it. Other human rights documents do offer definitions. For example, the 1984 UN Convention Against Torture supplies the following definition:

> Torture means any act by which severe pain or suffering, whether physical or mental, is intentionally inflicted on a person for such purposes as obtaining from him or a third person information or a confession, punishing him for an act he or a third person has committed or is suspected of having committed, or intimidating or coercing him or a third person, or for any reason based on discrimination of any kind, when such pain or suffering is inflicted by or at the instigation of or with the consent or acquiescence of a public official or other person acting in an official capacity. (http://www.hrweb.org/legal/cat.html)

If this definition is accepted, then torture interrogation as a practice continued after use of the five techniques was officially discontinued. That torture was used in the Guildford Four and Birmingham Six cases is beyond doubt (Woffinden 1987). In a classic case of British understatement, the Bennett Report (Report of the Committee of Inquiry into Police Interrogation Procedures in Northern Ireland) of March 1979 noted that

> the uncertainty, despite the standards upheld and applied by the courts, about what is permissible and what is not, short of the use of physical violence or ill-treatment, may tempt police officers to see how far they can go and what they can get away with. (Taylor 1980, p. 77)

Tragically for some, in many cases police seem to have acted in accordance with the motto once attributed to the Saigon police: 'If they are not guilty, beat them until they are' (Shue 1978, p. 135).

Shoot-to-Kill Executions

Shoot-to-kill executions as a method of counter-terrorism involve the extra-legal pre-emptive use of lethal force against individuals (alleged to be) carrying out, about to carry out, or in the planning stages of carrying out an act of terrorism. Nationalists have claimed that the security forces have a shoot-to-kill policy toward suspected republican paramilitaries such that individuals who could be arrested and taken into custody are instead summarily executed. For example, in three separate incidents between 11 November and 12 December 1982, six suspected republican paramilitaries were shot dead by members of a special RUC anti-terrorist unit. None of those killed was armed. John Stalker, a Deputy Chief Constable of the Greater Manchester Police, cautiously summed up his two-year investigation into these killings by concluding that 'the circumstances of these shootings pointed to a police inclination, if not a policy, to shoot suspects dead without warning rather than to arrest them' (Stalker 1988, p. 253). His account of how the RUC obstructed his investigation and attempted to suppress his findings lend credence to the stronger (policy) interpretation.

Although the RUC, the British army, MI5 and MI6 have all been accused of such killings, of those security forces said to be involved in shoot-to-kill executions none has attracted more attention than the SAS. The Special Air Service was founded in July 1941 to carry out sabotage and intelligence operations behind enemy lines. It continues to enjoy a reputation as one of the most elite Special Forces units in the world. As the veteran Northern Ireland journalist Martin Dillon notes, 'The SAS image of stealth, firepower, aggression and efficient killing power was such that successive British governments were reluctant to admit that the SAS played any role in Northern Ireland . . .' (Dillon 1990, p. 161). Nonetheless, that the SAS has been active and lethally effective in Northern Ireland is well documented (Murray 1990; Urban 1992). Two infamous SAS operations illustrate their lethal effectiveness.

On Friday, 8 May 1987, eight members of the East Tyrone Brigade of the IRA, all wearing body armour, set out to destroy the RUC station in Loughgall, County Armagh. The operation was part of a broader strategy of creating 'zones of liberation' – areas beyond the control of the security forces. South Armagh (so-called 'bandit country') already constituted such a zone. Although the British military had installations there, they could only be accessed by helicopter because the IRA ensured that travel along the roads was simply too dangerous. The attack on the Loughgall RUC station was intended to expand the zone of liberation by destroying another rural police station, and then following up by killing any building contractors who were bold enough to attempt to rebuild it. The plan involved placing a 200lb (91kg) bomb in the front bucket of a backhoe digger, driving the digger through the reinforced fences surrounding the RUC station, detonating the bomb to destroy the police station, and then shooting any police personnel who attempted to escape. The East Tyrone Brigade had successfully carried out similar operations twice before. The attack on the Loughgall RUC station was expected to simply repeat this successful strategy.

This time, however, the authorities had been tipped off and set an ambush. Twenty-four SAS soldiers took up concealed positions around the

RUC station, while another was placed inside the station. Shortly after 7:00 p.m. the eight-man IRA unit approached the station, three on the digger and five in a blue Toyota van. One man drove the backhoe digger through the perimeter fence, lit the fuse on the bomb and ran. The five men in the van leapt out and began spraying the police station with gunfire. At that point the SAS unleashed a fusillade of bullets, firing over 600 rounds and killing all eight IRA men with shots to the head. A local man who happened to be driving by as the shooting began was mistaken for part of an IRA backup unit and was shot dead when the SAS opened fire on the car. His brother, riding next to him in the car, was seriously wounded.

As a counter-terrorism operation, the SAS ambush at Loughgall was a dramatic victory. The bomb in the digger exploded, destroying the police station, but one of the IRA's most dangerous active service units had been wiped out. None of the SAS soldiers was injured. Politically, however, the SAS's success at Loughgall was more ambiguous. Many cheered the fact that the security forces had countered an IRA terrorist operation with overwhelming force, giving them as little opportunity to escape as they were prone to give to their own victims. Among republicans, however, the eight IRA men who had given their lives for 'the cause' became known as the 'Loughgall Martyrs'. Their funerals were among the largest in Northern Ireland since those of the 1981 hunger strikers. They were divinised in wall murals (and more recently on T-shirts, coffee mugs and refrigerator magnets). Their deaths are still commemorated by republicans every year.

The Loughgall ambush involved the SAS killing an IRA active service unit caught in the act of carrying out an attack on an RUC station. The most infamous shoot-to-kill incident attributed to the SAS, however, involved three members of an IRA active service unit in the British overseas territory of Gibraltar, none of whom was armed at the time. The Gibraltar killings thus raise in a more pointed way the justification for shoot-to-kill executions.

On Sunday, 6 March 1988, three members of an IRA active service unit crossed over from Spain into Gibraltar. At 12:30 p.m. Seán Savage drove a white Renault 5 automobile into the British overseas territory and parked near the Governor's mansion. Mairéad Farrell and Dan McCann crossed the border into Gibraltar on foot at 2:30 p.m. and met Savage near the parked car. A little over an hour later they split up. At 3:41 p.m., as Farrell and McCann walked toward the border, they were approached by two SAS soldiers in plain clothes. According to witnesses, Farrell and McCann raised their hands in surrender, at which point the soldiers opened fire. Forensic evidence indicated that Farrell had been killed by three bullets fired into her back at a distance of a few feet. She was shot eight times in total. McCann had two bullet holes in his back. The upward trajectory of a number of the bullet wounds in Farrell's and McCann's bodies indicated that they were shot either from a gunman firing his weapon from a kneeling position, or when their bodies were already on the ground or close to it. Savage had been walking toward the city centre when Farrell and McCann were killed. Upon hearing the gunshots, he turned around and was killed by another SAS soldier. Forensic evidence indicated that he had been shot sixteen to eighteen times, with at least four bullet wounds in his head as he lay on the ground, a conclusion verified by witnesses at the scene (Murray 1998).

Although some of the circumstances of the killings remain in dispute, certain facts are well established. The three were members of the IRA on active service who were in Gibraltar to stage an attack against British military personnel. Their plan had been to use the Renault automobile to hold a parking space near the parade grounds where a British army band and the Royal Anglian Regiment would be assembled the following Tuesday for the weekly changing of the guard ceremony at the Governor's residence. That car did not contain explosives, but across the border in Spain was another car containing 64kg of Semtex explosive, later identified as belonging to the three by keys found in Farrell's handbag. The plan had been to switch cars prior to the following Tuesday, and to detonate the bomb during the changing of the guard ceremony. Finally, McCann, Farrell and Savage were all unarmed at the time they were killed and presumably could have been arrested unharmed.

According to the official British version of the events, the Renault driven into Gibraltar was believed to have been packed with explosives to be detonated by remote control as the army band assembled on the parade grounds. Testimony from the soldiers responsible for the shootings indicated that when confronted each of the three IRA volunteers had made an 'aggressive move' toward bags they were carrying (in the case of Farrell and McCann) or toward a pocket (in the case of Savage), and therefore had to be killed before any of them could detonate the car bomb. The fact that the army band would not be assembled on the parade ground for two more days, and that no triggering devices were found in their possession, casts doubt on this claim. Nonetheless, a formal British inquest into the killings found them to have been 'lawful'. Whether the killings were also morally justified is a distinct question, to which we can now turn.

THE MORALITY OF COUNTER-TERRORISM

Internment without trial, torture interrogations and shoot-to-kill executions certainly do not constitute the bulk of British counter-terrorism efforts in Northern Ireland, and the discussion of them here should not be interpreted as suggesting that they are representative of those efforts. Throughout the 1980s and into the 1990s, the security forces became increasingly successful in containing the level of violence in Northern Ireland, mainly through improved technology, surveillance techniques, intelligence-gathering and agent-handling. As the Provisional IRA became more sophisticated, especially in devising remote-controlled bombs, the British army became more adept at jamming their detonation signals. The IRA killed more British soldiers in 1972 than it did in all of the 1980s. Despite the reorganisation of the IRA in the late 1970s into three- or four-man 'cells', British counter-terrorism units were increasingly successful in penetrating the IRA. In 1992 the IRA killed twice as many of its own members as 'touts' (informers) than it killed British soldiers. Increasingly, the IRA found itself in a bind. Attacks on 'hard targets' (military and security personnel) resulted in the loss of IRA volunteers; attacks on 'soft targets' (pubs frequented by soldiers) resulted in civilian casualties and loss of support for the movement. All of these factors contributed to the success of the security forces in containing IRA violence, but did not generate sustained moral criticism of British counter-terrorism strategies. Internment without trial, torture interrogations and shoot-to-kill executions, on the other hand, have been roundly condemned by the nationalist community in Northern Ireland as being grossly unjust and therefore obviously morally wrong. Whether, or under what conditions, this moral judgement is correct is another matter. In this section I want to address directly the morality of these three methods of counter-terrorism, again, without implying that these three practices constitute either the bulk or the most significant elements of British counter-terrorism in Northern Ireland. But because of their perceived significance in the context of the Troubles, the grievances they have spawned within the nationalist community, and the role they have been made to play in legitimising IRA violence, they are worth considering even if they are exceptions.

184

Internment without Trial

From a just war perspective, it could be argued that detention without trial was consistent with the way in which enemy soldiers are treated during wartime. By belonging to a terrorist organisation, the terrorist becomes like the enemy soldier. As Gerstein notes,

> Because of the danger he presents, he is subject to being captured and held prisoner without regard to his responsibility for particular acts of violence. His commitment to the terrorist group justifies this reversal of the usual presumption and warrants his imprisonment because he will do harm if left free. (Gerstein 1989, p. 299)

This presupposes that those interned have been reliably identified as members of a terrorist organisation. Unlike the capture of uniformed enemy soldiers on the battlefield, a broad sweep of communities believed to be sympathetic to the activities of a terrorist organisation is likely to net far more individuals who are not terrorists and who pose no threat to the common good – precisely what happened in August 1971.

The British government's main argument in support of internment without trial was based on a comparative consideration of likely benefits and costs, and thus was broadly consequentialist (Hennessey 2007). IRA terrorism had created an emergency situation in Northern Ireland. Given the difficulty, or rather impossibility, of separating those who had committed terrorist offences from those who had not, as well as the close association of the IRA with, and widespread support for it in, the Catholic community, the most effective method of containing the terrorist threat would be to sweep up as many potential IRA men as possible in fairly indiscriminate internment operations, and then to sort out the actual terrorists from those not involved in terrorism once those detained had been interrogated. If some of those interned were not IRA men but could supply information about the IRA and its activities, so much the better. Because internment was intended to contain the threat of terrorism, not to punish known terrorists, formal trials were irrelevant and hence unnecessary. That internment without trial did not have the uniformly beneficial consequences the British authorities might have hoped has already been noted. Not only did the initial internment sweep on 9 August 1971 fail to net many IRA men, but the brutality and perceived sectarian nature of the operation so angered and alienated the nationalist community that the IRA's ranks swelled as never before, with far-reaching consequences for subsequent violence in Northern Ireland.

185

Finally, it might seem obvious that internment without trial would be morally unjustified from a perspective that takes rights seriously. Being forcibly removed from one's home, taken to an interrogation centre and detained indefinitely without the benefit of legal counsel appears to be a blatant violation of one's basic rights. Could detention without trial ever be morally justified from a perspective that takes rights seriously? It could, if the suspension of the rights of some was necessary in order to respect the more fundamental rights of others. 'Internment', then Home Secretary Reginald Maudling said, when it was re-introduced in August 1971, 'is a very ugly thing, but political murder is even uglier' (Taylor 1980, p. 20). Arguably, the right to move around freely is an important right but is less important than the right to not be killed or maimed as a result of acts of terrorism. It could be argued that the individuals who were detained did not lose or forfeit their rights; their rights were temporarily overridden by the need to respect other more vital rights. Of course, the brutal manner in which the internment operations were conducted, the length of time they were held in custody without legal counsel, and the alleged treatment of many of those detained (including torture), raise even more serious moral questions that would make such detention difficult to justify from a perspective that takes rights seriously.

Torture Interrogation

Torture can be and has been used for a range of purposes, including deterrence, retribution, intimidation and information-gathering. Torture is expressly prohibited in a range of human rights conventions, including the 1948 Universal Declaration of Human Rights and the 1949 Geneva Conventions (Bellamy 2006). Most nations are signatories to these conventions and have their own laws making torture illegal. The broadly accepted legal prohibitions against torture reflect the widespread (though not universal) moral conviction that torture is morally impermissible. Nonetheless, that torture is generally illegal is only indirectly relevant to the moral issue, because what is illegal may nonetheless be morally justified. At issue here are two questions concerning the morality of torture exclusively as used to extract information from known or suspected terrorists. First, under what conditions, if any, is torture interrogation of suspected terrorists morally justified? Second, were these conditions satisfied in any of the (alleged) cases of torture interrogation discussed above?

186

Consider first the question of the morality of torture interrogation in relation to Just War Theory. Strictly speaking, this question will only arise within the context of a war already in progress with regard to the torture interrogation of an enemy combatant who is known or suspected to possess information that could lead to the thwarting of a terrorist attack – a conceivable albeit highly unlikely situation. Still, we can ask whether Just War Theory would prohibit the use of torture interrogation given these stipulations.

On the one hand, it appears that the use of torture is no worse than killing an enemy combatant in war, and that insofar as torture does not involve the complete destruction of the enemy combatant, it could be considered as less harmful. Thus it could be argued that torture is morally permissible, provided that it can satisfy the conditions of morally justified killing in Just War Theory. According to Henry Shue, it cannot. The problem arises with regard to the *jus in bello* requirement that, insofar as possible, violence not be directed at non-combatants, understood as those who are unable to defend themselves. The problem is that, unlike enemies in warfare, the victim of torture is unable to defend himself:

> In combat the other person one kills is still a threat when killed and is killed in part for the sake of one's own survival. The torturer inflicts pain and damage upon another person who, by virtue of now being within his or her power, is no longer a threat and is entirely at the torturer's mercy. (Shue 1978, p. 130)

Therefore, the torturer is attacking a non-combatant, and in so doing, Shue argues, violates the *jus in bello* 'discrimination' condition of Just War Theory.

Against this it could be argued, first, that in many combat situations, such as high-altitude bombing, the persons being killed are not a threat at all and are entirely at the mercy of the aerial bomber. Second, it could be argued that the captive *does* have a defence against torture – he can divulge to his captor the information being sought. For this to be effective it must be the case that the act of compliance is sufficient to produce the permanent cessation of the torture, and that this fact be known to the captive. Accordingly, any set of conditions for the morally justified use of torture interrogation, in order to avoid the problem Shue identifies, would need to include this requirement. I will return to this idea shortly.

From a consequentialist perspective, an act of torture would be morally permissible in a given situation if engaging in that act would produce effects at least as good as would any other alternative act available to the agent in that situation. If an act of torture in a given situation would produce *better* effects than any other act available to the agent in that situation, then committing an act of torture is morally obligatory in that situation. To take the stock example, if torturing a suspected terrorist would cause that person to divulge information permitting the deactivation of a bomb about to explode in a heavily populated area, and there was no other less drastic means for obtaining this information, then from a consequentialist perspective torturing the suspect would be morally obligatory. Whether an act of torture in any given situation *would* lead to the best overall consequences is a related but distinct issue that would need to be determined (fallibly, and with difficulty) on a case-by-case basis. A strong case could be built to show that in the vast majority of cases the use of torture would be likely to produce far more negative than positive effects (Sussman 2005). But at most this would show that torture is not *usually* morally justified from a consequentialist perspective. The fact would remain that a consequentialist perspective would not necessarily rule out the use of torture, and that there are conceivable situations in which such a perspective would actually require its use.

With regard to a non-consequentialist rights-based perspective, however, matters appear, at least at first, to be entirely different. If people have fundamental rights, it is never morally permissible to violate someone's fundamental rights, and torture necessarily violates one or more of a person's fundamental rights, then torture is necessarily morally impermissible. This argument presupposes that if persons have rights, those rights can never be forfeited. If rights can be forfeited (if, for example, being involved in terrorist activities forfeits one's right to not be killed, tortured and so on), then torture interrogation of terrorists would not involve a rights violation, and hence the conclusion that torture is always morally impermissible would not follow. How one can be sure that one is torturing a *terrorist* rather than a mere terrorist *suspect* is obviously critical. But as David Sussman points out,

> By itself, the mere possibility of torturing the ignorant is no more of an objection to the permissibility of torture than the mere possibility of killing a noncombatant is to just warfare or the bare chance of punishing the innocent is to legal sanctions. (Sussman 2005, p. 18)

Moral theory can provide us with insights into what sort of actions are right and wrong, but it cannot supply the empirical information so often needed in order to determine, in a particular situation, which action *is* right.

This argument also presupposes that it is never morally permissible, from a rights-based perspective, to violate someone's rights – an assumption that was challenged in Chapter 6. In cases of rights violation minimisation, rights have to be violated (or one must permit rights violations) in order to prevent even graver rights violations. The application to torture interrogation is straightforward. If torturing a terrorist is the only way to extract information from him necessary for preventing the violation of the rights of others, then even if the torture constitutes a violation of the terrorist's rights it may still, in certain circumstances, be morally justified. Hence, a non-consequentialist rights-based approach need not absolutely prohibit the use of torture. But this general conclusion leaves completely unspecified the exact conditions that would need to be satisfied in order for this abstract possibility to become a just policy.

One way to begin to identify such conditions is to reflect on the relationship between rights and consequences. Rights place limits or constraints on actions undertaken in the pursuit of beneficial consequences. Thus in any situation one ought to perform whatever action from among those available in that situation would result in the best overall consequences, so long as doing one does not violate any rights, or if one does violate rights, one does so in order to minimise rights violations overall. The question of the morality of torture interrogation then concerns the limits or constraints that ought to be placed on the use of torture interrogation in situations in which the use of this method is likely to produce the best overall results.

Fritz Allhoff (2005) identifies four conditions that he believes must be satisfied in order for torture interrogation to be morally justified: 'the use of torture aims at acquisition of information; the captive is reasonably thought to have the relevant information; the information corresponds to a significant and imminent threat; and the information could likely lead to the prevention of the threat' (Allhoff 2005, p. 255). Specifying the general conditions under which the use of torture interrogation in counter-terrorism would be morally justified is one thing. Implementing such a practice in a way that consistently satisfies these conditions is quite another. Given the history of the use of torture, it might seem foolhardy to even open the door to the consideration of conditions for the morally justified use of torture. As Shue emphasises, there are significant risks involved in any officially approved policy of torture interrogation, no matter how well intentioned. 'There is', as he says, 'considerable evidence of all torture's metastatic tendency' (Shue 1978, p. 143). What begins as limited and subject to constraints may well become unlimited and uncon-strained. The ramifying costs of the institutionalisation of torture interro-gation satisfying these (or other similar) conditions must also be taken into account (Casebeer 2005). Such concerns should not be minimised, and whether a policy of torture interrogation embodying the conditions out-lined above *should* be put in place, given our knowledge of human nature, is itself a moral question whose answer would depend on carefully formed judgements about how likely they *would*, not just possibly could, be honoured.

Finally, none of the cases of the torture interrogation of terrorist suspects discussed in this chapter comes close to satisfying all of Allhoff's condi-tions. All involved the use of torture to force confessions of, and to impli-cate others in, terrorist activity. None involved the use of torture to acquire information necessary for thwarting an imminent terrorist attack. Accordingly, none can be considered morally justified according to these conditions.

Shoot-to-Kill Executions

The shoot-to-kill practice of covert RUC and SAS squads was widely per-ceived within the Catholic working class community as cold-blooded murder – and sectarian murder at that, because the practice seemed to be directed exclusively at republican paramilitaries rather than also at the loyalist paramilitaries who were killing ordinary Catholics (Newsinger 2002). However, this moral outrage depended on overlooking the fact that it was republican paramilitaries who had declared a 'war' on the British army. In war, soldiers are permitted to kill enemy soldiers at any time whether or not those enemy soldiers pose an immediate threat. If the self-description of IRA volunteers as members of an *army* is accepted, then pre-emptively killing them would be no different in principle than pre-emptively killing other enemy combatants who do not pose an imme-diate threat to one's own safety (for example, by dropping bombs on them from high altitude). Significantly, this seems to have been precisely the view taken by the IRA with respect to *its own* operational standards during much of the Northern Ireland conflict. Any IRA volunteer who encoun-tered a British soldier, a policeman or other member of the security forces (for example, a member of the UDR), whether armed or unarmed, in uniform or in civilian clothes, on duty or off duty, combat-ready or stand-ing down, and could fire on him with a reasonable chance of escape, was encouraged to do so (Stevenson 1996). The bulk of IRA attacks on security personnel took the form of hit-and-run sniping attacks, rather than more conventional military engagements – in other words, as essentially shoot-to-kill operations. Against the claim that shoot-to-kill executions against republican paramilitaries was cold-blooded murder, it could be pointed out that it was the IRA (supported in part by the Catholic community) that set the ruthless terms of engagement in the conflict that led to a shoot-to-kill practice on the part of the security forces in the first place. As Stevenson (1996, p. 57) sardonically observes, 'For the terrorists themselves [or their supporters] to castigate the other side for adopting those terms recalls the casuistry of the man who murders his parents and then pleads for judicial clemency on the grounds that he's an orphan.'

Two arguments could be offered against this line of reasoning. First, the applicability of just war criteria to shoot-to-kill executions presupposes that the two sides are involved in a bona fide war, which seems to contradict the British policy, dating from March 1976, to treat the conflict in Northern Ireland as an internal security problem to be dealt with by law enforcement agencies, rather than as an insurgency to be dealt with by military force (Neumann 2003). But if so, then SAS units have no more moral justification for killing unarmed terrorists, in terms of Just War Theory, than do law enforcement personnel. Second, it is not quite true that soldiers in war have carte blanche to kill enemy soldiers wherever and whenever they encounter them. They are not authorised to kill enemy soldiers who have surrendered or been taken prisoner. In the Loughgall Martyrs case the enemy combatants were not given an opportunity to surrender. In the Gibraltar case those killed were in the process of surrendering when they were killed. Viewed from a just war perspective, therefore, these killings would be violations of the rules of war, hence morally unjustified.

From a consequentialist perspective, a shoot-to-kill execution is morally justified if it produces consequences better than or equal in overall benefits to the consequences resulting from any alternative act available to the agent(s) in that situation. Obviously it will matter whether the execution was the only way to prevent a terrorist from carrying out a significantly destructive act, or whether it kills a terrorist who could have been captured without significant risk of loss of life. Admittedly, such calculations will typically be difficult to make with any degree of precision. But at a very coarse level of granularity, it is reasonable to assume that the chances of a shoot-to-kill execution being morally justified in consequentialist terms are dramatically greater in the former than in the latter case. In the case of the Loughgall Martyrs, although they were killed in the very act of carrying out a terrorist attack, the SAS unit was lying in ambush, and presumably could have attempted to intercept the IRA bombers prior to their arrival at the Loughgall RUC station as they drove along a country road with a 91kg bomb in the bucket of a backhoe digger. In the Gibraltar killings it would have been relatively easy to arrest the three IRA volunteers without bloodshed, and had the British authorities done so, it would have been hailed as a successful counter-terrorism operation that few, including nationalists, could have criticised. In fact, their being killed as they attempted to surrender instead set in motion a tragic train of events that resulted in many more deaths, including (arguably) the death the following year of the Catholic solicitor Pat Finucane.[2]

Finally, from a rights perspective it could be argued that shoot-to-kill executions are morally wrong because they violate the rights of those killed. For example, Khatchadourian maintains that such killings can never be morally justified because they necessarily violate a person's right to life. Moreover, the right to life is inalienable: it cannot be forfeited or even voluntarily given up by a person (Khatchadourian 2005, pp. 178–9). No argument is given for this position. Against this is the view that through one's actions one may forfeit one's rights, including the right to life. According to James Rachels,

> if a person is himself responsible for bringing upon others a great evil or injustice, then we may regard ourselves as released from any obligation that we might have had toward him in virtue of his 'rights' when it is necessary to treat him badly in order to eliminate that evil or injustice. (Rachels 1984, p. 329)

Resolving this disagreement would require understanding when, if ever, fundamental rights may be forfeited – a topic beyond the scope of this chapter. What is clear, however, is that simply invoking 'rights' is not sufficient, *by itself*, to settle the moral question of shoot-to-kill executions. It is significant that in 1995 the European Court of Human Rights in Strasbourg, France, found the British government to be guilty of breaching Article 2 of the European Convention on Human Rights in connection with the Gibraltar killings in virtue of using an excessive degree of force. But it *also* ruled that because the three IRA volunteers had been involved in planning an act of terrorism, no compensation for their deaths was owed to those who had sought the inquest. As a Solomonic judgement weighing both sides of the case, this verdict could hardly be improved upon.

CONCLUSIONS

My concern in this chapter has been with the morality of a subset of British counter-terrorism efforts in Northern Ireland that have condemned by many within the nationalist community as obviously immoral. Internment without trial, Diplock courts, criminalisation and supergrass trials were each attempts to deal with an unprecedented terrorist threat. In reactions that have contemporary resonance, counter-terrorism legislation created a de facto alternative legal system for dealing with terrorist offences that arose out of, and was sustained by, a heightened sense that an ongoing emergency required extraordinary measures to combat it. In its zeal to put away terrorists, internal security often took precedence over respect for human rights, as evidenced in the indiscriminate nature of the initial internment sweep, the setting aside of normal standards of evidence in Diplock Court trials, the reliance on untrustworthy witnesses in supergrass trials, and in numerous cases of miscarriages of justice, only the best-known of which were discussed in this chapter. Criminalisation, introduced in 1976, marked a shift in emphasis from treating the Northern Ireland conflict as an insurgency requiring a military solution, to an internal security problem requiring a more aggressive law enforcement response. Yet this hardly meant that British counter-terrorism efforts consisted solely of policies and practices authorised by counter-terrorism legislation. Allegations of torture interrogations and shoot-to-kill executions led to further criticism by the nationalist community of the brutal methods apparently condoned by the British authorities. However, from a moral perspective matters were far from simple. The same is true of charges that the British government practised and condoned 'state terrorism' in its war against the IRA.

CHAPTER 8

When the Law Makers are the Law Breakers:
State Terrorism

> The major part of violence is created and maintained by Britain. All other vio-
> lence is a counter to the state violence of the security forces. The real terrorists
> are the UDR and the Police.
>
> (Republican Owen Carron, Westminster MP, *Irish News*, 22 August 1981;
> in Wright 1990, p. 32)

INTRODUCTION

The previous chapter examined British counter-terrorism policies and
practices in Northern Ireland without considering the accusation, often
levelled against the British government by the nationalist community,
that some of these policies and practices individually, or all of them collectively, constitute terrorism – that is, *state terrorism*. It is just as frequently
assumed that if terrorism is morally wrong, then terrorism practised by the
state is necessarily even worse. To evaluate this accusation of state terrorism and the moral judgement commonly attached to it, reasonable answers
must be given to three fundamental questions: (1) What is 'state terrorism'? (2) To what extent has the British government engaged in state terrorism in Northern Ireland? (3) Is state terrorism necessarily morally worse
than terrorism practised by non-state agents? Answering each of these
questions will require examining a number of subsidiary issues as well,
including the vexed question of whether, or to what extent, loyalist terrorism should be regarded as state-terrorism-by-proxy. I will argue that
state terrorism has occurred in Northern Ireland, but there is little evidence to suggest state terrorism has been pursued as a policy. Although
state terrorism frequently is morally worse than terrorism undertaken by

194

non-state actors, this is not a necessary characteristic of state terrorism per se. Finally, although there are conceivable situations in which acts of state terrorism can be morally justified, there are vastly more opportunities for it to be morally wrong.

WHAT IS STATE TERRORISM?

'State terrorism' is terrorism carried out by the state's agents acting *as* agents of the state. It follows from this definition that an act of terrorism carried out by a government employee for purely personal reasons would not be an act of *state* terrorism. Likewise, a private individual who carries out an act of terrorism because he believes doing so will benefit the state, but whose action is in no way sanctioned by state authorities, would not have committed an act of state terrorism. State terrorism could be further distinguished into 'internal' and 'external' state terrorism. The former would be terrorism directed against members of the same state; the latter would be terrorism directed against other states or their members. Despite the fact that nationalists reject the legitimacy of UK jurisdiction in the Six Counties, they nonetheless remain citizens of the British state. The discussion that follows will therefore be concerned exclusively with *internal* state terrorism in Northern Ireland, and not with the quite different issue of the moral status of 'terrorist states', understood as states that routinely engage in terrorism against other states or their members, perhaps as an element of foreign policy.

Is State Terrorism Possible?

Given the negative connotations associated with the word, it is in the interests of governmental agencies to define terrorism such that a state's employment of violence or intimidation can never qualify as terrorism. For example, the US State Department defines terrorism as necessarily involving '*sub-national* groups or clandestine agents' (emphasis added). Other governmental definitions (for example, those of the FBI and of the US Vice-President's Task Force on Terrorism) make state terrorism virtually impossible by defining terrorism as involving the *unlawful* use of force or violence. Insofar as actions undertaken by governments can always (somehow) be interpreted as lawful, they necessarily fail to be acts of terrorism, regardless of whether such acts resemble acts of terrorism in all other respects. Such definitions are not restricted to governmental agencies. Louise Richardson writes that 'terrorism simply means deliberately and violently targeting civilians for political purposes', and then goes on to assert that 'by definition, terrorism is the behaviour of substate groups' (Richardson 2006, pp. 5, 50), thus rendering 'state terrorism' conceptually incoherent.[1] Rüdiger Bittner is exceptionally explicit on this point: 'States do not use terrorist means – mind you, not thanks to their virtue, but thanks to [the] concept: state terrorism is, on my understanding of the words, a square circle' (Bittner 2005, p. 207).

Bittner's claim is nothing if not clear. Unfortunately, there seems to be no way to establish the *truth* of this claim except by definitional fiat. But even stipulative definitions must be responsive to the ways in which words are normally used and understood. In the Prologue I proposed a specific definition of 'terrorism' that does not limit terrorism to non-state or subnational agents acting unlawfully. Because that definition focuses on methods and general aims rather than on the identity of the agents involved, I see no reason to reject the *possibility* of states engaging in terrorism. State terrorism, as I will discuss it, is the strategically indiscriminate harming or threat of harming others within a target group, carried out by the state's agents acting *as* agents of the state, in order to advance some political, ideological, social, economic or religious agenda by influencing members of an audience group in ways believed to be conducive to the advancement of that agenda. With this definition in mind, we can now proceed to consider state terrorism in Northern Ireland.

State Terrorism as Policy in Northern Ireland

Defining state terrorism is one thing. Identifying instances of state terrorism so defined is another. In the preface to his investigation of British counter-terrorism activities in Northern Ireland, the journalist Martin Dillon writes, 'In a few instances I uncovered evidence which pointed to the involvement of members of the security forces in terrorism but the overwhelming evidence indicated that such involvement was personal and not part of a stated policy' (Dillon 1990, p. xx). Given the negative connotations generally associated with terrorism, it would be quite surprising if the use of terrorism by the security forces was part of a *stated* policy. To explicitly state such a policy would be to invite moral censure. The issue is rather whether the British government has in fact employed a policy of terrorism against those it considers its enemies in Northern Ireland, and if so, how extensively and in what way(s).

It could be argued that the counter-terrorism practices discussed in the previous chapter de facto amount to a policy of state terrorism. Internment, torture interrogation and shoot-to-kill executions carried out by the state could each be viewed as serving a dual purpose. The primary purpose would be to remove suspected terrorists from circulation, to extract valuable information from suspected terrorists and to destroy terrorist cells, respectively. A secondary purpose would be to use these practices to threaten similar harm to others in order to influence them in ways believed to be conducive to the advancement of the government's agenda. To the extent that these practices were strategically indiscriminate with respect to the individuals targeted, and undertaken with this secondary purpose in mind, they would constitute state terrorism. If instances of such practices were as widespread as much of the literature and the anecdotal evidence suggests, then the extent of state terrorism in Northern Ireland would be immense. As important as all of these policies and practices are, however, if the allegations of many nationalists are correct, then in importance they pale in comparison with the *primary* locus of state terrorism in Northern Ireland.

Is Loyalist Terrorism State-Terrorism-by-Proxy?

A common view in the nationalist community, encouraged by the republican movement, is that loyalist paramilitaries in collusion with the state's security forces constitute the most pernicious instrument of state terrorism (http://www.sinnfein.ie/peace/collusion). This is a view shared by some scholars. John Newsinger maintains that

> in the 1980s British covert agencies began to make increasing use of the loyalist paramilitaries, providing them with intelligence and giving their activities direction. The . . . collusion between the Forward [sic; actually, Force] Research Unit (FRU) and UFF . . . points quite clearly to the loyalist death squads acting as proxies for the British. (Newsinger 2002, p. 192)

Jeffrey Sluka (2000, p. 127) goes further by describing loyalist paramilitary attacks against Catholics as an 'important aspect of the culture of British state terror in Northern Ireland'. According to Sluka, the random killings of Catholics by loyalist paramilitaries has in fact been 'an integral part' of the British authority's counterinsurgency strategy since 1972 (Sluka 2000,

p. 128). Officially, of course, the British authorities vehemently deny that they sponsor loyalist death squads. When evidence of collusion between the security forces and loyalist paramilitaries surfaces, the authorities distance themselves from such incidents by describing them as 'individual acts by rogue soldiers and policemen – and not a reflection of government policy or military strategy'. Sluka summarily dismisses such patently absurd claims as 'political lies' (Sluka 2000, p. 128).

A serious weakness of Sluka's analysis, in addition to the fact that the sources he relies upon for his data are Sinn Féin, *An Phoblacht/Republican News* and the *Irish News* (a nationalist newspaper in Northern Ireland), is that he takes for granted that loyalist paramilitaries are 'pro-government death squads' whose interests are identical to those of the British government (Sluka 2000, p. 141). Despite being widely accepted as an incontrovertible truth in much of the nationalist community, this assumption is certainly false, not least because many of these loyalist paramilitaries ended up in the state's prisons for carrying out acts that they, but not the state, perceived to be in the state's interest. In addition, some denials of widespread collusion with loyalist paramilitaries by well-placed members of the security forces have the ring of truth. Consider the following statement by a former RUC Special Branch officer:

> We never dreamed of aiding their twisted cause. There may have been some bad apples within the intelligence services who leaked files to the UDA and the UVF but the overwhelming majority of intelligence officers had nothing but contempt for the Loyalist terrorists. Not only were their actions morally reprehensible but they also put an extra burden on an already-overstretched police force. Imagine if we had been able to divert all of our resources to combating republican terrorism in the event of the inactivity of Loyalists. Surely more lives would have been spared as a result. (Barker 2004, p. 222)

This suggests that a more nuanced account of the relationship between loyalist paramilitaries and the British state is required.

Pro-State Terrorism and Conservative Terrorism

That loyalist paramilitaries and the British government shared a common goal of containing or eliminating militant republicanism is undeniable. Ironically, however, this common goal is in large measure why loyalist paramilitaries should not (*pace* Sluka) be uncritically classified as 'pro-government death squads'. Loyalist paramilitary groups were constituted by working-class Protestants who concluded that the state's security forces were not adequately responding to the republican threat, and thus that more direct action was required – including using the terrorists' own methods against them. In other words, the very raison d'être of loyalist paramilitary groups was to fill a perceived *lacunae* that the state's security forces appeared to them unable or unwilling to fill. Although the agendas of the state and of loyalist paramilitary groups could be expected to generally coincide, the fact that one group saw itself as remedying a deficiency in the other also meant that conflicts could and would arise.

This possibility was demonstrated in 1974 when loyalists judged the state to be promoting initiatives that threatened to compromise the integrity of Northern Ireland as a part of the United Kingdom. Acknowledging that a military solution to the problems in Northern Ireland was ineffectual, in 1973 the British government undertook a series of political initiatives intended to de-escalate the violence. The Sunningdale Agreement of November 1973 proposed a power-sharing initiative that included a North-South Council of Ireland responsible for economic and social matters, a commitment by the Irish government to recognise the right of the majority in Northern Ireland to remain part of the UK for as long as it wished, and a promise on the part of the Irish government to intensify its offensive against the Provisionals. In return, Britain would agree to review internment and would take steps to make the RUC more acceptable to Catholics.

Many Protestants saw these initiatives as 'the supreme sell-out, the supreme betrayal' that would constitute a first step down a slippery slope to a united Ireland (Taylor 1999, p. 127). As they saw it, the 'stupid, blind, blundering Unionist politicians' were 'letting our heritage and everything our forefathers ever fought for slowly slip away'. The choice was clear: they could do nothing and relinquish Ulster to the republicans, or they could 'take to the streets' and defend Ulster (Wood 2006, p. 30). They chose the latter. At 6:08 p.m. on 14 May 1974 the Ulster Workers' Council (UWC) announced that it was calling a general strike to begin the following day. Major industries, including essential utilities, would be suspended. The strike succeeded thanks to UVF and Ulster Defence Association (UDA) blockage of main roads and the intimidation of business owners. Workers were turned away from factories at gunpoint. The port of Larne was completely shut down. Shipyard workers were told in no uncertain terms that unless they let their tools lay idle they would find their cars to be smouldering shells when they returned to the car park. In other words, loyalist paramilitaries used terrorism to enforce the strike. After the first two days of 'discouraging' some of those who were tempted to go to work, further intimidation was hardly necessary. Others had gotten the message loud and clear. The strike also attracted widespread support among Protestants who decided that living without electricity for a few days was preferable to living with the prospect of a united Ireland. The strike lasted two weeks, crippling the economy of the province and forcing the collapse of the Sunningdale Agreement, precisely as the strike's organisers had intended. The success of the 1974 UWC strike proved, as the journalist Peter Taylor aptly put it, that 'what the British Government thought was best for Northern Ireland was seldom viewed in that light by most of its citizens' (Taylor 1999, p. 127) – that is, by working-class Protestants, ably represented in the strike by loyalist paramilitary organisations.

Reflection on the extent to which the state's security forces have opposed loyalist paramilitaries should also temper any temptation to identify the two as one force in different clothing. When the British army first arrived in 1969, it showed considerable sympathy for the Catholic minority and equal ambivalence toward Protestants. After the IRA's campaign swung into high gear in 1971, its stance was one of wariness of both sides in the conflict – a prudent attitude because by that time both sides were taking shots at them. For its part, the RUC was quite willing to use the emergency powers granted to it to take loyalist paramilitaries off the streets, and when convicted, loyalists were sentenced as severely as republicans. Finally, although the UDR has a worse record of convictions of its members for terrorist offences than does the regular British army or the RUC, from 1970 to 1989 around 30,000 men and women served in the UDR, and only 23 (0.076%) have been convicted of murder or manslaughter, compared to the very large number of UDA and UVF men convicted for terrorist offences during that same period. In sum, 'despite sharing a common enemy, recruiting from the same population, and living in the same areas, the security forces and the paramilitaries have not enjoyed a cosy relationship' (Bruce 1992, p. 225).

The relationship between the state and loyalist terrorism is therefore more complex than some have supposed. A more fine-grained classification of types of terrorism is necessary. Steve Bruce (1992, p. 269) usefully distinguishes between 'state terrorism' and 'pro-state terrorism'. State terrorism involves agents of the state engaging in terrorism to protect the state from its enemies, whereas pro-state terrorism involves non-state agents engaging in terrorism to protect the state from its enemies. To the extent that loyalist paramilitary groups, in common cause with the British authorities, sought to contain or eliminate militant republicanism, they can be considered to be agents of pro-state terrorism. During the UWC strike, however, loyalists used terrorism to *oppose* the state's political initiatives. 'Pro-state terrorism' does not quite capture their actions in this case.

Drake (1996) makes a persuasive case that loyalist paramilitaries are better described as engaging in 'conservative terrorism' rather than in 'pro-state terrorism' because the *primary* motivation for their acts of terrorism (whether against Catholics or in opposition to the British authorities) was to preserve the existing social order rather than to support the state per se, about whose commitment to maintaining the union they were often suspicious. It is perhaps a not insignificant irony that the first RUC officer to die from Troubles-related violence was shot dead by loyalists rioting in Belfast on 16 October 1969 in response to an announced plan to disband the mainly Protestant B Special part-time police force. This incident was in a way emblematic of loyalist terrorism. On those occasions where loyalist and state agendas were judged as not coinciding, loyalist paramilitaries were willing to *oppose* the state through acts of violence, including acts of terrorism. 'Conservative terrorism' nicely captures this important aspect of loyalist terrorism. The safest general statement might be that loyalist terrorism is always conservative terrorism, but where the aims of loyalist paramilitaries and those of the authorities were judged by loyalists to coincide, they engaged in pro-state terrorism as well.

State-Sponsored Terrorism

In this account, not being agents of the state, loyalist paramilitaries qua loyalist paramilitaries cannot engage in state terrorism per se, although they can and frequently have engaged in pro-state terrorism. Even when loyalist paramilitaries engage in pro-state terrorism, however, it does not follow that such terrorism is necessarily *state-sponsored terrorism*. The latter implies a degree of deliberate active assistance from the state that need not be present in the former. More precisely, in order for an act of terrorism carried out by loyalist paramilitaries to be judged as an instance of state-sponsored terrorism, loyalist paramilitaries must have been intentionally aided in carrying out that act, or aided in carrying out kinds of acts of which the act in question is an example, by agents of the state acting on behalf of the state. To the extent that the British government, including members of its security forces, provided resources to loyalist paramilitaries in order to enable the latter to carry out acts of terrorism, to that extent acts of loyalist terrorism can be considered to be acts of state-sponsored terrorism. State-sponsored terrorism in this sense is simply state-terrorism-by-proxy, whereby the state uses loyalist paramilitaries (rather than the police or military) to carry out acts of terrorism. The distinction between pro-state and state-sponsored terrorism is essential for understanding the extent to which certain alleged cases of state or state-sponsored terrorism really are so. Consideration of a range of different cases in order of increasing state participation in terrorism will help to clarify this important point.

First, there are acts by loyalist paramilitaries that are arguably acts of terrorism that do not appear to have any state involvement whatsoever. On a number of occasions loyalist paramilitaries have targeted prominent republicans. On 28 October 1976, loyalist gunmen dressed as doctors shot dead Máire Drumm, the Vice President of Sinn Féin, as she lay in a hospital bed in Belfast's Mater Hospital recovering from eye surgery. On 26 June 1980, Dr Miriam Daly, a lecturer in Social and Economic History at Queen's University, Belfast, and a founder of the Irish Republican Socialist Party (IRSP), was murdered in her home in Andersonstown, Belfast. Her body was found with her hands and feet bound. She had been killed by six 9mm shots to the head from a semi-automatic pistol. Although her killers were never identified, the nationalist community blamed the UDA. On 16 October 1992, Sheena Campbell, a Queen's University student and Sinn Féin activist, was assassinated by the UVF in the bar of the York Hotel in Belfast. Those who allege collusion between the killers and the security forces note that in the weeks prior to her murder Campbell had several times been stopped at checkpoints manned by the RUC and the British army as she drove from her home in Lurgan to Belfast, and claim that the UVF used information acquired from security force members to target her. This remains speculation. In none of these cases is there any clear evidence that loyalist paramilitaries were actively assisted by the state's security forces, although that possibility is not definitively ruled out. The fact that such individuals were prominent in the republican movement means that they would have been relatively easy to identify, track and kill without special assistance. The many random killings of ordinary Catholics in revenge for IRA attacks on individual Protestants, and/or in order to deter further IRA attacks, would be acts of this first sort.

Second, the state undoubtedly has on occasion unintentionally provided assistance to loyalist paramilitaries through sheer carelessness, as well as by the very existence of military forces equipped with weapons whose possession would be a dream-come-true for many terrorist groups. RUC and UDR officers frequented loyalist pubs where information about local Catholics might flow as freely as the pints, thereby inadvertently providing loyalist paramilitaries with information enabling them to plan attacks. The very existence of heavily armed security forces also meant that the weaponry sought after by paramilitary groups would often be close at hand. In March 1988, three UDA men were convicted of participating in an arms raid on a military camp in Coleraine, County Londonderry (Jackson 1999).

Third, because the state's locally recruited security forces and loyalist paramilitary groups drew their members from the same community, their memberships often overlapped. Consequently, resources in the form of information, weapons and uniforms available to the former could easily become available to the latter, which could then be used to carry out acts of terrorism. An infamous loyalist attack illustrates this sort of case. In the early morning hours of 31 July 1975, eight heavily armed men in uniform flagged down a Volkswagen van carrying five members of the popular musical group the Miami Showband just outside of Loughbrickland in County Down. The band had just played a successful gig at the Castle Ballroom in the mainly Protestant town of Banbridge the night before, and was on its way to Dublin. Although the band was based in the Republic of Ireland, and all of its members were Catholic, it refused to be restricted to playing in Catholic venues. A man in a UDR uniform flagged down the van and directed the driver to park the vehicle on the side of the road. The band was then ordered to line up along a ditch with their backs to the van. A loud explosion knocked Des McAlea, the band's saxophonist, and his bandmates into the ditch. Then the shooting began. When police arrived they found the body of the band's heartthrob lead singer, Fran O'Toole, lying twenty feet from the roadside, his body riddled with bullets. He had been shot twenty-two times in the face. The bodies of Brian McCoy, the band's trumpet player, and Tony Geraghty, the guitar-player, were found nearby, also riddled with bullets. Another guitar-player, Stephen Travers, managed to survive by pretending to be dead – made easier by being covered with blood. Fifty feet from the burned-out wreck of the van police found a man's body blown in two. Another body in similar condition was found ninety feet from the vehicle, plus a human arm tattooed with the inscription 'UVF Portadown'. An investigation into the incident revealed that the operation had been planned weeks in advance by the UVF. The appearance of a military roadcheck had been created in order to get the musicians out of their van and facing away from it. While they were being questioned by some of the UVF men, others would be planting a bomb under the driver's seat, timed to explode after the vehicle had crossed the border into the Republic, perhaps to make it look as if the band was in fact transporting explosives (Dillon 1990). Five of the eight UVF gunmen involved in the murders were also soldiers on active duty in the UDR who had used their military uniforms to create the appearance of an official military roadcheck to flag down the musicians' van. This particular case is perhaps best described as a case of 'passive collusion' between the state and loyalist paramilitaries, although to the extent that the state in general did not actively seek to identify and discharge soldiers with membership in loyalist paramilitary groups, it could be considered in active collusion with such groups.

Fourth, there are cases in which the state has intentionally provided loyalists with tacit permission to stage attacks on Catholics, perhaps the most notorious instance being in August 1969 when RUC officers stood by as loyalist mobs burned to the ground entire Catholic neighbourhoods in West Belfast, and following clashes between police and Catholic rioters in the 'Battle of the Bogside' in Derry. In these cases the state permitted loyalist terrorism to proceed unopposed but (for the most part) did not actively assist it. A more controversial case involves the attack on Bernadette Devlin McAliskey, a prominent republican activist, on 16 February 1981. She and her husband were shot and seriously wounded by loyalist gunmen who broke into their home in Coalisland, County Tyrone. British soldiers watching the McAliskey home at the time did nothing to prevent the assassination attempt, although they did administer first aid immediately after the shooting and apprehended the three-man UFF team that had carried out the operation. Active collusion between the attackers and the military remains unproven. It seems clear that the soldiers could have prevented the attack had they chosen to intervene, yet they also could have simply left after the shooting rather than remaining to administer first aid and possibly saving the McAliskeys' lives.

Fifth, there are cases in which it is alleged that agents of the British government have been instrumental in actively assisting loyalist paramilitaries in carrying out acts of terrorism. On 17 May 1974, three days into the UWC strike, three car bombs exploded in Dublin, killing twenty-six people, and a fourth car bomb exploded in Monaghan town, killing another seven and injuring hundreds more. Although forensic evidence indicated that some of the UVF members involved in the Miami

Showband murders were also responsible for the Dublin and Monaghan bombings, among nationalists the suspicion remained that the attacks *must* have been carried out with the assistance of the British state. Loyalist paramilitaries rarely conducted operations in the Republic, and the sophistication of the attacks indicated coordination by British security forces (it being assumed that loyalists acting alone were responsible for ordinary or bungled operations, but necessarily received significant assistance from governmental agents for successful difficult operations). In March 2004, the Irish government released the findings of an exhaustive four-year inquiry into the bombings. It explicitly addressed the charge of collusion between loyalist paramilitaries and British security forces. Despite some circumstantial evidence that emerged, such collusion could not be established.

A clearer case of collusion between the state and loyalist paramilitaries concerns the murder of the Catholic solicitor Patrick ('Pat') Finucane. On Sunday, 12 February 1989, two masked gunmen broke into his home in North Belfast as he and his wife and three children were sharing a meal. He was shot fourteen times. The UDA/UFF claimed responsibility for the killing, asserting that Finucane was a high-ranking officer in the Provisional IRA, a claim denied by his family and, significantly, by the police. Human rights groups alleged that his murder by loyalist paramilitaries had been carried out in collusion with RUC Special Branch officers who were displeased with his success in frustrating their attempts to prosecute IRA terrorists. In September 1989, Sir John Stevens began the first of three official British government inquiries into the killing of Finucane and other Catholics killed by loyalist death squads. After a four-year investigation, the Stevens Report was released on 17 April 2003. It concluded that members of the Force Research Unit (FRU) of the British army and members of the RUC's Special Branch had actively helped a loyalist paramilitary group to murder Catholics in the late 1980s, including many who were not involved in terrorism. It reported evidence that some police officers wanted Finucane killed and that a number of loyalist paramilitary suspects who had been questioned at the RUC's Castlereagh holding centre had been told that Finucane was a member of the IRA. Ken Barrett, a member of the UDA, served three years of a twenty-two-year sentence for the murder of Finucane. He was released from prison in 2006 under the conditions of the Good Friday Agreement. Although a fourteen-year investigation headed by Lord John Stevens, the ex-head of London's Metropolitan Police, determined that rogue elements in the

Northern Ireland security forces had colluded in Finucane's murder, no other individuals were ever arrested in connection with the crime. On 25 June 2007, the Public Prosecution Service for Northern Ireland announced that there was insufficient evidence to charge former members of the RUC and military intelligence with the murder, and that the investigation had come to an end.

Where does this leave the issue of state-sponsored terrorism in Northern Ireland? Steve Bruce (1992, p. 200) puts the question this way: 'Have the army and police treated the loyalist paramilitaries as wayward but useful adjuncts to state policy or as enemies of the state?' Taken as a whole the evidence suggests that although there was some collusion between individual members of the security forces with the UVF and the UDA, this is a far cry from the assertion that loyalist paramilitaries were merely puppets of the British state, or that there was *systematic* collusion between the state's security forces and loyalist paramilitaries. It seems rather that loyalist paramilitaries were often assisted by the state, either through passivity or negligence, in carrying out acts of conservative terrorism.

THE LOGIC OF LOYALIST 'COUNTER-TERROR'

If loyalist paramilitaries are *not* best thought of as merely puppets of the British state, this leaves open the question of how their violence *should* be conceptualised. In an attempt to find rationality in loyalist violence, various theories have been advanced. According to one theory, by killing Catholics indiscriminately loyalists hoped to alienate the nationalist community from the republican movement by exposing the IRA as manifestly incapable of discharging its self-declared mission of defending the Catholic community. According to another theory, the security forces actually encouraged loyalists to carry out attacks on randomly selected Catholics because it would involve the IRA in a sectarian war against loyalists, thus diverting republicans from waging their guerrilla war against the security forces. A third theory explains at least some loyalist attacks, such as those in the Dublin and Monaghan bombings, as intended to force the Irish government to deny the IRA what amounted to a safe haven in the south, thus cutting off one of its most valuable resources.

All of these theories probably capture aspects of loyalist violence. But the reality for typical acts of loyalist violence is probably much more prosaic. The story of those who joined loyalist paramilitary organisations is strikingly similar to the stories told by those who joined the IRA after

1969. Some local outrage perceived as directed against oneself, one's family or one's community instilled an intense desire to defend oneself and, if possible, to strike back. Michael Stone, perhaps the most infamous loyalist gunman, joined the UDA after witnessing an IRA bombing on the Shankill Road on 11 December 1971. The no-warning bomb destroyed the Balmoral furniture store, killing four persons, including two children aged two years and one year old. Hundreds of residents joined police and troops in digging through the rubble with their bare hands, looking for survivors. (The bombing of the furniture store was itself in retaliation for a loyalist bombing a week earlier of McGurk's Bar, a Catholic pub on North Queen Street.) Such incidents led some, like John White, to conclude that the only adequate response was to pay back the IRA (or rather, the community that was seen as supporting it) in a similar coin: 'I'd seen the results of IRA operations, babies, children, pensioners beheaded, blown apart. I thought we should fight fire with fire' (Wood 2006, p. 6). Like many of those who joined the IRA between 1969 and 1971, the young men who joined loyalist paramilitary groups were originally interested in defending their neighbourhoods. Only later did they conclude that the best defence was a strong offence, and that this meant taking the fight to the enemy by using many of the same tactics that had been used against them.

There were also some significant differences between loyalist and republican violence. Because republican paramilitaries were waging a war against the state and its representatives, its primary targets were often readily identifiable (for example, by being uniformed). Loyalist paramilitaries, by contrast, often targeted randomly selected Catholics for attack because of the difficulty of identifying actual IRA members, the greater availability (and vulnerability) of ordinary Catholics as targets, and the close identification in the minds of many loyalists between ordinary Catholics and the IRA who together constituted a terrorist network. A high-ranking UDA man explained,

> When we decided we had no choice but to take on the Provos we had to find them, target them, and that wasn't easy . . . We wanted to go for the IRA and republicans but we couldn't locate them, we didn't know who they were. (Wood 2006, p. 112)

The solution to this problem was ready at hand: 'The bottom line was that if the IRA killed us, some of us were going to kill them' (Wood 2006, p. 115). 'Them' here, of course, meant ordinary Catholics. As a loyalist who bombed a Catholic pub in 1974 explained later, 'If we couldn't get the IRA, we would have to slaughter members of the Catholic community who after all seemed to support them' (Drake 1996, p. 36).

That ordinary Catholics were in league with the IRA early on became an article of faith for many loyalists. In July 1976 the UDA announced, 'We can say without fear of contradiction that 98 per cent of "innocent Catholic" victims have in fact contributed, by their actual presence or giving information, to assisting the murder of Loyalists' (Wood 2006, p. 112). Needless to say, the '98 per cent' figure was not based on careful social science research. But loyalists could appeal to an indisputable fact to corroborate their interpretation of the relationship between ordinary Catholics and the IRA: the significant support Sinn Féin received from the Catholic community. As one middle-aged Protestant Tyrone farmer interviewed in 1992 by Steve Bruce explained:

> Twenty years now people has been telling us that ordinary Catholics is not gunmen, that they is like us . . . Well I ask you, who was it that voted for Bobby Sands MP IRA man? Thirty and a half thousand of ordinary decent Catholics in this con-stituency [Fermanagh and South Tyrone] who are not gunmen and voted for a gunman. And who still votes for Sinn Féin? I am not a bitter man and I have raised five children not to be bitter and I can tell you that the ordinary Catholic does not mind benefiting from the work of the gunman . . . The ordinary Catholic tolerates the IRA and votes for the IRA and takes the benefits from the IRA because they want us out of our country. (Bruce 1994, pp. 42–3)

Whether a vote for Sinn Féin *always* indicated support for the IRA is ques-tionable. What is not questionable is that many Protestants tended to draw that conclusion.

For loyalist paramilitaries the identification of the Catholic community with the IRA was even tighter, with tragic consequences for many ordi-nary Catholics. The 'logic' of much loyalist violence against ordinary Catholics resembles that of the ethical sorites argument of the ancient Greek philosopher Sextus Empiricus (c. 200 CE), who argued that touch-ing his mother's toe with his finger was tantamount to incest because there is a whole series of other less innocent actions intermediate between that gesture and sexual intercourse. For example, in response to the IRA bombing of the Four Step Inn on the Shankill Road on 29 September 1971, the UVF retaliated on 4 December 1971 by bombing McGurk's Bar, a Catholic-owned pub in North Queen Street in Belfast city centre. Fifteen people were killed, mostly elderly men who frequented the pub to discuss horse racing. The attack was justified because the victims were IRA men. Or, if they weren't all IRA men, then some of them were. But even if none of them were active members of the IRA, then they were certainly IRA supporters. If they didn't actively support the IRA, then at the very least they silently acquiesced in the IRA's activities and didn't do enough to root out the IRA from their community. At a minimum, they were nationalists who were willing to benefit from the IRA's atrocities, which made them equally guilty of the IRA's crimes, and therefore deserving of retribution. Using this logic, the distinction between the IRA and ordinary Catholics could be blurred and dissolved, making those killed in McGurk's Bar, like all Catholics, legitimate targets (Bruce 1994, p. 45). Of course, something very much like this logic was also at work in the minds of republican paramilitaries, who could in good conscience kill not only full-time or part-time, on-duty or off-duty, uniformed or plains clothed members of the security forces (military, police, prison guards), but also civilians who worked for the security forces (building contractors, suppliers, maintenance workers) and anyone who associated with any of the foregoing (for example in mainly Protestant pubs), in an ever-expanding ripple of association until virtually all Protestants (and some Catholics) became legitimate targets.

It is worth noting that loyalist violence was more 'reactive' during some periods of the conflict than during others. Although republican violence claimed far more lives than loyalist violence, during some periods loyalist violence actually exceeded republican violence (Wood 2006), a fact that is difficult to square with the loyalist claim that their violence was *always* in response to IRA violence. Levels of loyalist violence also tended to be related to the sense that the British government was about to abandon them to a united Ireland, either through some new political initiative or by merely talking with the IRA. Such loyalist violence was the mirror-image of republican violence – the latter being violence intended to change the status of Northern Ireland, the former being violence to prevent such change.

Although many loyalist attacks on Catholics were motivated by nothing more than a desire to 'even the score' in response to republican attacks on security forces or bombings of Protestant pubs, other attacks had a more clearly pro-active motivation: 'counter-terror' (Wood 2006, p. ix). As Stevenson (1996, p. 60) notes, 'Loyalist violence was only partly reactive. Loyalists, as much as republicans, appreciate the stark efficiency of the terrorist act as an instrument of preemptive deterrence'. The explanation that loyalist terrorism was intended to compel the IRA to quit recurs repeatedly in interviews with loyalist paramilitaries. As a high-ranking UFF member explained, 'It was a message to the Roman Catholic community that if youse [sic] continue to slaughter our people, this is what's going to happen to youse, so youse put pressure on your people to stop, and we'll stop' (Stevenson 1996, p. 60). Another UFF member put it this way: 'We are out to terrorise the terrorists. To get to the stage when old grannies up the Falls will call on the IRA to stop, because it is ordinary Catholics that are getting hit, not the provos behind steel doors' (Drake 1996, p. 37). A UDA man confided: 'I always felt the only way to beat terrorism was to terrorize the terrorist – and be better at it' (Taylor 1999, p. 97). Another confessed that retribution was a major motivation: 'I joined the UDA for revenge and to take a real war to the IRA. We thought that we could do it better than the security forces and we did' (Wood 2006, p. 109).

A final cause of loyalist violence was simple resentment. Many loyalists saw the reforms enacted in the wake of the civil rights movement and the republican violence of the early 1970s as unfairly favouring Catholics over Protestants in terms of economic and social resources. As already mentioned, they also saw the British government as bending over backwards to accommodate the demands of the 'disloyal' Catholics while ignoring their own grievances. Catholics often had legitimate grievances with regard to housing, to be sure, but whether priority for housing went to Catholics or to Protestants was a local affair. Andy Tyrie, who later assumed command of the UDA, recalls discrimination against Protestants when he growing up in the Moryard estate in West Belfast: 'What I found behind the scenes was that everything was being done to block Protestants from getting houses in the area. Protestants were being encouraged to leave the district and I became suspicious of people involved in housing allocation' (Wood 2006, p. 2). Striking out at the primary recipients of this favouritism was far more convenient, and perhaps more immediately psychologically satisfying, than attempting to strike at the more remote and inaccessible bureaucrats ultimately responsible for the perceived injustice.

BLOODY SUNDAY AS STATE TERRORISM

A range of different cases in order of increasing (alleged) state participation in terrorism have been discussed, from the random shooting of Catholics by loyalist paramilitaries, in which there is no discernable state involvement, to cases such as the murder of Pat Finucane, in which members of the state's security forces actively assisted loyalist paramilitaries in the murder of an individual considered detrimental to the state's

interests. The endpoint on the continuum of state involvement in terrorism would be cases in which the state unequivocally engaged in terrorism
directly through its authorised personnel, rather than indirectly through
sponsorship of non-governmental groups such as loyalist paramilitaries. A
case could be made that the shoot-to-kill executions discussed in the previous chapter would be examples of such direct state terrorism, although
the sense in which such killings were 'indiscriminate' is questionable,
aimed as they were at the members of a paramilitary organisation on active
service. But to many nationalists it is obvious that the events of Bloody
Sunday constitute the most glaring example of British state terrorism. The
essential details of this incident are worth reviewing briefly before critically evaluating this interpretation.

Despite a ban on civil rights marches in Northern Ireland, on 30 January
1972 a NICRA march against internment went ahead in Derry's Catholic
Bogside area, to be followed by speeches from civil rights activists. The
march had originally been planned to end at the Guildhall, but army barricades redirected it to Free Derry Corner. A small group of teenagers broke
away from the main march and insisted on marching to the Guildhall
anyway. En route they threw stones at British troops positioned in William
Street. Meanwhile, the army command centre was informed that an IRA
sniper had been spotted in the area.

Just before 4:00 p.m., as the crowd gathered at Free Derry Corner to hear
the speakers, British paratroopers from the First Battalion of the Parachute
Regiment were sent in to arrest rioters. According to eyewitnesses, the
'Paras' instead opened fire into the crowd. During the next thirty minutes
over a hundred rounds were fired, wounding fourteen people and killing
thirteen (a fourteenth person died from his wounds four months later).
Many of those killed were shot in the back as they attempted to flee, were
crawling to safety, or were aiding others who had been shot. Eyewitnesses
including marchers, local residents and British and Irish journalists later
testified that none of those who were shot had been armed. The official
Army account stated that the paratroopers had come under sustained gun
and nail-bomb attack by the IRA, and had only returned fire at people seen
to be in possession of weapons. Nonetheless, not a single paratrooper was
injured, and no bullets or nail-bombs were recovered to support their
claim. Two official British government investigations failed to find any of
the paratroopers culpable for the killings and injuries inflicted that day.

In light of the definition proposed earlier, the case for considering
Bloody Sunday to be an example of state terrorism is straightforward. The

soldiers of the First Battalion of the Parachute Regiment had acted as instruments of the state in order to both harm and threaten harm to civil rights demonstrators agitating for an end to internment without trial, one of the state's chief weapons against a resurgent and increasingly dangerous Irish Republican Army dedicated to the violent overthrow of the government of Northern Ireland. According to some accounts, they had been instructed to 'teach the Catholic population of Derry a lesson' (Hennessey 2007, p. 348). By firing indiscriminately into the crowd of fleeing demonstrators, a clear message was conveyed that no distinction would be drawn between members of the IRA and its ordinary supporters, and that challenging the rule of law in Northern Ireland by participating in illegal demonstrations would simply not be tolerated. This interpretation seems to be confirmed by the response of the British government in the aftermath. Rather than taking full responsibility, the British government appeared committed to whitewashing the killings by refusing to hold the soldiers culpable. In this view, the shootings on Bloody Sunday were a naked example of brutal state terrorism.

Against this interpretation, it could be argued that far from being *strategically* indiscriminate in order to advance some political, ideological, social, economic or religious agenda – which requires that a good deal of advance planning went into the assault – the shootings that day represented no deliberate strategy at all. The paratroopers' task had been to arrest rioters. But because of the high level of IRA activity in and around Derry during the prior two week period, coupled with the belief that the IRA would be present during the demonstration, plus the fact (only recently disclosed) that shots had been fired (probably by members of either the Official IRA, or the Provisional IRA, or both) *prior* to the paratroopers commencing their arrest operation (Hennessey 2007), the most reasonable conclusion is that the shootings that day simply represented an army unit trained for combat rather than crowd control, made to expect violence, poised on a razor's edge of anticipation, coming under fire and then running amok. It was not uncommon for individual soldiers on the ground to act outside the rules of engagement specified by their senior military and political masters (Hennessey 2007). This is probably what happened that tragic day. Rather than intended to advance some agenda, the killings per se resulted simply from an unfortunate confluence of causes that came together to produce horrific effects. Although the killings were undoubtedly cold-blooded murder, to call this 'state terrorism' is to impute more high-level political intentionality to the events of that day than is probably warranted.

Despite the fact that these two interpretations of Bloody Sunday appear to be incompatible with one another, the truth probably lies in some combination of the two. The paratroopers had been instructed beforehand to take an 'aggressive' approach to the demonstrators, and especially to the rioters. Although presumably they had not been instructed to shoot unarmed demonstrators in the back as they fled, doing so was an unforeseen but not unforeseeable consequence of the vague instructions that they had received, which included, in addition to simply rounding up rioters for questioning, conveying a strong message to those engaged in an illegal civil rights demonstration. Given the high level of anticipation of violence, coupled with the belief that they had come under attack, they overreacted in a way that appears difficult to comprehend in light of their unit's reputation for a high level of training and discipline, but is made perhaps somewhat more comprehensible by considering the difficult situation into which they had been placed and by their apparent proclivity to 'go in hard' (Wood 2006, p. 104). Bloody Sunday may not have been a *clear-cut* example of state terrorism, but its aftermath at the very least lends support to the widespread belief in the nationalist community that in its unqualified condemnation of the IRA's use of indiscriminate violence in pursuit of political goals, the British government employed a glaring and untenable double-standard.

THE MORALITY OF STATE TERRORISM

Bloody Sunday involved the murder of fourteen innocent persons and ruined lives for many more, and is rightly considered a terrible act of injustice. The events of that day have received unprecedented scrutiny. They have been the subject of innumerable books, a feature film, a docudrama, several documentaries and at least half a dozen songs. The Bloody Sunday Centre was established in Derry to commemorate those who died and to seek justice for them. Under intense pressure from human rights organisations, two official British government inquiries were undertaken to resolve what really took place that day. By December 2007 the total cost of the Saville Inquiry into Bloody Sunday had reached £181.2 million, and was projected to continue costing £500,000 a month – financed at taxpayers' expense – until its anticipated conclusion in the latter half of 2008.

Why so much attention? Some members of the unionist community have complained that other massacres of comparable or greater magnitude for which republican paramilitary groups are responsible have received

213

scant attention compared to the enormous media and judicial attention given to the killings of Bloody Sunday, suggesting to them that republicans have succeeded in converting the admitted tragedy of Bloody Sunday into an obscene media propaganda bonanza. Republican outrages, such as the IRA bombing of the La Mon House Hotel in County Down on 17 February 1978, and the IRA bombing of the Remembrance Day ceremonies on 8 November 1987 in Enniskillen, County Fermanagh, have received no such scrutiny. For those who lost loved ones in these attacks they were no less significant than were the killings on Bloody Sunday for its victims' families. But neither of these operations, nor any of the innumerable others undertaken by the IRA, has received anything close to the attention paid to Bloody Sunday. How is this asymmetrical attitude to be explained?

Part of the explanation, no doubt, concerns the unique causal effects of Bloody Sunday. Whereas the IRA's bombings mentioned above were simply two of a seemingly endless series of attacks intended to 'sicken the British' into withdrawing from the Six Counties, Bloody Sunday was unique in its effect of consolidating the IRA's support base in the Catholic community and in attracting volunteers to its ranks. Still, this seems secondary from a moral point of view, because Bloody Sunday had this profound impact *precisely because it was viewed as morally egregious to an extent unmatched by other attacks upon innocent persons*. In this sense, the perceived moral distinctiveness of Bloody Sunday is logically *prior* to its distinctive causal influence. Therefore, the perceived moral distinctiveness of Bloody Sunday itself requires closer examination and evaluation.

Is State Terrorism Necessarily Morally Worse than Non-State Terrorism?

The killing of fourteen unarmed civil rights demonstrators was terribly unjust and wrong; but is there some reason to judge these killings to be *especially* morally wrong compared to other unjust killings? More generally, if we suppose (for the sake of argument) both that the killings on Bloody Sunday were an act of terrorism perpetrated by the state, and that acts of terrorism are always (or at least always prima facie) morally wrong, is there some reason to suppose that state terrorism is *by its very nature* morally worse than non-state terrorism?

Igor Primoratz (2004) claims that there is. He gives four arguments in support of this commonly held view. First, terrorism carried out by states has been enormously more destructive, and has caused more deaths,

214

injuries and ruined lives, than have all the terrorist acts ever committed by non-state agents combined. The RAF's night-time firebombing of Hamburg on 27 July 1943 (the second of four raids on that city) left some 40,000 civilians dead. The US Army Air Force's atomic bomb dropped on Hiroshima on 6 August 1945 took the lives of some 140,000 civilians. The atomic bomb dropped on Nagasaki three days later took the lives of roughly 74,000 civilians. The asymmetry between state and non-state agents in their respective abilities to wreak destruction through terrorist acts lies in the fact that states have at their disposal resources for committing terrorism far in excess of anything available to non-state agents. Primoratz adds:

> Now this asymmetry is not just another statistical fact; it follows from the nature of the state and the amount and variety of resources that even a small state has at its disposal. No matter how much non-state terrorists manage to enrich their equipment and improve their organization, planning, and methods of action, they stand no chance of ever significantly changing the score. (Primoratz 2004, p. 118)

Second, 'state terrorism is bound to be compounded by secrecy, deception, and hypocrisy. When involved in terrorism . . . a state will be acting clandestinely, disclaiming any involvement, and declaring its adherence to values and principles that rule it out' (Primoratz 2004, p. 118). Alternatively, if it cannot plausibly deny involvement, 'it will do its best to present its actions to at least some audiences in a different light: as legitimate acts of war, or as acts done in defence of state security' (Primoratz 2004, p. 118). Those engaging in non-state terrorism, on the other hand, need not (except at the operational level) be secretive, deceptive or hypocritical. They can be open and forthright about their use of terrorism and can even embrace terrorism as a method of achieving the supremely valuable goals whose attainment renders their acts morally justified.

Third, states that engage in terrorism act in breach of the international human rights declarations, agreements and conventions to which they are signatories. By committing acts of terrorism they violate their solemn international commitments. Non-state agents who commit terrorism are presumably not bound by such agreements and so this charge cannot be levelled against them (Primoratz 2004).

Fourth, whereas some non-state agents (representing, for example, groups subjected to oppression, persecution and injustice) can claim, sometimes plausibly, that there was no alternative to terrorism for remedying the plight of those they represent, this defence will seldom or never be available to states for whom, with their superior resources and power, other alternatives will always exist (Primoratz 2004).

These four arguments taken together are intended to show that state terrorism is morally worse than terrorism by non-state agents. It is unclear, however, whether Primoratz intends to argue that (1) state terrorism has, *as a matter of fact*, been morally worse than non-state terrorism, or that (2) state terrorism, *by its very nature*, is necessarily worse than non-state terrorism. In asserting that the asymmetry between states and non-state agents in the destruction wrought through terrorism by each is not just another statistical fact but instead 'follows from the nature of the state and the amount and variety of resources that even a small state has at its disposal', he seems to be endorsing the second interpretation. But if so, then the argument is vulnerable to the objection that this is merely a *contingent* feature of state terrorism, rather than something essential to state terrorism per se that makes it morally worse than non-state terrorism. Should non-state terrorists find a way to acquire nuclear weapons and detonate them in heavily populated urban centres, the resulting destruction could easily exceed the destruction of any specific act of state terrorism to date, and could even exceed the total destruction resulting from all acts of state terrorism to date. Hence whether state terrorism turns out to be more destructive than non-state terrorism is a contingent matter rather than an essential feature of state terrorism per se.

Similarly, there is no reason why a state's use of terrorism must necessarily involve more secrecy, deception and hypocrisy than the use of terrorism by non-state agents. Given the fact that terrorism tends to be morally condemned by most people, there will be a strong incentive for state and non-state agents alike who engage in terrorism to deny that they are doing so. For example, the IRA has never admitted to carrying out acts of terrorism even though, by virtually any reasonable definition of terrorism, that it what its operations were. It is true that states that engage in terrorism act in breach of the international human rights declarations, agreements and conventions to which they are signatories, whereas non-state agents, not being signatories to such agreements, cannot violate them. But this does not make the *acts of terrorism* committed by states worse than the acts of terrorism committed by non-state agents. It simply indicates that states that do so are duplicitous and hence cannot be trusted to abide by their solemn agreements, which is a distinct (and important) issue.

Finally, despite their greater resources, or sometimes precisely because of their greater resources, states may find themselves in situations in which they have no practical alternative but to engage in acts of terrorism.

During the Cold War, the US and the Soviet Union each amassed large stockpiles of nuclear weapons in the service of the deterrence policy known as 'mutually assured destruction' (MAD). Each state in a nuclear standoff threatens the population centres of the other side with destruction as a deterrent to the other side launching a first strike. Such actions satisfy the conditions for (external) state terrorism, yet given the capabilities of the other side, there appears to be no alternative to threatening a nuclear counter-strike. Ironically, in such cases it is precisely the states' superior resources and power that give them no alternative but to employ terrorism in the protection of their citizens.

If the purported asymmetries between state and non-state terrorism Primoratz emphasises represent contingent and variable features of each type of terrorism rather than necessary differences that would underwrite an *essential* moral difference between the two types of terrorism, then there is (as yet) no reason to conclude that state terrorism *by its very nature* is morally worse than non-state terrorism. What, then, explains the perceived moral distinctiveness of Bloody Sunday (again, assuming for the sake of argument that it was an instance of state terrorism)?

One possibility is that the state could be understood to have the formal responsibility of protecting the rights of its citizens to enjoy order, security and justice. To the extent that acts of internal state terrorism violate these rights in such a way that there is no compensating increase in respect for rights, then from a rights-based perspective such terrorism would be morally problematic in a way that terrorism by non-state agents in principle cannot be.

This observation might explain why the killings on Bloody Sunday are so often treated as more morally egregious than many other killings during the conflict in Northern Ireland. Bloody Sunday involved the killing of innocent persons by highly trained professionals of the British army, whose actions were callously excused by government officials – the very people whose collective duty was to protect life and to uphold the law. It is thought that they should be responsible to a higher standard, and that their actions that day and after were especially morally reprehensible because they subverted the most essential function of the state to support the rule of law, one of the foundations for promoting order, security and justice. As such, Bloody Sunday and its aftermath struck at the very foundation of the common good in a way that acts of non-state terrorism, even if morally wrong, even in principle could not. At stake was the very existence of a law-governed society. As graffiti scrawled on the Derry city wall

217

facing the site of the Bloody Sunday killings once pointedly declared in large, rough-drawn letters, 'When the law makers are the law breakers their [sic] is no law'.

The Morality of State Counter-Terrorist Terrorism

These considerations raise a final question about the morality of state terrorism. Can a state consistently condemn terrorism by non-state agents while itself engaging in counter-terrorist activities that involve the use of terrorism? Primoratz endorses the common-sense view that the answer to this question is an unequivocal 'No'. In addition to the four arguments intended to show that state terrorism is necessarily morally worse than non-state terrorism, he advances an additional argument intended to show that state terrorism *as a method of counter-terrorism* is intrinsically problematic from a moral point of view. He locates this special problem for the morality of state terrorism in the concept of 'moral standing':

> A thief does not have the moral standing required for condemning theft and preaching about the paramount importance of property. A murderer does not have the moral standing necessary for condemning murder and pontificating about the sanctity of life. By the same token, a state which has made use of terrorism, or sponsored it, or condoned it, or supported governments that have done any of the above – in a word, a state which has itself been involved in or with terrorism to any significant degree – lacks the moral standing required for bona fide moral criticism of terrorism. (Primoratz 2004, p. 122)

Although at first glance this perhaps sounds plausible enough as a moral critique of a state's use of terrorism to combat terrorism, and indeed perhaps seems too obvious to require explication, when considered more carefully it appears to commit what introductory logic texts call the *argumentum ad hominem tu quoque* fallacy, namely, the mistake in reasoning of attempting to discredit a person's *conclusion* by pointing out that some aspect of the person's *behaviour* is inconsistent with either the premises or the conclusion of his argument. That this *is* a fallacy is clear. Whereas we might not want to rely solely on a murderer's judgements concerning the morality of taking human lives, because such a person's credentials for making such judgements are dubious, the claim 'murder is morally wrong' is not invalidated as a moral judgement just because it is uttered by a murderer. Likewise, states that morally condemn all terrorism but also engage in terrorism as a method of counter-terrorism are guilty of *hypocrisy*, and ought to be criticised as such. But nothing whatsoever logically follows concerning the moral justification of states using terrorism as a method of counter-terrorism. That issue can only be settled by an examination of the *arguments* for and against the morality of a state's use of terrorism as a method of counter-terrorism; a state's *behaviour* is simply not relevant to deciding that issue. A limited use of terrorism as a method of counter-terrorism could, in principle, be morally justified, at least from a consequentialist perspective. As Jonathan Glover observes, 'The use of a small dose of state terrorism might have short-term gains that outweighed the losses. It might cripple a terrorist organization, and save many more lives than it took' (Glover 1991, p. 273). This will not be a popular conclusion. It might, nevertheless, be true.

Conclusions

State terrorism has occurred in Northern Ireland, but there is little evidence to suggest state terrorism has been pursued as a policy. The claim that loyalist terrorism is simply state-terrorism-by-proxy is a considerable over-simplification. The distinctions between state, pro-state, conservative, and state-sponsored terrorism are critical to understanding the nature and extent of the British government's involvement in terrorism in Northern Ireland. Determining whether state terrorism is necessarily morally worse than non-state terrorism requires distinguishing between different kinds of state terrorism, as well as the careful application of moral theories. Although state terrorism, as judged from a consequentialist moral perspective, typically is morally worse than non-state terrorism, it need not be. It is also not necessarily morally worse from a rights-based perspective except when the state through acts of terrorism violates rights in such a way that overall respect for rights is not enhanced. Although there are conceivable situations in which acts of state terrorism can be morally justified, there are vastly more opportunities for it to be morally wrong, as history demonstrates only too well.

Epilogue

It is patently obvious after decades of conflict that there can be no military solution to what is essentially a political problem.
(Sinn Féin President Gerry Adams, addressing a press conference in Jerusalem, 5 September 2006)

THE MORALITY OF TERRORISM

At Sinn Féin's 1983 *Ard Fheis*, Gerry Adams boldly declared that 'armed struggle is a morally correct form of resistance in the six counties' (*An Phoblacht/Republican News*, 17 November 1983). Despite the confident tone of this declaration, its truth is hardly self-evident. I have been concerned to critically evaluate this and related republican claims about the Provisional IRA's armed struggle. But doing so raises broader questions about the use of force to achieve political ends. When is a resort to violence in the pursuit of political goals morally justified?

Two clear and consistent answers are 'never' and 'always'. The 'total pacifist' asserts the former, claiming that violence is never morally justified, even in the pursuit of worthy political goals. The proponent of 'total *realpolitik*' asserts the latter, maintaining that violence is morally justified whenever it will be or has been effective in achieving the desired political goal (Govier 2002, pp. 84–5). Such positions can be clear and consistent because they lie on the endpoints of a continuum of views about the morality of political violence. Those who crave clarity and simplicity will be attracted by such positions.

Most people, quite reasonably, will find both answers too extreme to be acceptable, and will instead find themselves drawn to an intermediate

220

position according to which a resort to political violence is 'sometimes' morally justified. This 'moderate moralist' answer has the virtue of attempting to find a middle ground between the extremes of 'never' and 'always', but the price to be paid for this gain is a problem of daunting difficulty: under what precise conditions is a resort to violence in the pursuit of political goals morally justified?

Moral intuitions may be essential as sources of moral data, but by themselves they cannot answer such questions in an intellectually satisfying way. The three moral theories applied in this book, however, can each provide a theoretical framework for addressing this question in a principled manner, although obviously doing so requires considerable effort. Unless one is willing to embrace one of the extremes (total pacifism or total *realpolitik*), or (what might amount to the same thing) to just turn away from the problem entirely because it seems too difficult, a view based on these or other principled approaches is unavoidable.

The specific focus of this book has been on the morality of the use of violence (including terrorism) by the Provisional Irish Republican Army. Richard English concludes his book on the IRA with a personal moral assessment of its armed struggle: 'I myself – in the end – am not really persuaded by the IRA's argument that their violence was necessary or beneficial. But nor am I satisfied with a depiction of the IRA which casually or myopically condemns them' (English 2003, p. 384). I think that there are sufficient grounds for going beyond this cautious conclusion while avoiding the charge of myopia either in celebrating or in condemning IRA violence. If the applications of several different fundamental moral theories all yield the conclusion that acts of a certain sort are morally justifiable, then it would be reasonable to conclude that such acts *are* morally justifiable. Likewise, if the applications of several different fundamental moral theories all yield the conclusion that acts of a certain sort are not morally justifiable, then it would be reasonable to conclude that such acts are *not* morally justifiable. After all, we have no higher or better standard for the rational adjudication of such issues. The three moral theories applied in the foregoing discussion to the Provisional IRA's armed struggle all lead to the conclusion that the IRA's armed struggle, including its use of terrorism, was not morally justified. This conclusion is unlikely to surprise many readers. Its value may lay primarily in the detailed *arguments* given in its support.

The Provisional IRA's armed struggle has come to an end, but the general sorts of problems (social, economic and political) that gave rise to it, as well as ideas about the sorts of goods (of cultural self-realisation, of security and of nationhood) that are commonly thought to be obtainable only through armed struggle, are likely to recur. The historical circumstances and agents necessarily will be different, but the basic structural features of the Northern Ireland conflict are likely to be replicated elsewhere at other times. The chief agents in these other conflicts will not speak with a distinctive Northern Irish accent, but they will believe as passionately in the justice of their causes, and will be as willing to shed blood to advance them, as were the volunteers of the IRA. We will still be faced with the challenge of understanding the circumstances (if any) under which a resort to violence, including terrorism, is morally justifiable. To what extent, then, can the results obtained in relation to the IRA's armed struggle be said to have more general applicability in the moral assessment of the use of terrorism? Can the results arrived at in this study responsibly be generalised?

I believe that they can, provided that due care is taken to recognise the specific ways in which other contexts are like, and unlike, the context of the Provisional IRA's armed struggle. The on-going (as I write) Israeli-Palestinian conflict is a case in point. Opinions on the moral rightness of the Israeli occupation of Palestine, and of the moral justifiability of Palestinian violence against Israelis, are sharply divided, and frequently split along political lines. Elsewhere I have attempted to show, through the application of Just War Theory, consequentialist and rights-based moral theories, that Palestinian terrorism isn't *necessarily* morally unjustified simply by virtue of employing terrorist tactics; nevertheless, given the details of that conflict, it is in fact morally unjustified (Shanahan 2008). There is no reason why this same approach could not be extended to better understand the morality of other structurally similar situations, past, present or future.

A particular danger of this approach, of course, is the failure to take into consideration the differences in the use of terrorism from one context to the next. Many have succumbed to the temptation of lumping all acts of political violence of which one disapproves into the category of 'terrorism' and then condemning them all equally. Former Israeli prime minister Ariel Sharon (perhaps echoing Margaret Thatcher's mantra during the 1981 republican hunger strikes) asserted that 'terrorism is terrorism is terrorism anywhere in the world' (*The New York Times*, 19 March 2002, p. A12), implying that there are no relevant differences, moral or otherwise, between the terrorism carried out by Palestinians and that carried out by al Qaeda. Yet clearly there are different motivations for terrorism just as there are different motivations for wars. The sort of terrorism carried out by Palestinians against the Israeli occupation of their land, as well as republican terrorism aimed at establishing a thirty-two-county Irish republic, are both best understood as a tactic used by disadvantaged minority populations aimed at the establishment of sovereign political states believed (correctly or not) to be essential for the good of their people. Republican and Palestinian political aspirations are of a sort that would be shared by many people with no inclination toward violence. As former British Prime Minister Tony Blair noted, 'the political demands of republicanism are demands that would be shared by many perfectly law-abiding people who are nationalists in the north, or citizens of the south in Ireland'. The demands are easily stated: 'in its broadest definition during most of the 36 years of the IRA's war, armed struggle was depicted as a means to national self-determination'. Drawing a contrast with the aspirations of some Islamic terrorist groups, he went on to note that 'the IRA never claimed to be the voice of international Catholicism in a campaign to restore the medieval papacy and the Inquisition' (*The Houston Chronicle*, 30 July 2005).

In contrast, the motives of terrorist groups such as al Qaeda, whose ambition, apparently, is to destabilise the West in order to usher in a new worldwide Islamic caliphate, are shared only by those whose concerns can perhaps best be described as 'apocalyptic' (Harte 2005). Clearly, terrorism, like political violence more generally, can be employed for different reasons, and it makes sense to ask whether some of these reasons provide greater moral justification than others. Ariel Sharon notwithstanding, there are important differences between various acts of terrorism, and some of these differences bear on the moral evaluation of such acts. The terrorism of al Qaeda, or of Timothy McVeigh for that matter, which includes no specific demands and is in the service of no struggle to secure the basic goods of some community, are unlikely to be morally justified in terms of either Just War Theory or the morality of rights. Like other forms of terrorism, the best chance of moral justification for such terrorism is in terms of its consequences; but it is very difficult to conceive of a convincing argument that acts such as flying airplanes into buildings in New York and Washington, DC, or blowing up the Alfred P. Murrah Federal Building in Oklahoma City, have in fact resulted in better consequences than would have resulted from any alternative acts available to those agents. Remaining *open* to the possibility of the moral justifiability of

nationalist struggles that use terrorism as a tactic, such as those of republicans in Northern Ireland and of Palestinians in Palestine, obviously does
not entail the moral justifiability of every form of terrorism. Each use of
terrorism must be examined in its historical and political context. In addition, even when the use of terrorism *is* morally justified, it does not follow
that there are no *moral limits* on its use, just as the fact that war is sometimes morally justified doesn't entail that there are no moral limits to the
prosecution of wars. Terrorism and war are both, by their very nature,
destructive activities. It is this very power to destroy that requires careful
moral consideration of their deployment. As 'Dora' eloquently expresses
this essential point in Albert Camus' play, *The Just Assassins*, 'Even in
destruction, there is a right way and a wrong way – and there are limits'
(Camus 1958, p. 258).

THE MORALITY OF COUNTER-TERRORISM

It is perhaps natural to look to Britain's extensive experience in combating terrorism in Northern Ireland for lessons that could be applied to
counter-terrorism efforts in other contexts. In practice what this usually
means is examining British responses to IRA terrorism to determine what
'worked' and what was counter-productive, where these terms refer to
efficacy in re-establishing security – in other words, for clues about how to
'defeat', or at least contain, terrorist threats (Richardson 2006). My discussion of British counter-terrorism in this book, by contrast, has focused
on the *moral evaluation* of such efforts rather than on counter-terrorism
strategy per se. The two issues are not unrelated, because the morality (or
perhaps more precisely, the perceived morality) of counter-terrorism
strategies often bear directly on their effectiveness. Yet they are fundamentally distinct because it is conceivable that the most pragmatically
effective way of combating terrorism may not be the most morally
justifiable way. It is perhaps a sad fact about our world that the domains of
the practical (taken in a narrow instrumental sense) and of the moral do
not always, or even usually, coincide.

The question here, then, is whether the moral evaluation of British
counter-terrorism offered in this book can be generalised to morally evaluate other counter-terrorism efforts, past, present or future. As with the
morality of terrorism, so too with the morality of counter-terrorism: meaningful moral analysis must take into account the specific details of each situation, and can responsibly generalise only to the extent that different

situations are structurally similar in relevant ways. This suggests that general pronouncements (for example, 'shoot-to-kill executions are necessarily wrong because they violate the victims' rights') cannot but be facile judgements of very dubious warrant. Nonetheless, with these important caveats in mind it is worthwhile to consider some of the broader implications of this study for the morality of counter-terrorism. This is especially so because many of the issues discussed here remain critical issues in current counter-terrorism efforts.

British counter-terrorism efforts in Northern Ireland included at least three distinct (albeit interrelated) elements: the use of military force, the introduction of special counter-terrorism legislation and the routine use of various extra-legal practices to make headway against a resilient and determined Irish Republican Army. Perhaps predictably, military force turned out to be a blunt instrument whose use, while not guaranteeing morally questionable actions, nonetheless made such actions extremely likely. To the extent that the Falls Road curfew and internment were counter-terrorism operations (intended to take terrorists' weapons and terrorists themselves, respectively, out of circulation), they resulted both in the violation of individuals' rights and in consequences (to those on the immediate receiving end of these military operations and to those who would suffer from the IRA's increased strength resulting from these operations) that can only be judged to be negative. Although the military operation that resulted in the tragedy of Bloody Sunday was not a counter-terrorism operation per se, it resulted from a chain of causation extending back to the military enforcement of internment without trial, and further underlines the moral risks inherent in using troops that have been trained to kill enemy combatants in security operations in civilian settings.

Criminalisation, introduced in 1976, marked a shift in emphasis from treating the Northern Ireland conflict as an insurgency requiring a military solution, to an internal security problem requiring a more aggressive law enforcement response. The introduction of special counter-terrorism legislation, intended to give the security forces and the judicial system greater latitude in subverting terrorist activities and in prosecuting suspected terrorists, essentially extended a de facto separate legal system created for dealing with individuals accused of terrorist offences. In its zeal to put away terrorists, internal security often took precedence over respect for human rights, as evidenced in a number of cases of miscarriages of justice. Security and respect for individual rights often exist in a delicate balance, such that the greater the emphasis placed on the former, the greater the danger to the latter. In this case, emphasising greater security led to disregard for individual rights, which then created a backlash that made the sought-for security more difficult to obtain. It is not extravagant to suppose that a greater concern with protecting individual rights might well have ultimately enhanced rather than comprised security, while staying on firmer moral ground. In other words, the moral and the pragmatic, although by no means identical, need not be in conflict.

Similarly, the use of military force, draconian counter-terrorism legislation and the use of extra-legal counter-terrorism practices, besides often being counter-productive from a counter-terrorism perspective, often involved actions that would have to be judged, according to one or more fundamental moral theories, as morally unjustified. Far more effective, as well as being on safer ground morally, was the use of intelligence to subvert terrorist activities. To the extent that those engaged in counter-terrorism can maintain the moral high ground, not just in word but in deed, to that extent the terrorists' activities might come to seem morally unacceptable to the communities upon whose support they depend. Because there is no *necessary* connection between the morally justifiable and the pragmatically expedient, there is no reason to suppose that taking the moral high road will *always* issue in consequences that are effective from a perspective that is concerned with effective counter-terrorism per se. Yet to the extent that counter-terrorism is ultimately supposed to bring about some *good* or at least *better* state of affairs, the normative and the practical can never be completely separated, thus making a philosophical inquiry into the morality of counter-terrorism an important, albeit frequently overlooked, element of a more comprehensive response to terrorist threats.

Endnotes

PROLOGUE

1. Following standard practice both in the media and in most scholarship, 'the IRA' and 'Sinn Féin' will henceforth be used as synonymous with 'the Provisional IRA' and 'Provisional Sinn Féin', respectively, unless otherwise noted.

2. Data are from Malcolm Sutton's 'Index of Deaths from the Conflict in Ireland', at http://cain.ulst.ac.uk/sutton/index.html. Of the 3,523 deaths directly linked to the conflict in Northern Ireland between July 1969 and 31 December 2001, 93 per cent took place in Northern Ireland, with the remainder in the Republic of Ireland, England and other parts of Europe.

CHAPTER I

1. For example, on the various Sinn Féin websites (http://www.sinnfein. ie/history and http://www.sinnfein.ie/introduction), and in Sinn Féin publications such as 'Freedom' and 'A Scenario for Peace' (at http://sinnfein.org/). The composite 'standard republican narrative' reported here closely tracks these official sources, although all the elements of it cannot be found in precisely this form in any single official republican source.

2. Curiously, this version of the republican narrative lists internment without trial as one of the catalysts leading the Provisional IRA to shift to offensive action in 1969, even though internment without trial was not introduced until 9 August 1971 in response to, and long after the beginning of, the Provisionals' offensive campaign. In other words, this version gets the temporal and causal order backwards – unless we can suppose that the Provisional IRA went on the offensive *in anticipation of* the introduction of internment without trial two years later.

227

3. Something like this interpretation is suggested by O'Doherty, who writes: 'It is . . . important to see that the IRA campaign was honed to be an efficient party political instrument for preventing reconciliation, rather than delude ourselves that it is merely a symptom of the pain of excluded people' (O'Doherty 1998, p. 200). Here I attempt to build on this basic insight.

CHAPTER 2

1. In Finneran 2002, p. 76.
2. Yeats himself apparently felt ambivalent about the value of the sacrifices made. In his biography of Yeats, R. F. Foster notes that, 'the last stanza of the poem took up the question of martyrology. While the names are "told" at midnight like the beads of a rosary, the poem subtly links the rebels' sacrifice to a life of dreams and delusion' (Foster 2003, p. 62).
3. Consider an analogy: when one catches a head-cold, one can rest, drink plenty of fluids, and stay warm in the belief that such practices are pleasing to Apollo, the god of healing, who will reward one with a speedy recovery. But if those embracing this belief do not, on average, recover any sooner than those lacking it, this strongly suggests that the belief in question is seriously deficient in explanatory power.
4. Moran says that there were five, but in fact there appear to have been just four: Thomas Ashe (in 1917), and Terence MacSwiney, Michael Fitzgerald and Joseph Murphy (in 1920).
5. Denis Barry, Andrew Sullivan and Joseph Whitty all died on hunger strike in 1923 (White 1993, p. 117).
6. It is *possible* that statements such as those quoted earlier do not represent authentic republican thinking, but instead represent a form of 'metaphysical propaganda'. By repeatedly describing the IRA's armed struggle *as if* it were the necessary, inevitable, unavoidable consequence of the British occupation of Ireland, questions about the truth of that claim are discouraged so that listeners' attention can be redirected and focused on what really matters, namely, the problem of how to get 'the Brits' to leave. I do not doubt that republican rhetoric involves the use of metaphysical propaganda in this way. However, the pervasiveness of this kind of language in republican publications and presentations suggests that it is more than that – namely, that it represents a core republican belief. In what follows, therefore, I will adopt this hypothesis in order to further explore its philosophical cogency.

CHAPTER 3

1. The formulation of the ultimate republican goal that appears as the title for this chapter is taken from a poster purchased in the Sinn Féin office/shop on the Falls Road in Belfast, July 1998. It is a variation on a statement made by then Sinn Féin Vice President Gerry Adams on Sunday, 17 June 1979 as he

delivered the annual Wolfe Tone commemoration address at Bodenstown Cemetery in County Kildare: 'We stand for an Ireland free, united, socialist, and Gaelic' (*An Phoblacht/Republican News* 23 June 1979; in English 2003, p. 224). By 1998 the 'socialist' part of the republican agenda had been dropped, at least from its merchandise.

2. According to some writers, this is the core conviction of 'nationalism', namely, 'a belief that humanity is divided into culturally distinctive communities which should be politically autonomous' (Hutchinson 1996, p. 109). Because 'nationalism' has other connotations as well, for clarity I will continue to refer to the core idea at issue here as 'the nation-state principle'.

3. Other, slightly different, formulations appear in earlier publications, for example in Smith (2001, 2003). This formulation, however, perhaps best captures the character of the Provisional IRA's armed struggle on behalf of Irish nationhood as situated 'between history and destiny'.

4. International Covenant on Civil and Political Rights, Article 1; adopted by the United Nations General Assembly on 16 December 1966.

CHAPTER 4

1. The full text of the Pope's remarks appeared in *The Irish Times*, 1 October 1979, p. 14. Responses by the IRA and Sinn Féin appear in *The Irish Times* for Wednesday 3 October, 1979, pp. 5 and 6, respectively.

2. Just War Theory originated in the writings of St Augustine (354–430 CE), was further developed by St Thomas Aquinas (1225–74), and received perhaps its fullest classical development in *The Laws of War and Peace*, by Hugo Grotius (1583–1645). The correct formulation of Just War Theory continues to be controversial. In addition to *jus ad bellum* and *jus in bello* conditions, some contemporary theorists (Evans 2005, pp. 13, 19–20) also include various *jus post bellum* (justice after war) conditions requiring that those engaged in war establish just conditions of peace, address the material consequences of the war, and take an active role in post-war reconciliation between the previously warring parties. Space prohibits me from discussing this and, indeed, many other important aspects of contemporary Just War Theory.

3. Apologists for the Provisional IRA typically neglect to mention that as it became clear in 1986 that Provisional Sinn Féin planned to drop abstention from Leinster House from its constitution, Maguire (then 94 years old) formally retracted the authority he had previously vested in the Provisional Army Council and transferred it the following year to the Continuity IRA, the paramilitary wing of rival 'Republican Sinn Féin' (White 2006, pp. 301, 327).

4. As US Secretary of Defense Donald Rumsfeld famously remarked at a press briefing on 12 February 2002: 'As we know, there are known knowns. There are things we know we know. We also know there are known unknowns. That is to say we know there are some things we do not know. But there are also unknown unknowns, the ones we don't know we don't know'.

5. The account here follows that of Wallace (1989) who provides a useful summary of the considerations that led to the adoption of a policy of area bombing in 1940–1.

CHAPTER 5

1. Excellent treatments of consequentialism include Hooker 2000, Darwell 2002, and Mulgan 2005.
2. Unlike Nielsen, however, Corlett is not committed to a strictly consequentialist analysis of terrorism. This does not, however, affect the particular point Corlett is making in this passage.

CHAPTER 6

1. This apparently straightforward claim is complicated by the fact that Khatchadourian also wants to maintain that acts which violate someone's human rights *can* be morally justified where overriding *consequentialist* considerations justify the violation. This would make him a 'threshold deontologist', in Kamm's (2004, p. 664) terminology. In order to assess distinctively rights-based approaches to the morality of terrorism in this chapter, I will focus on the rights-based argument against terrorism he gives, and ignore this complication.
2. In contrast to this description of human rights, some rights theorists maintain that human rights are simply human conventions. According to this 'conventionalist' view, human rights are contingent upon particular social and historical conditions. It is hardly surprising that rights-based arguments against terrorism typically presuppose an objectivist rather than a conventionalist interpretation of human rights. In evaluating rights-based arguments for and against terrorism, therefore, I will focus exclusively on the view that treats human rights as grounded in trans-historical, trans-cultural, non-socially contingent features of the world.
3. Some rights theorists (for example, Kamm 1989, 1992; Applbaum 1998) prefer to speak of rights as *constraints* on action. In my discussion of their views, I have substituted the word 'rights' for their word 'constraints' whenever doing so contributes to understanding how their views bear on the central issues of this chapter.

CHAPTER 7

1. Hennessey (2007, pp. 214–26, 345) balances this judgement somewhat by detailing the significant intelligence gains the security forces obtained through internment combined with interrogation in depth along with the disruption internment caused to the IRA's leadership.
2. On 16 March 1988, mourners assembled in Milltown Cemetery in Belfast for the funeral of the three IRA volunteers killed in Gibraltar. Michael Stone, a

rogue loyalist paramilitary, attacked the mourners. Throwing grenades and shooting into the crowd of 10,000, he killed three people before he was caught by an angry mob and nearly beaten to death. Three days later at the funeral for those killed by Stone, two British army corporals inadvertently drove into the funeral cortège at Milltown Cemetery. Believing that they were under attack again, the crowd pulled the two soldiers from their car, beat them and dragged them away where they were killed by IRA gunmen, one of whom was alleged to be Patrick McGeown. The Catholic solicitor Patrick Finucane, who had already gained a reputation for his fearless legal representation of republican paramilitaries, successfully defended McGeown by arguing that there was insufficient evidence against him. On Sunday, 12 February 1989, two masked gunmen of the UDA/UFF broke into Finucane's home in North Belfast as he was sharing a meal with his family They shot him fourteen times. Thus, the SAS's killing of the three IRA volunteers in Gibraltar set in motion a train of events resulting in Finucane's murder.

CHAPTER 8

1. Other definitions of 'terrorism' would preclude the possibility of state terrorism in more subtle ways. According to Bruce Hoffman, 'terrorism' is the deliberate creation and exploitation of fear through violence or the threat of violence in the pursuit of political change (Hoffman 2006, p. 40). Insofar as those holding power in government wish to *prevent* political change, their actions cannot (according to this definition) be acts of terrorism.

References

Adams, Gerry (1986), *The Politics of Irish Freedom*, Dingle: Brandon.

Adams, Gerry (1988), *A Pathway to Peace*, Cork: Mercier.

Adams, Gerry (1995), *Free Ireland: Towards a Lasting Peace*, Dingle: Brandon.

Allhoff, Fritz (2005), 'Terrorism and torture', in Timothy Shanahan (ed.), *Philosophy 9/11: Thinking about the War on Terrorism*, Chicago, IL: Open Court Publishing, pp. 243–59.

Alonso, Rogelio (2001), 'The modernization of Irish republican thinking toward the utility of violence', *Studies in Conflict & Terrorism*, 24:131–44.

Alonso, Rogelio (2007), *The IRA and Armed Struggle*, London and New York: Routledge.

Anderson, Benedict (2006), *Imagined Communities: Reflections on the Origin and Spread of Nationalism*, revised edn, London and New York: Verso.

Applbaum, Arthur Isak (1998), 'Are violations of rights ever right?', *Ethics* 108:340–66.

Arendt, Hannah (1970), *On Violence*. New York: Harvest Books.

Barker, Alan (2004), *Shadows: Inside Northern Ireland's Special Branch*, Edinburgh: Mainstream.

Barritt, D. and C. Carter (1962), *The Northern Ireland Problem*, Oxford: Oxford University Press.

Beiner, Ronald (1999), 'Nationalism's challenge to philosophy', in Ronald Beiner (ed.), *Theorizing Nationalism*, Albany, NY: SUNY Press, pp. 1–25.

Bell, J. Bowyer (1976), *On Revolt: Strategies of National Liberation*, Cambridge, MA: Harvard University Press.

Bell, J. Bowyer (1990), *IRA: Tactics and Targets*, Dublin: Poolbeg Press.

Bellamy, Alex J. (2006), 'No pain, no gain? Torture and ethics in the war on terror', *International Affairs* 82:121–48.

Bennett, Jonathan (1981), 'Morality and consequences', in Sterling M. McMurrin (ed.), *The Tanner Lectures on Human Values*, Salt Lake City, UT: University of Utah Press, vol. 2, pp. 95–105.

Bittner, Rüdiger (2005), 'Morals in terrorist times', in Georg Meggle (ed.), *Ethics of Terrorism and Counter-Terrorism*, Frankfurt: Ontos/Verlag, pp. 207–13.

Bonner, David (1988), 'Combating terrorism: Supergrass trials in Northern Ireland', *The Modern Law Review* 51:23–53.

Boyce, D. George and Alan O'Day (eds) (1996), *The Making of Modern Irish History: Revisionism and the Revisionist Controversy*, London and New York: Routledge.

Brady, Ciaran (ed.) (1994), *Interpreting Irish History: The Debate on Historical Revisionism, 1938–1994*, Dublin: Irish Academic Press.

Brilmayer, Lea (1991), 'Secession and self-determination: a territorial interpretation', *Yale Journal of International Law* 19:177–202.

Brownlie, Ian (1972), 'Interrogation in depth: the Compton and Parker reports', *The Modern Law Review* 35:501–7.

Bruce, Steve (1992), *The Red Hand: Protestant Paramilitaries in Northern Ireland*, Oxford: Oxford University Press.

Bruce, Steve (1994), *The Edge of the Union: the Ulster Loyalist Political Vision*, Oxford: Oxford University Press.

Buchanan, Allen (1991), 'Toward a theory of succession', *Ethics* 101:322–42.

Calvert, J. (1972), 'Housing problems in Northern Ireland: a critique', *Community Forum* 2:18–20.

Camus, Albert (1958), *The Just Assassins*, in A. Camus, *Caligula and Three Other Plays*, trans. Stuart Gilbert, New York: Alfred A. Knopf, pp. 233–320.

Casebeer, William D. (2005), 'Torture interrogation of terrorists: a theory of exceptions (with notes, cautions, and warnings)', in Timothy Shanahan (ed.), *Philosophy 9/11: Thinking about the War on Terrorism*, Chicago, IL: Open Court Publishing, pp. 261–72.

Coady, C. A. J. (2004), 'Terrorism and innocence', *The Journal of Ethics* 8:37–58.

Colley, Linda (1992), 'Britishness and otherness: an argument', *The Journal of British Studies* 31:309–329.

Corlett, J. Angelo (1996), 'Can terrorism be morally justified?', *Public Affairs Quarterly* 10:163–84.

Corlett, J. Angelo (2003), *Terrorism: a Philosophical Analysis*, Dordrecht: Kluwer Academic Publishers.

Darwell, Stephen (ed.) (2002), *Consequentialism*, Malden, MA: Wiley-Blackwell.

Dillon, Martin (1990), *The Dirty War*, London: Hutchinson.

Dixon, Paul (2001), *Northern Ireland: the Politics of War and Peace*, New York: Palgrave.

Douglas, Roy, Liam Harte and Jim O'Hara (1999), *Ireland Since 1690: a Concise History*, Belfast: Blackstaff.

Drake, C. J. M. (1996), 'The phenomenon of conservative terrorism', *Terrorism and Political Violence* 8:29–46.

Eagleton, Terry (1999), 'Nationalism and the case of Ireland', *New Left Review* 234:44–61.

Edwards, Ruth Dudley (2006), *Patrick Pearse: the Triumph of Failure*, Dublin: Irish Academic Press.

Ellis, Steven G. (1986), 'Nationalist historiography and the English and Gaelic worlds in the late Middle Ages', *Irish Historical Studies* xxv:1–18.

English, Richard (2003), *Armed Struggle: the History of the IRA*, London: Macmillan.

English, Richard (2006), *Irish Freedom: the History of Nationalism in Ireland*, London: Macmillan.

Evans, Mark (2005), 'Moral theory and the idea of a just war', in Mark Evans (ed.), *Just War Theory: a Reappraisal*, Edinburgh: Edinburgh University Press, pp. 1–21.

Feeney, Brian (2004), *A Pocket History of the Troubles*, Dublin: O'Brien Press.

Finneran, Richard J. (ed.) (2002), *The Yeats Reader*, New York: Scribner Poetry.

Foster, Robert Fitzroy (2003), *W. B. Yeats: a Life*, Oxford and New York: Oxford University Press, vol. 2.

Foster, Robert Fitzroy (2007), *Luck and the Irish: a Brief History of Change c. 1970–2000*, London: Allen Lane.

Fotion, Nicholas (1981), 'The burdens of terrorism', in B. M. Leiser (ed.), *Values in Conflict: Life, Liberty, and the Rule of Law*, New York: Macmillan, pp. 463–70.

Freeman, Michael (2003), *Freedom or Security: the Consequences for Democracies Using Emergency Powers to Fight Terror*, Westport, CT: Praeger.

Frey, R. G. and C. W. Morris (1991), 'Violence, terrorism, and justice', in R. G. Frey and C. W. Morris (eds), *Violence, Terrorism, and Justice*, Cambridge: Cambridge University Press, pp. 1–17.

Gallagher, Frank (1957), *The Indivisible Island: the History of the Partition of Ireland*, London: Gollancz.

Gallagher, Michael (1990), 'Do Ulster unionists have a right to self-determination?', *Irish Political Studies* 5:11–30.

Gallagher, Michael (1995), 'How many nations are there in Ireland?', *Ethnic and Racial Studies* 18:715–39.

Gans, Chaim (2001), 'Historical rights: the evaluation of nationalist claims to sovereignty', *Political Theory* 29:58–79.

Garrett, S. A. (1993), *Ethics and Airpower in World War II: the British Bombing of German Cities*, New York: St. Martin's Press.

George, D. A. (2000), 'The ethics of IRA terrorism', in Andrew Valls (ed.), *Ethics in International Affairs: Theories and Cases*, Lanham, MD: Rowman & Littlefield, pp. 81–97.

Gerstein, Robert S. (1989), 'Do terrorists have rights?', in D. C. Rapoport and Yonah Alexander (eds), *The Morality of Terrorism: Religious and Secular Justifications*, 2nd edn, New York: Columbia University Press, pp. 290–307.

Gilbert, Paul (1993), 'Criteria of nationality and the ethics of self-determination', *History of European Ideas* 16:515–20.

Gilbert, Paul (1998), *The Philosophy of Nationalism*, Boulder, CO: Westview Press.

Gillon, Steven M. (2000), *That's Not What We Meant to Do: Reform and Its Unintended Consequences in the Twentieth Century*, New York: W. W. Norton & Co.

Glover, Jonathan (1991), 'State terrorism', in R. G. Frey and C. W. Morris (eds), *Violence, Terrorism, and Justice*, Cambridge: Cambridge University Press, pp. 256–75.

Govier, Trudy (2002), *A Delicate Balance: What Philosophy Can Tell Us about Terrorism*, Boulder, CO: Westview Press.

Grotius, Hugo [1631] (1925), *The Laws of War and Peace*, translated by F. W. Kelsey, Indianapolis, IN: Bobbs-Merrill.

Harris, Charles Edwin, Jr (2006), *Applying Moral Theories*, 5th edn, Belmont, CA: Wadsworth.

Harte, Liam (2005), 'A taxonomy of terrorism', in Timothy Shanahan (ed.), *Philosophy 9/11: Thinking about the War on Terrorism*, Chicago, IL: Open Court Publishing, pp. 23–50.

Hayden, Tom (2001), *Irish on the Inside: In Search of the Soul of Irish America*, London and New York: Verso.

Held, Virginia (1991), 'Terrorism, rights, and political goals', in R. G. Frey and C. W. Morris (eds), *Violence, Terrorism, and Justice*, Cambridge: Cambridge University Press, pp. 59–85.

Held, Virginia (2004), 'Terrorism, rights, and political goals' [revised version], in Igor Primoratz (ed.), *Terrorism: the Philosophical Issues*, New York: Palgrave-Macmillan, pp. 65–79.

Hennessey, Thomas (2005), *Northern Ireland: the Origins of the Troubles*, Dublin: Gill & Macmillan.

Hennessey, Thomas (2007), *The Evolution of the Troubles, 1970–72*, Dublin: Irish Academic Press.

Hewitt, Christopher (1981), 'Catholic grievances, Catholic nationalism and violence in Northern Ireland during the Civil Rights period: a reconsideration', *British Journal of Sociology* 32:362–80.

Hoffman, Bruce (2006), *Inside Terrorism*, revised and expanded edn, New York: Columbia University Press.

Holland, Jack (1999), *Hope Against History: the Course of Conflict in Northern Ireland*, New York: Henry Holt.

Hooker, Brad (2000), *Ideal Code, Real World: a Rule-Consequentialist Theory of Morality*, Oxford: Clarendon Press.

Hutchinson, John (1996), 'Irish nationalism', in D. George Boyce and Alan O'Day (eds), *The Making of Modern Irish History: Revisionism and the Revisionist Controversy*, London and New York: Routledge, pp. 100–19.

Jackson, Alvin (1999), *Ireland 1798–1998: Politics and War*, Oxford: Blackwell.

Jackson, Brian A. (2007), 'Counterinsurgency intelligence in a "long war": the British experience in Northern Ireland', *Military Review*, January–February, pp. 74–84.

Jennings, Sir Ivor (1956), *The Approach to Self-Government*, Cambridge: Cambridge University Press.

Kamm, Frances M. (1989), 'Harming some to save others', *Philosophical Studies* 57:227–60.

Kamm, Frances M. (1992), 'Non-consequentialism, the person as an end-in-itself, and the significance of status', *Philosophy and Public Affairs* 21:354–89.

Kamm, Frances M. (2004), 'Failures of just war theory: terror, harm, and justice', *Ethics* 114:650–92.

Khatchadourian, Haig (1988), 'Terrorism and morality', *Journal of Applied Philosophy* 5:131–45.

Khatchadourian, Haig (1998), *The Morality of Terrorism*, New York: Peter Lang.

Khatchadourian, Haig (2005), 'Counter-terrorism: torture and assassination', in Georg Meggle (ed.), *Ethics of Terrorism and Counter-Terrorism*, Frankfurt: Ontos/Verlag, pp. 177–96.

Knight, David B. (1985), 'Territory and people or people and territory? Thoughts on postcolonial self-determination', *International Political Science Review* 6:248–72.

Krejci, Jaroslav and Vitezslaw Velimsky (1981), *Ethnic and Political Nations in Europe*, London: Croom Helm.

Lansing, Robert (1921), 'Self-determination', *Saturday Evening Post*, 9 April 1921, p. 9.

Leiser, Burton M. (ed.) (1981), *Values in Conflict: Life, Liberty, and the Rule of Law*, New York: Macmillan.

Lennon, Brian (2004), *Peace Comes Dropping Slow: Dialogue and Conflict Management in the Northern Ireland Conflict*, Belfast: Community Dialogue.

Lichtenberg, Judith (1999), 'How liberal can nationalism be?', in Ronald Beiner (ed.), *Theorizing Nationalism*, Albany, NY: SUNY Press, pp. 167–88.

MacStiofáin, Seán (1975), *Memoirs of a Revolutionary*, Edinburgh: Gordon Cremonesi.

Makinson, David (1989), 'On attributing rights to all peoples: some logical questions', *Law and Philosophy* 8:53–63.

Martin, F. X. (1968), 'The 1916 Rising – *coup d'état* or a "bloody protest"', *Studia Hibernica* 8:106–37.

McBride, Ian (2001), 'Memory and national identity in modern Ireland', in Ian McBride (ed.), *History and Memory in Modern Ireland*, Cambridge: Cambridge University Press, pp. 1–42.

McCann, Eamonn (1992), *Bloody Sunday in Derry*, Dingle: Brandon.

McIntyre, Anthony (1995), 'Modern Irish republicanism: the product of British state strategies', *Irish Political Studies* 10:97–121.

McIntyre, Anthony (2000), 'Interview with Brendan Hughes', *The Blanket: a Journal of Protest and Dissent* (http://lark.phoblacht.net/BH50208.html).

McKittrick, David et al. (2001), *Lost Lives: the Stories of the Men, Women and Children who Died as a Result of the Northern Ireland Troubles*, Edinburgh: Mainstream.

McKittrick, David and David McVea (2002), *Making Sense of the Troubles: the Story of the Conflict in Northern Ireland*, Chicago, IL: New Amsterdam Books.

Mill, John Stuart (1868), 'The contest in America', in *Dissertations and Discussions: Political, Philosophical, and Historical*, 2nd edn, London: Longmans & Company, vol. 1. [First published in *Fraser's Magazine*, 1862.]

Miller, David (1995), *On Nationality*, New York: Oxford University Press.

Moloney, Ed (2002), *A Secret History of the IRA*, New York: W. W. Norton & Co.

Moore, Margaret (2001), *The Ethics of Nationalism*, Oxford: Oxford University Press.

Moran, Seán (1991), 'Patrick Pearse and patriotic soteriology: the Irish republican tradition and the sanctification of political self-immolation', in Yonah Alexander and Alan O'Day (eds), *The Irish Terrorism Experience*, Aldershot: Dartmouth Publishing Co., pp. 9–29.

Moran, Seán (1994), *Patrick Pearse and the Politics of Redemption: the Mind of the Easter Rising, 1916*, Washington, DC: The Catholic University of America Press.

Mulgan, Tim (2005), *The Demands of Consequentialism*, new edn, New York: Oxford University Press.

Mulholland, Marc (2002), *The Longest War: Northern Ireland's Troubled History*, Oxford and New York: Oxford University Press.

Murphy, Séamus (1993), '"I don't support the IRA, but . . .": semantic and psychological ambivalence', *Studies* 82:276–86.

Murray, Gerard and Jonathan Tonge (2005), *Sinn Féin and the SDLP: from Alienation to Participation*, New York: Palgrave-Macmillan.

Murray, Raymond (1990), *The SAS in Ireland*, Dublin: Mercier.

Murray, Raymond (1998), *State Violence in Northern Ireland: 1969–1997*, Dublin: Mercier.

Nagel, Thomas (1995), 'Personal rights and public space', *Philosophy and Public Affairs* 24:83–107.

Nelson, William R. (1991), 'New developments in terrorist trials in Northern Ireland', in Yonah Alexander and Alan O'Day (eds), *The Irish Terrorism Experience*, Aldershot: Dartmouth Publishing Co., pp. 155–70.

Neumann, Peter R. (2003), *Britain's Long War: British Strategy in the Northern Ireland Conflict, 1968–98*, London: Palgrave.

Newsinger, John (2002), *British Counterinsurgency: From Palestine to Northern Ireland*, New York: Palgrave.

Nickel, James W. (1987), *Making Sense of Human Rights*, Berkeley, CA: University of California Press.

NICRA (Northern Ireland Civil Rights Association) (1978), *We Shall Overcome: the History of the Struggle for Civil Rights in Northern Ireland, 1968–1978*, Belfast: NICRA.

Nielson, Kai (1981), 'Violence and terrorism: its uses and abuses', in B. M. Leiser (ed.), *Values in Conflict: Life, Liberty, and the Rule of Law*, New York: Macmillan, pp. 435–49.

Nozick, Robert (1974), *Anarchy, State, and Utopia*, New York: Basic Books.

O'Boyle, Michael (1977), 'Torture and emergency powers under the European Convention on Human Rights: Ireland v. the United Kingdom', *American Journal of International Law* 71:674–706.

O'Brien, Brendan (1999), *The Long War: the IRA and Sinn Féin*, updated edn, Dublin: O'Brien Press.

O'Brien, Brendan (2004), *O'Brien Pocket History of the IRA*, Dublin: O'Brien Press.

O'Connor, Ulick (1996), *Michael Collins and the Troubles: the Struggle for Irish Freedom 1912–1922*, London and New York: W. W. Norton & Co.

Ó Dochartaigh, Niall (2005), *From Civil Rights to Armalites: the Birth of the Troubles*, 2nd edn, New York: Palgrave-Macmillan.

O'Doherty, Malachi (1998), *The Trouble with Guns: Republican Strategy and the Provisional IRA*, Belfast: Blackstaff.

O'Doherty, Shane (1993), *The Volunteer: a Former IRA Man's True Story*, London: Fount.

O'Leary, Brendan and John McGarry (1996), *The Politics of Antagonism: Understanding Northern Ireland*, 2nd edn, London: Athlone.

O'Mahony, Patrick and Gerard Delanty (1998), *Rethinking Irish History: Nationalism, Identity and Ideology*, London: Macmillan.

O'Malley, Padraig (1983), *The Uncivil Wars: Ireland Today*, Belfast: Blackstaff.

Patterson, Henry (1990), 'Gerry Adams and the modernisation of republicanism', *Conflict Quarterly* 10:5–23.

Patterson, Henry (1997), *The Politics of Illusion: a Political History of the IRA*, London: Serif.

Philpott, Daniel (1995), 'In defense of self-determination', *Ethics* 105:352–85.

Primoratz, Igor (1997), 'The morality of terrorism', *Journal of Applied Philosophy* 14:221–33.

Primoratz, Igor (2004), 'State terrorism and counter-terrorism', in Igor Primoratz (ed.), *Terrorism: the Philosophical Issues*, New York: Palgrave-Macmillan, pp. 113–27.

Purdie, Bob (1988), 'Was the civil rights movement a republican/communist conspiracy?', *Irish Political Studies* 3:33–41.

Purdie, Bob (1990), *Politics in the Streets: the Origins of the Civil Rights Movement in Northern Ireland*, Belfast: Blackstaff.

Quinn, Dermot (1993), *Understanding Northern Ireland*, Manchester: Baseline.

Rachels, James (1984), 'Political assassination', in J. P. White (ed.), *Assent/Dissent*, Dubuque: Kendall/Hunt Publishing Company, pp. 323–33.

Rees, Phil (2005), *Dining with Terrorists: Meetings with the World's Most Wanted Militants*, London: Macmillan.

Richardson, Louise (2006), *What Terrorists Want*, New York: Random House.

Sands, Bobby (1981), *The Diary of Bobby Sands*, Dublin: Sinn Féin Publicity Department.

Schelling, Thomas C. (1966), *Arms and Influence*, New Haven, CT: Yale University Press.

Schmid, Alex P. and Albert J. Jongman (1988), *Political Terrorism: a New Guide to Actors, Authors, Concepts, Data Bases, Theories, and Literature*, New Brunswick, NJ: Transaction Books.

Shanahan, Timothy (2003), *Reason and Insight: Western and Eastern Perspectives on the Pursuit of Moral Wisdom*, 2nd edn, Belmont, CA: Wadsworth Publishing.

Shanahan, Timothy (2008), 'The morality of Palestinian terrorism', in Stephen Law (ed.), *Israel, Palestine and Terror*, London: Continuum Publishing, pp. 34–46.

Shue, Henry (1978), 'Torture', *Philosophy and Public Affairs* 7:124–43.

Similansky, Saul (2004), 'Terrorism, justification, and illusion', *Ethics* 114:790–805.

Simpson, Peter (1986), 'Just war theory and the IRA', *Journal of Applied Philosophy* 3:73–88.

Simpson, Peter (2005), 'The war on terrorism: its justification and limits', in Georg Meggle (ed.), *Ethics of Terrorism & Counter-Terrorism*, Frankfurt: Ontos/Verlag, pp. 197–205.

Sluka, Jeffrey A. (2000), 'For God and Ulster: the culture of terror and loyalist death squads in Northern Ireland', in Jeffrey A. Sluka (ed.), *Death Squad: the Anthropology of State Terror*, Philadelphia, PA: University of Pennsylvania Press, pp. 127–157.

Smith, Anthony D. (1986), *The Ethnic Origins of Nations*, Oxford: Blackwell.

Smith, Anthony D. (2001), *Nationalism: Theory, Ideology, History*, Oxford: Blackwell.

Smith, Anthony D. (2003), *Chosen Peoples*, Oxford: Oxford University Press.

Smith, David J. and Gerald Chambers (1991), *Inequality in Northern Ireland*, Oxford: Oxford University Press.

Smith, M. L. R. (1995), *Fighting for Ireland? The Military Strategy of the Irish Republican Movement*, London and New York: Routledge.

Smyth, Jim (1991), 'Weasels in a hole: ideologies of the Irish conflict', in Yonah Alexander and Alan O'Day (eds), *The Irish Terrorism Experience*, Aldershot: Dartmouth Publishing Co., pp. 135–53.

Soule, John W. (1989), 'Problems in applying counterterrorism to prevent terrorism: two decades of violence in Northern Ireland reconsidered', *Terrorism* 12:31–46.

Stalker, John (1988), *The Stalker Affair*, New York: Viking.

Steinhoff, Uwe (2004), 'How can terrorism be justified?', in Igor Primoratz (ed.), *Terrorism: the Philosophical Issues*, New York: Palgrave-Macmillan, pp. 97–109.

Stevenson, Jonathan (1996), *We Wrecked the Place: Contemplating an End to the Northern Ireland Troubles*, New York: Free Press.

Sussman, David (2005), 'What's wrong with torture?', *Philosophy & Public Affairs* 33:1–33.

Sutton, Malcolm (1994), *Bear in Mind these Dead . . . An Index of Deaths from the Conflict in Ireland 1969–1993*, Belfast: Beyond the Pale Publications.

Sweeney, George (1993), 'Irish hunger strikes and the cult of self-sacrifice', *Journal of Contemporary History* 28:421–37.

Taylor, Peter (1980), *Beating the Terrorists: Interrogation at Omagh, Gough, and Castlereagh*, New York: Penguin.

Taylor, Peter (1997), *Provos: the IRA and Sinn Féin*, London: Bloomsbury.

Taylor, Peter (1999), *Loyalists: War and Peace in Northern Ireland*, New York: TV Books.

Taylor, Richard (1992), *Metaphysics*, 4th edn, Englewood Cliffs, NJ: Prentice Hall.

Tenner, Edward (1997), *Why Things Bite Back: Technology and the Revenge of Unintended Consequences*, New York: Vintage Books.

Thompson, Janna (2001), 'Historic injustice and reparation: justifying claims of descendents', *Ethics* 112:114–35.

Tonge, Jonathan (1998), *Northern Ireland: Conflict and Change*, London: Prentice Hall Europe.

Toolis, Kevin (1996), *Rebel Hearts: Journeys within the IRA's Soul*, New York: St. Martin's Press.

Townshend, Charles (1986), *Britain's Civil Wars: Counterinsurgency in the Twentieth Century*, London: Faber & Faber.

Townshend, Charles (1999), *Ireland: the Twentieth Century*, London: Arnold.

Urban, Mark (1992), *Big Boys' Rules: the SAS and the Secret Struggle Against the IRA*, London: Faber & Faber.

Valls, Andrew (2000), 'Can terrorism be justified?', in A. Valls (ed.), *Ethics in International Affairs: Theories and Cases*, Lanham, MD: Rowman & Littlefield, pp. 65–79.

Waldron, Jeremy (1992), 'Superseding historic injustice', *Ethics* 103:4–28.

Wallace, Gerry (1989), 'Area bombing, terrorism, and the death of innocents', *Journal of Applied Philosophy* 6:3–15.

Walzer, Michael (2000), *Just and Unjust Wars*, 3rd edn, New York: Basic Books.

Warner, Geoffrey (2006), 'The Falls Road curfew revisited', *Irish Studies Review* 14:325–342.

Webster, Sir Charles and Noble Frankland (1961), *The Strategic Air Offensive Against Germany, 1939–45*, London: HMSO.

Whelan, Anthony (1994), 'Wilsonian self-determination and the Versailles Settlement', *International and Comparative Law Quarterly* 43:99–115.

White, Robert W. (1988), 'Commitment, efficacy, and personal sacrifice among Irish republicans', *Journal of Political and Military Sociology* 16:77–90.

White, Robert W. (1993), *Provisional Irish Republicans: an Oral and Interpretive History*, Westport, CT: Greenwood Press.

White, Robert W. (2006), *Ruairí Ó Brádaigh: the Life and Politics of an Irish Revolutionary*, Bloomington, IN: Indiana University Press.

Whyte, John (1983), 'How much discrimination was there under the Unionist regime, 1921–1968?', in T. Gallagher and J. O'Connell (eds), *Contemporary Irish Studies*, Manchester: Manchester University Press.

Whyte, John (1990), *Interpreting Northern Ireland*, Oxford: Oxford University Press.

Wilkins, Burleigh T. (1992), *Terrorism and Collective Responsibility*, London: Routledge.

Williams, Bernard (1973), 'A critique of utilitarianism', in J. J. C. Smart and Bernard Williams, *Utilitarianism: For and Against*, Cambridge: Cambridge University Press.

Wilson, T. (1989), *Ulster: Conflict and Consent*, Oxford: Blackwell.

Woffinden, Bob (1987), *Miscarriages of Justice*, London: Hodder & Stoughton.

Wood, Ian S. (2006), *Crimes of Loyalty: a History of the UDA*, Edinburgh: Edinburgh University Press.

Wright, Joanne (1990), 'PIRA propaganda: the construction of legitimacy', *Conflict Quarterly* 10:24–41.

Young, Robert (2004), 'Political terrorism as a weapon of the politically power-less', in Igor Primoratz (ed.), *Terrorism: the Philosophical Issues*, New York: Palgrave-Macmillan, pp. 55–64.

Zohar, Noam J. (2004), 'Innocence and complex threats: upholding the war ethic and the condemnation of terrorism', *Ethics* 114:734–51.

Index